In Memory of

Karen Ann Watkins

Granddaughter

of

Jane and Leonard

Frank

Elizabeth Barrett Browning
Selected Poetry and Prose

Meredith B. Raymond and Mary Rose Sullivan

The Labyrinth Press
Durham, North Carolina

Library of Congress Cataloging in Publication Data

Browning, Elizabeth Barrett, 1806-1861.
    [Selections. 1993]
    Elizabeth Barrett Browning: selected poetry and prose /
Meredith B. Raymond and Mary Rose Sullivan.
          p.   cm.
    ISBN 0-939464-52-7
    I. Raymond, Meredith B.   II. Sullivan, Mary Rose.
        III. Title.
PR41182.R38 1993
821' .8–dc20   91-45540
                                              CIP

Printed in the United States of America

CONTENTS

ACKNOWLEDGEMENTS

The authors wish to thank Labyrinth Press editors, Dr. Virginia Steinmetz, Debra H. Weiner, and Nancy L. Zingrone who worked on this manuscript at various stages of its preparation.

The editors and Labyrinth Press wish to make acknowledgement for the kind permission to publish the following letters of Elizabeth Barrett Browning, or selections therefrom, manuscripts of which are located in the English Poetry Collection, Wellesley College Library: 17 July 1841 to Miss Mitford, 14 January 1843 to Miss Mitford, 15 January 1845 to Robert Browning, [16–17 July 1845] to Robert Browning, November [1850] to Miss Mitford, February [1857] to Mrs. Martin. We also acknowledge the kind permission of the Huntington Library to publish the manuscript of a letter dated 22 September 1844 to Hugh Stuart Boyd and also permission of The Henry W. and Albert A. Berg Collection, The New York Public Library, Astor and Tilden Foundations to publish the manuscript of the letter of 21 April [1861] to William Thackeray.

Copyright and permission to quote from previous publications have been obtained from Wellesley College, the publishing house of John Murray, The President and Fellows of Harvard College, and Wedgestone Press. The text is based on the following publications:

Elizabeth Barrett to Mr. Boyd: Unpublished Letters of Elizabeth Barrett Browning to Hugh Stuart Boyd. Ed. Barbara P. McCarthy. New Haven: Yale University Press, 1955, for Wellesley College.

The Letters of Elizabeth Barrett Browning. Ed. Frederic G. Kenyon. 2 vols. New York and London: The Macmillan Co., 1898.

The Letters of Elizabeth Barrett Browning to Mary Russell Mitford, 1836–1854. Ed. Meredith B. Raymond and Mary Rose Sullivan. 3 vols. Winfield, Kansas: Armstrong Browning Library of Baylor University, The Browning Institute, Wedgestone Press and Wellesley College, 1983.

The Letters of Robert Browning and Elizabeth Barrett, 1845–1846. Ed. Elvan Kintner. 2 vols. Cambridge, Mass.: The Belknap Press of Harvard University Press, 1969.

Cue Titles

EB to HSB   *Elizabeth Barrett to Mr. Boyd*, ed. Barbara P.
             McCarthy (New Haven, 1955).

HUPS   *Elizabeth Barrett Browning: Hitherto Unpublished
             Poems and Stories with an Inedited Autobiography*,
             ed. H. Buxton Forman, 2 vols. (Boston, 1914).

LBGB   *Letters of the Brownings to George Barrett*, eds. Paul
             Landis and Ronald E. Freeman (Urbana, Illinois,
             1958).

LEBB   *The Letters of Elizabeth Barrett Browning*, ed.
             Frederic G. Kenyon, 2 vols. (New York and
             London, 1899).

LRB and EBB *The Letters of Robert Browning and Elizabeth Barrett
             Browning, 1845–1846*, ed. Elvan Kinter, 2 vols.
             (Cambridge, Massachusetts, 1969).

LMRM   *The Letters of Elizabeth Barrett Browning to Mary
             Russell Mitford, 1836–1854*, eds. Meredith B.
             Raymond and Mary Rose Sullivan, 3 vols.
             (Winfield, Kansas, 1983).

The text of the poems and prose commentary, except where noted by cue title following the poem, is taken from *The Complete Works of Elizabeth Barrett Browning*, edited with Introduction and Notes by Charlotte Porter and Helen A. Clarke, 6 vols. (New York, 1900. Reprint: New York: AMS Press Inc., 1973). The text of the letters is from the volume indicated by cue title at the end of each selection.

Introduction

I

The works included in this volume were chosen to illustrate the range of Elizabeth Barrett Browning's poetic career over the course of her lifetime (1806–61). Even for a career which from the juvenilia to her last poems spanned almost half a century, the variety of genres and themes in her works is striking. Although her early poetry was, as is the case with most young poets, uneven in quality and often highly derivative, with the publication of her 1844 volume her authentic voice is heard. From first to last, her poetry is marked by a vigor of expression and intensity of feeling, by an interest in formal experimentation, and by an unswerving confidence in the moral significance of art and a conviction that a woman's voice belonged in the mainstream of literary tradition, especially poetry. In these ways, her voice was distinctive among nineteenth-century British poets.

A very young Elizabeth Barrett began as an imitator of eighteenth-century epics written in the heroic couplet; in the 1820s and early 1830s she turned to writing lyrical nature poetry in the Wordsworthian vein and then to verse drama which was Aeschylean in format and Miltonic in theme. In the next decade she worked in the pseudo-medieval narrative ballad form, before turning in the 1840s to the sonnet and producing a long sequence, reminiscent of Renaissance poetry in diction and imagery. By 1850 she had adopted a declamatory style for passing judgment on public and social issues, and in 1857—at the peak of her career—she published her major work, a blank-verse "novel" about the growth of a woman artist and the contemporary treatment of women. Just before her death she was writing brief psychological studies of passion suggestive of Robert Browning's shorter dramatic monologues.

The selections included here demonstrate each of these major phases of her development. Included also is some prose, mainly in the form of excerpts from her prefaces and letters, which sheds light on her intentions and her poetic theory and reveals how faithfully she held throughout her life to the belief that to be a poet—a role as appropriate to a woman as to a man—was a solemn, even a sacred, responsibility.

It may be difficult for a present-day reader, who knows of Elizabeth Barrett Browning mainly as the author of the "Sonnets from the Portuguese," to conceive of the magnitude of her poetic reputation at the height of the Victorian era. By 1850, her poetic reputation surpassed that

of her husband and by 1857 John Ruskin was hailing the newly pub-
lished *Aurora Leigh* as the greatest poetic work of the age. Edition after
edition of her poems appeared in England and America and she was
considered a bold defender of liberal causes, a daring stylistic innovator,
and a greater artist than her husband and fellow-poet Robert Browning.

Time did not sustain that reputation. By the beginning of the twen-
tieth century, public attention had shifted away from her poetry and
toward her life, radically altering her public image from that of social
protester to romantic heroine. Publication in 1899 of the correspondence
between her and Browning (the so-called "love letters") and, later, the
production of Rudolf Besier's popular *The Barretts of Wimpole Street*—
performed in London and New York and in World War II for thousands
of troops and subsequently made into a film—both worked to imprint
on the public mind the image of a sequestered invalid who escaped
from her father's tyranny to domestic bliss with the dashingly romantic
Robert Browning. Such an image prevails; when dramatists like Eugene
O'Neill and Tennessee Williams wanted to suggest the "gentility"
of a female character, they showed her reading "Mrs. Browning's"
love sonnets rather than her poems protesting mistreatment of women
or other injustices.

Despite the range of her work, the liberality of her views, and the
abundant evidence that she has influenced other important women
writers—most notably Emily Dickinson—twentieth-century anthologies
of English literature have generally presented the image of Elizabeth
Barrett Browning as "minor poet." Recently, however, under the impetus
of feminist criticism, her poetry is being reassessed in its totality. The
selections in the present volume illustrate a variety of poetic techniques
and themes in striking contrast to those traditionally considered typical-
ly Victorian. The treatment in these poems of such topics as sexual pas-
sion, rape, and prostitution—topics generally considered taboo by Vic-
torian standards—is remarkably modern in its outspokenness. The
depiction of a desperate black slave, for example, strangling her half-
white child, who "moaned and struggled, as well might he, / For the
white child wanted his liberty—," and, in another instance, of a betrayed
woman excoriating the rival who "lied and stole, / And spat" out "The
rank saliva of her soul" is thoroughly at odds with conventional Vic-
torian expressions of women's emotions. Besides dramatizing the plight
of individual women, Elizabeth Barrett Browning was also quick to
attack—in a voice ringing with implacable moral authority—other in-
stances of injustice, whether by the hand of politician, emperor, or
pope. It is her clarity of vision, honesty, and courage, qualities long
acknowledged to be manifest in her letters, that are now attracting
renewed attention and admiration from readers of her poetry.

Elizabeth Barrett (or EBB, as she habitually signed herself, for "Elizabeth Barrett Barrett") was convinced from her earliest years that she was destined to be a poet. As the oldest of eleven children in a close-knit, upper-middle-class household, she was encouraged to act as family laureate, marking birthdays and other ceremonial occasions with appropriate verses. Almost entirely self-taught, she read avidly in eighteenth-century poetry and fiction as well as Romantic poetry, and pursued the study of Hebrew with the aid of a lexicon and grammar. Under the tutelage of Hugh Stuart Boyd, a blind classical scholar who encouraged her to translate *Prometheus Bound*, she read the Greek dramatists. Her father, a country magistrate and a devout Dissenter (as was EBB), had *The Battle of Marathon* privately printed in 1820; EBB wrote this imitation of a neo-classical epic at the age of 12. By the age of 15, she had written her youthful autobiography, *Glimpses into My Life and Character*, and had published verses on Greek freedom in the *New Monthly Magazine*. At 20, still writing in the neo-classical poetic tradition, she published *An Essay on Mind*, a philosophical argument in the style of Alexander Pope. In 1833 she published her translation of *Prometheus Bound* in a volume with "miscellaneous poems," many of them suggestive of Byron, on liberty and the heroic ideal.

The different kind of poetry that emerged in the next decade reflected changed family circumstances. Her mother, a self-effacing, gentle woman to whom EBB was devoted, died in 1828 and shortly thereafter her father, pressed by financial difficulties, sold the palatial estate of Hope End near the scenic Malvern Hills and moved the family to more modest quarters in Sidmouth on the English Channel, a location considered beneficial to Elizabeth who by that time had contracted chronic tuberculosis. It was here that EBB began a friendship with the Rev. George Barrett Hunter, a Dissenter, whose generally high-minded ethical views but narrow-minded attitudes towards woman's place in society probably influenced the characterization of Romney Leigh in her later work, *Aurora Leigh*. In 1835, Mr. Barrett settled the family permanently in London and EBB, her health improved, began to write with renewed vigor.

In 1838, she brought out her first volume of poetry under her own name, *The Seraphim, and Other Poems*. The title poem is an ambitious dramatic lyric portraying, as a Christianized Aeschylus might have, the reaction of angelic hosts to the Crucifixion. Like many of the poems in this volume, it grapples with the dilemma of human loss by looking to religion for consolation. The speaker in "The Deserted Garden," for example, feels drawn closer to God through suffering so that, remembering lost childhood joys, she can conclude that "I who was, would shrink to be / That happy child again." A more problematic attitude toward loss appears in "The Romaunt of Margret," a long narrative using the ballad formula to tell the story of the lady Margret who drowns in despair at her lover's death. The loss of him is the last of a series of separations—from sister, brother, father—that force Margret to face the transiency of human relationships. In pairing this poem with "The Poet's Vow," which is about a poet who tried to live apart from humankind, EBB said that as the poet's failure proves that "the creature cannot be *isolated* from the creature," so "Margret" proves that "the creature cannot be *sustained* by the creature." Besides the poem's biographical interest—its strange prefiguring of EBB's loss of brother and father by death and estrangement—"The Romaunt of Margret" is of interest on two other counts: first, the role of the poet who narrates the lady's story and becomes so involved in her melancholy fate that his creative powers are suspended ("Hang up my harp again! / I have no voice for song") and second, the hint of a Jungian archetype of evil latent in the lady's persona in the form of a mocking "shadow" which seduces Margret into surrendering to the principle of doubt and negation. Writing to her friend Mary Russell Mitford, EBB defended herself against charges of romantic posturing in this poem by saying that she was sure "I had not written in affectation or *out* of my own nature." In another work from this volume, the short meditative lyric "A Sea-side Walk," EBB invokes, with subdued power, the same sense of loss; however, she looks not to the supernatural but to the natural world for consolation.

EBB's reputation rose steadily during the late 1830s and early 1840s. Her friend Mary Russell Mitford, editor of *Findens' Tableaux*, featured her poems, many of them pseudo-medieval ballads in the style of "The Romaunt of Margret;" James Russell Lowell, the prominent American poet and editor, offered generous terms for anything she would send him; the *Athenaeum* published her critical review of English poets, and R. H. Horne used her critical commentaries on Carlyle and Tennyson in his *A New Spirit of the Age*. Her circle of friends and correspondents also widened to include the prominent political economist Harriet Martineau and art historian Anna Jameson, both of whom provided EBB with models of women writers wielding influence far beyond the conventional feminine sphere.

By the time *Poems*, 1844 appeared, a number of other events also contributed to EBB's altering her poetic tone. A lung hemorrhage in 1838 had forced a move from London to the milder climate of Torquay where in 1840 her beloved brother "Bro" drowned in a boating accident. Since the autocratic Mr. Barrett had only reluctantly consented to Bro's staying with EBB, the remorse she felt about his death plunged her into a near-fatal illness. When she recovered physically—she never fully recovered psychologically from this trauma—and joined the family in London in

1841, she resumed work in a new vein, one more directly engaged with human relationships. The initial poem in the 1844 volume, "A Drama of Exile," the last of her spiritual dramas, treats the expulsion of Adam and Eve from Eden after the Fall, but it is notable for its emphasis on Eve as a woman who embodies hope as well as guilt. EBB calls attention to Eve's grief, her self-sacrifice, and her consciousness of originating the Fall. In addition, EBB calls attention in her preface to her own role as writer, saying that Eve's grief "imperfectly apprehended hitherto" is "more expressible by a woman than a man." The remaining poems turn away from Aeschylean/Miltonic themes toward more earthbound and realistic subjects, and suffering is more positively defined as a potentially exalting burden borne by the poet who serves God through man. "A Vision of Poets," for example, describes the role of the true poet as that of service to mankind through suffering and self-sacrifice: " . . . his songs in troops / Walk up and down our earthly slopes."

In this 1844 volume, EBB found the sonnet's disciplined formality congenial to her chastened state. "Grief," for example, through its spare diction and imagery, conveys the sensation of unrelenting and inexpressible sorrow. It is:

> Most like monumental statue set
> In everlasting watch and moveless woe
> Till itself crumble in the dust beneath.
> Touch it; the marble eyelids are not wet:
> If it could weep, it could arise and go.

Two sonnets addressed to George Sand in the 1844 volume reflect an increasing assertiveness in EBB. Sand, the bohemian novelist known for her masculine dress and numerous love affairs, was considered a writer no "self-respecting" woman would acknowledge reading; EBB's decision to praise her publicly shows courage as well as an unexpected breadth of taste. More importantly, these sonnets addressed to Sand show her already defining the ideal poet's nature as one balancing a "feminine" capacity for feeling with a "masculine" independence of thought—a combination of qualities she admired in Robert Browning. Years later she would develop more completely this concept of the ideal poetic nature in *Aurora Leigh*. In another work, "The Cry of the Children," she adapts a ballad-like refrain to a topic entirely new to her. Inspired by parliamentary reports on child labor, it is the first of her many protests against political and social abuses.

Poems, 1844, which marks her maturation as a lyric and narrative poet and established her reputation, stands as a focal point in EBB's poetic career. The most popular poem was, to her chagrin, "Lady Geraldine's Courtship," a ballad-like narrative subtitled "A Romance of the Age," hurriedly completed when one volume of *Poems* fell short in length. It delighted such severe critics as Thomas Carlyle and Harriet Martineau and encouraged her to consider a major "verse-novel" in a similar vein. "Lady Geraldine's Courtship" touches lightly on many of the themes and concerns developed more comprehensively in *Aurora Leigh*: lovers overcoming misunderstandings and class division as well as topical and prophetic commentary on technology and aesthetics. Tennyson had recently combined such themes in "Locksley Hall," a poem EBB deeply admired ("it burns with life and passion"); she, however, went beyond Tennyson in "Lady Geraldine's Courtship" to make the love story more dramatic and the topical allusions more specific—from indictments of "rotten boroughs" to encomiums on the steam engine. In spite of a certain facileness, the poem was crucial to EBB's career. It proved to her the longer narrative afforded the possibilities for mingling dramatic action and philosophical commentary so that she could at once satisfy her readers' taste for romance and her own desire to explore contemporary social and moral issues.

"Lady Geraldine's Courtship" has biographical significance as well; its graceful praise of poet Robert Browning (for his "heart within blood-tinctured, of a veined humanity") led to their introduction. John Kenyon, Browning's friend and EBB's cousin, had long wanted the poets to meet, but it was not until January 1845, when Browning wrote to thank EBB for her poetic compliment, that their correspondence began. The sympathy between them was instant and total. By May he was visiting her once or twice a week as their correspondence continued without interruption; within the year they had declared their love to each other. Despite the age difference (she was six years older than he) and her precarious health, in September 1846 they married (secretly, to avoid her father's wrath) and left England for Italy. Their hopes that the warmer climate would restore EBB's health were spectacularly realized, and in the fifteen years of their married life both EBB and Browning produced the best work of their careers.

Although the question of how much these married poets affected each other's poetry has yet to be fully explored, evidence in their courtship letters and from poems written by both during their years together points to a greater reciprocal influence than has been generally recognized. Of the traits they shared—strong family ties, wide reading in the classics, a devotion to evangelical religion and liberal causes—none was so pronounced as their commitment to the poetic vocation. Their life in Florence, where they lived in comparative ease thanks to John Kenyon's financial help, was devoted almost entirely to reading and composing poetry. After the birth in 1849 of their child, Robert Wiedemann, called "Pen," they traveled more extensively, to Siena and Rome and to Paris and England, and entertained the James Russell Lowells, the Tennysons, Thackeray, Fanny Kemble and Margaret Fuller Ossoli. In 1852, EBB managed at last to meet her long-admired George Sand.

The 1850 volume of *Poems* contained what she called the "ferocious" anti-slavery poem, "The Runaway Slave at Pilgrim's Point," written two years earlier for the *Liberty Bell*, a Boston journal, and also several lyrics revealing an interest in the psychology of the sexes. "A Woman's Short-comings" and "A Man's Requirements," for example, both question con-ventional attitudes toward love in a manner reminiscent of Browning in "A Woman's Last Word" and "Two in the Campagna." The major work in *Poems* (1850) was, however, "Sonnets from the Portuguese." This son-net sequence, which for decades after her death continued to be EBB's most highly regarded work, records her transformation from "A poor, tired, wandering singer" on "the dreadful outer brink" of death to one who stands erect, "transfigured, glorified aright" through the power of love. Placing the intensely personal story of her courtship within the framework of the traditional Petrarchan sonnet structure and the con-cept of the Platonic ladder-of-love allowed EBB to achieve and sustain a new control and clarity. Besides its aesthetic success, the sonnet se-quence is significant for the way it shows EBB assuming the role of sub-ject as well as object in the love relationship. Like her lover, she too is a singer, and the restorative power of his song enables her to realize her full human and creative potential. The sequence moves toward integra-tion on several levels—of the natural and supernatural, the ideal and real, the subjective and objective—and culminates with EBB, lover as well as beloved, giver as well as recipient, offering to her poet the gift of her own poetry.

Her next volume, *Casa Guidi Windows* (1851), reflects on recent events of the Italian revolution, some of which the Brownings viewed from the windows of their Casa Guidi apartment opposite the Pitti Palace. In this long lyrical-philosophical poem, EBB forthrightly claims to speak as the conscience of the nation, exercising the traditional vatic role even as she voices her personal concern for the future of her child and all children threatened by tyranny. In Part I, she exults at the over-throw of the Grand Duke in 1848 and calls for a hero to lead the forces of freedom; in Part II, written some three years later, she bitterly con-demns the betrayal of the revolution by statesmen and churchmen alike. Her intense identification with the cause of Italian independence was still evident a decade later: in *Poems Before Congress* (1860), a volume en-tirely political, she vents her sympathy for victims of the Italian struggle and her hopes for Napoleon III as their savior. As the revolution faltered, however, disappointment and frustration took their toll on EBB; "A Tale of Villafranca" illustrates her loss of aesthetic distance, as the speaker moves uncertainly between high rhetoric and personal expression, to end—as in the earlier "The Romaunt of Margret"—in grief-stricken silence ("Ah child! ah child! I cannot say / A word more"). A more effective expression of a poet's struggle to reconcile public and private roles is "Mother and Poet," from this same period; here EBB speaks dramatically, in the voice of an actual patriot-poet who sees her two sons lost in the war she advocated. The most controversial poem in *Poems Before Congress* was directed toward America: in "A Curse for a Nation," an uncompromising condemnation of slavery, EBB once again assumes the authoritative bardic voice of *Casa Guidi Windows*. She claims the right to speak for the downtrodden not only as a poet but as a woman: "A curse from the depths of womanhood / Is very salt, and bitter, and good."

Between these two political volumes came the long verse-novel *Aurora Leigh* (1857). EBB dedicated this, her major work, to her staunch friend of many years, John Kenyon, and was able to show it to him shortly before his death. It was a resounding success—hailed by critics as different as Landor and Ruskin, who praised its strong poetical expression, and Swinburne, who felt every character so "original and natural" that the poem "rivals the male Browning's character-drawing." It was the last extended work she undertook. Of the miscellaneous pieces completed in the remaining years (arranged by Robert Browning for publication in 1862 as *Last Poems*), several were dramatic lyrics marked by a psychological complexity reminiscent of Browning's own poems: the elaborate unmasking of male hypocrisy in "Lord Walter's Wife," for example, recalls "The Glove," and the speaker's choice in "Bianca Among the Nightingales"—better a lover dead than unfaithful—recalls "Porphyria's Lover." Perhaps, having exploited in *Aurora Leigh* the possibilities of the extended first-person speech for revealing character in action, EBB was being drawn to the potential of the brief dramatic monologue for revealing intense internal conflict.

Her last years brought a series of painful losses: of the father who had never become reconciled to her marriage, of her close friend Anna Jameson, of her sister Henrietta after a long illness. Disillusionment with the course of the Italian revolution and with the fraudulent practitioners of spiritualism, to which she had been strongly attracted, contributed to her declining health. Her lung disease recurred and, after a brief illness at Casa Guidi, she died on 29 June 1861, at the age of 55. She was buried in the Protestant Cemetery in Florence amid demonstrations of grief by many Italians who regarded her not merely as a famous poet but as a great spokeswoman for the cause of freedom.

II

Writing to her friend Mary Russell Mitford late in 1844 about having composed "Lady Geraldine's Courtship" on the Mitford principle of realism rather than on her own romantic principle, EBB confided: "and I mean to write a poem of length on your principle, — a sort of novel-poem! I am looking about for a story—Something not too complex, & admitting of high application." To Browning, shortly afterward, she wrote: "But my chief *intention* just now is the writing of a sort of novel-poem—a poem as completely modern as 'Geraldine's Courtship,' running into the midst of our conventions, & rushing into drawing-rooms & the like 'where angels fear to tread'; & so meeting face to face and without mask the Humanity of the age, & speaking the truth as I conceive of it, out plainly." In the 11,000–line narrative *Aurora Leigh*, EBB did speak out "plainly" on topics ranging from sexual hypocrisy and exploitation of the poor to the nature and function of art. Moreover, she wrote about women in general, and herself in particular, in a spirit and style different from anything she had done before. As Kathleen Hickok says in *Representations of Women: Nineteenth-Century British Women's Poetry*, EBB's previous "poetical representations of women, though sometimes subtly critical, had remained well within conventional expectations and traditional forms." By creating in *Aurora Leigh* three female characters representative of different social, intellectual, and moral levels, she could generalize about roles imposed by society and the differing responses of women to such roles. Thus Marian Erle, lowborn and powerless against exploitation, is saved from ruin only by the chance intervention of friends; Lady Waldemar by her self-serving schemes wastes the considerable powers inherent in her social position; Aurora Leigh by her self-reliance, courage, and dedication to her craft challenges society's expectations for her and achieves moral independence. By linking all three women romantically with the same man, the social reformer Romney Leigh, EBB could dramatize each woman's situation in a highly involved plot, replete with sensational incidents—from rape to mob violence—of the kind popular in melodramatic novels of the day. More important, by making her heroine a poet, EBB could portray in detail the difficulties and rewards involved in the search for fulfilment as artist and woman. It was the latter aspect of *Aurora Leigh* that EBB had in mind when she described the poem as the culmination of her life's work, into which she had poured her "highest convictions upon Life and Art."

In her 1844 preface EBB had set forth her enduring belief in the necessity of integrating Life and Art:

Poetry has been as serious a thing to me as life itself; and life has been a very serious thing: there has been no playing at skittles for me in either. I never mistook pleasure for the final cause of poetry; nor leisure, for the hour of the poet. I have done my work, so far, as work, —not as mere hand and head work, apart from the personal being, — but as the completest expression of that being to which I could attain.

That exalting of the poet's solemn moral responsibility—a concept implicit in all EBB's works—lies at the heart of *Aurora Leigh* and constitutes the heroine's constant goal and her ultimate achievement. The primary and perennial value of Art, according to Aurora, lies in its unique power to represent the ideal in the material so compellingly that the unique worth of every created thing is "fully recognised":

> Thus is Art
> Self-magnified in magnifying a truth
> Which, fully recognised, would change the world
> And shift its morals. If a man could feel,
> Not one day, in the artist's ecstasy,
> But every day, feast, fast, or working-day,
> The spiritual significance burn through
> The hieroglyphic of material shows,
> Henceforward he would paint the globe with wings,
> And reverence fish and fowl, the bull, the tree,
> And even his very body as a man—
> Which now he counts so vile, that all the towns
> Make offal of their daughters for its use,
> On summer-nights, when God is sad in heaven
> To think what goes on in His recreant world
> He made quite other. . . .
>
> (VII, 854–69)

But even Art, with all its power to illuminate the material world, is not the final goal or highest good. That preeminence belongs to Love which, transcending finite language and reason, can truly transform the world:

> Art itself
> We've called the larger life, must feel the soul
> Live past it. For more's felt than is perceived,
> And more's perceived than can be interpreted,
> And Love strikes higher with his lambent flame
> Than Art can pile the faggots.
>
> (VII, 889–94)

The first book of *Aurora Leigh* has been included here because, as a portrait of the artist as a young woman, it describes the shaping influences on the creative imagination and portends the mature poet's integrating of art and life. Clearly, Aurora Leigh's burgeoning consciousness of her poetic vocation reflects EBB's own experience: the frustration at the constricted "genteel" education, offset by exposure to the benevolent influence of nature and by solitary adventuring into books and ideas. The natural way Aurora takes her place in the traditional line of serious poets—un-self-consciously comparing herself, in precocity, to Pope and Byron and making no allowances for her writing efforts on grounds of her sex—reflects the youthful EBB's idea of herself as a born poet. The first book also demonstrates in brief the range of styles and techniques EBB employs in succeeding books of *Aurora Leigh*: dramatic passages, like those describing Aurora's departure from Italy; lyrical sections, like her rhapsodies over English fields and hills; satirical touches, like those that assess the gentlewoman's "education." This book also presents a potent symbol: corollary to Aurora's growing sense of herself as a poet is her growing sense of what it is to be a woman, a consciousness of female identity first aroused by the portrait of her dead mother. The portrait that so fascinates the child Aurora is an icon of Woman in all her mythical, culturally imposed aspects—Muse, Fate, angel, witch—a portrait that the mature Aurora will replace with a more realistic image after encountering authentic womanhood and motherhood, individualized in the character of Marian Erle.

The central message of *Aurora Leigh*—that art cannot exist apart from life and love—reminds us that, for all its unconventionality of form and treatment, this poem represents more a shift of emphasis than a new departure in EBB's work. Consistent from first to last in her poetry is the conviction that the poet's function is essentially religious. This concept, sometimes more, sometimes less obvious at different stages of her career, is essentially a Romantic fusion of Platonic and Christian ideals, affirming ultimate redemption through human and divine love. It underlies all her depictions of evil, metaphoric and literal. In portraying the causes and effects of evil, whether through the biblical view of sin in "The Seraphim" and "A Drama of Exile," the psychological temptations and doubts in "The Romaunt of Margret," the social prejudices of "Lady Geraldine's Courtship," or the political injustices in *Casa Guidi Windows*, EBB's moral stance is rooted in religious values. Even her poems on relations between the sexes, like "Sonnets from the Portuguese" and *Aurora Leigh*, achieve a resolution based ultimately on the Christian concept of redemption. Understanding the persistence and depth of EBB's conviction that the artist is by definition a moral teacher and guide helps us to grasp the apparent paradox of her defiant feminism flourishing within a framework of religious conservatism. Oppression in any form—of slaves, of the poor, of factory workers, of women—and the pride and prejudice behind such oppression must be attacked uncompromisingly, but with the Christian armor of righteous indignation, optimism, and love. The conclusion of *Aurora Leigh*, in which Romney comes to understand the true meaning of "reform"—that the renewal of the world will come through, but not alone by, the work of men and women—is rendered in explicitly religious terms:

> "It is the hour for souls,
> That bodies, leavened by the will and love,
> Be lightened to redemption. The world's old,
> But the old world waits the time to be renewed,
> Toward which, new hearts in individual growth
> Must quicken, and increase to multitude
> In new dynasties of the race of men;
> Developed whence, shall grow spontaneously
> New churches, new œconomies, new laws
> Admitting freedom, new societies
> Excluding falsehood: HE shall make all new."
>   (IX, 939–49)

In the light of her preeminently moral stance, it is easy to see why a note of exasperation creeps into EBB's responses (as in the letter included here to Mrs. Martin) to readers who professed to being "offended" by the frankness of passages in *Aurora Leigh*. Another kind of criticism lodged against her work is more likely to concern today's readers: the charge of technical and aesthetic lapses. To accusations that she was careless with rhyme and meter, EBB responded that she broke the rules deliberately—"in cold blood," as she said—and certainly evidence in such works as the neo-classic *Battle of Marathon* proves that she was quite capable of observing the proprieties of meter and rhyme. She told R. H. Horne, who objected to her near-rhymes in the 1844 volume (like "Hellas" with "tell us" and "islands" with "silence"), that she was determined to experiment with variations in sound patterns, and the paucity of true double rhymes in the language required the use of near-rhymes. To John Kenyon, who complained about the "roughness" of meter in "Lady Geraldine's Courtship," she replied that it was intentional, a way of "playing at ball with the pause." Clearly, she felt entitled to be as unconventional in her techniques as she was in her themes; what is less clear is that she worked to make the irregularities functional as, for instance, Emily Dickinson did. Nevertheless, within the relative freedom of blank verse, EBB put to good use her penchant for the irregular foot and unexpected phrase to convey something of her heroine's spontaneity and ardor. The wondrous intricacies hidden in nature's forms, for example, are suggested by Aurora's paraphrase of a fellow-poet (Robert Browning in *Pippa Passes*), lines in which extra syllables suddenly vary the pattern:

> "There's nothing great
> Nor small," has said a poet of our day,
> Whose voice will ring beyond the curfew of eve
> And not be thrown out by the matin's bell:
> And truly, I reiterate, nothing's small!
> No lily-muffled hum of a summer-bee,
> But finds some coupling with the spinning stars;
> No pebble at your foot, but proves a sphere;
> No chaffinch, but implies the cherubim;
> And (glancing on my own thin, veinèd wrist)
> In such a little tremor of the blood
> The whole strong clamour of a vehement soul
> Doth utter itself distinct. Earth's crammed with heaven,
> And every common bush afire with God;
> But only he who sees, takes off his shoes—
> The rest sit round it and pluck blackberries,
> And daub their natural faces unaware
> More and more from the first similitude.
>   (VII, 809–26)

For the most part, we are carried along in *Aurora Leigh*, through the occasional strained analogy and improbable incident, by the sheer velocity of EBB's narrative and the force of her bold imagery and emphatic opinions. Filtering everything in the poem through the heroine's vivid imagination gave EBB the framework she had been seeking, ever since "Lady Geraldine's Courtship," for freely mingling subjective and objective modes of expression—the dramatic scene, the lyrical outpouring, the critical commentary. A passage will often exhibit a dramatic immediacy and a retrospective cast at one and the same time:

> Then at last
> I do remember clearly how there came
> A stranger with authority, not right
> (I thought not), who commanded, caught me up
> From old Assunta's neck; how, with a shriek,
> She let me go,—while I, with ears too full
> Of my father's silence to shriek back a word,
> In all a child's astonishment at grief
> Stared at the wharf-edge where she stood and moaned,

My poor Assunta, where she stood and moaned!
The white walls, the blue hills, my Italy,
Drawn backward from the shuddering steamer-deck,
Like one in anger drawing back her skirts
Which suppliants catch at. Then the bitter sea
Inexorably pushed between us both
And, sweeping up the ship with my despair,
Threw us out as a pasture to the stars.

(I, 222-38)

Whatever the final critical verdict on *Aurora Leigh*, the poem's emotional force is beyond dispute. EBB herself always held that the hallmark of a "true poet" was not technical proficiency but depth of feeling and seriousness of purpose; by these criteria she was justified in calling *Aurora Leigh* her "most mature" work. The poem projects, through the consciousness of its protagonist, EBB's supreme confidence in the significance of her poetic task and in her ability to carry out that task. The self-assurance she felt and projects onto her alter ego Aurora—an assurance that rises to a note of triumph at the poem's end—seems to reflect the extraordinary equilibrium she was experiencing between her public and private lives in the years of *Aurora Leigh*'s composition. Not only did she enjoy widespread acceptance as a poet-prophet, but she knew deep satisfaction in the personal relationships most important to her—with husband, child, sisters, friends. Especially satisfying to her was the emergence of Robert Browning's poetic reputation, at long last, with publication in 1855 of *Men and Women* (a volume dedicated to EBB). In short, what EBB envisioned as an ideal future for her heroine at the close of *Aurora Leigh*—autonomy as a woman and an artist, emotional fulfilment in an equal partnership—was for her a reality. She had indeed reached her lifelong goal of integration—of subjective and objective, Art and Life—and *Aurora Leigh* was public testimony to that achievement. No wonder that in an age of the "divided mind," marked by poets' ambivalence about whether to indulge romantic sensibilities or assume vatic responsibilities, Elizabeth Barrett Browning's confident voice rang out so distinctly. And no wonder that in our own age, when the task of integrating art and life, public and private domains, seems more urgent than ever, her voice resounds so compellingly.

Elizabeth Barrett Browning

CHRONOLOGY

1806	Born 6 March at Coxhoe Hall near Durham, eldest of eleven surviving children of Edward Moulton-Barrett and Mary Graham-Clarke
1809–10	Family moved to palatial estate of Hope End in Herefordshire
1815	October–November, visited France
1817–18	Wrote *The Battle of Marathon* which was privately printed in 1820
1821	Published two poems in *New Monthly Magazine* on the loss of freedom in Greece. First signs of lifelong disease of the lungs
1823–24	Spent seven months with her family in Boulogne
1826	Published *An Essay on Mind, with Other Poems*; began study of Greek under tutelage of the blind scholar Hugh Stuart Boyd
1828	Mother died
1832	Hope End sold because of financial difficulties; family moved to Sidmouth
1833	Published translation of *Prometheus Bound*
1835	Moved with family to Gloucester Place, London
1837	Contributed to *Findens' Tableaux*, edited by her friend Mary Russell Mitford
1838	Moved to 50 Wimpole Street. Published *The Seraphim, and Other Poems* to favorable notice. In September went to Torquay to recuperate from a lung hemorrhage
1840	Suffered a near-fatal illness after her eldest brother ("Bro") drowned in a sailing accident in Tor Bay
1841	Acquired the spaniel Flush; September, returned to Wimpole Street
1842	Wrote critical series on the Greek Christian poets and the English poets for the *Athenaeum*
1843	Collaborated with R. H. Horne on *A New Spirit of the Age*
1844	Published *Poems*
1845	January, began correspondence with Robert Browning; May, began receiving him
1846	12 September, married Robert Browning, moved to Italy
1847	April, moved to Florence from Pisa
1848	Settled in Casa Guidi as permanent residence

1849	9 March, gave birth to son, Robert Wiedemann Barrett Browning ("Pen")
1850	Published *Poems*
1851	May, to London via Venice and Paris; published *Casa Guidi Windows*; September, to Paris
1852	Winter and spring in Paris; July–October, London; October, to Florence
1853	November, to Rome
1854	May, returned to Florence
1856	June, to London; October, returned to Florence
1857	*Aurora Leigh* published. April, father died.
1858	July, to Paris; October, returned to Florence; November, to Rome
1859	May, returned to Florence
1860	Published *Poems Before Congress*
1861	Returned from Rome to Casa Guidi 5 June; died 29 June; buried 1 July in Protestant Cemetery, Florence
1862	*Last Poems* posthumously published

JUVENILIA

ON HEARING CATALANI SING, AND BEING TOLD HER STORY[1]

Here Catalani[2] in a convent lies,
Virtuous, beauteous, good and wise,
Her parents thought that there she had better stay,
They can't support her any other way.
The night before she took the Veil,
She did in tears and beauty wail. —
An English singer heard her voice
And felt 't would make the World rejoice;
He to her Father went to beg and pray
That she with him a month might stay.   10
Cheered with bright Hope, her genius rose,
In tones sublime, her talent glows —
Proud monarchs listen to her strain
And on her, treasures shower like rain;
She to Newcastle came to sing,
The playhouse with her Voice did ring —
O! sweet inspirer of my lay
I could not too much of thy genius say,
For when you raise your warbling throat,
The Nightingale is humbled by your note.   20

[Composed 1814]

HUPS, I

THE BATTLE OF MARATHON[3]
1820

Preface

That Poetry is the first, and most celebrated of all the fine arts, has not been denied in any age, or by any philosopher. The culture of the soul, which Sallust[4] so nobly describes, is necessary to those refined pleasures, and elegant enjoyments, in which man displays his superiority to brutes. It is alone the elevation of the soul, not the form of the body, which constitutes the proud distinction; according to the learned historian, "Alterum nobis cum diis, alterum cum belluis commune est."[5] The noblest of the productions of man, that which inspires the enthusiasm of virtue, the energy of truth, is Poetry: Poetry elevates the mind to Heaven, kindles within it unwonted fires, and bids it throb with feelings exalting to its nature.

This humble attempt may by some be unfortunately attributed to vanity, to an affectation of talent, or to the still more absurd desire of being thought a *genius*. With the humility and deference due to their judgments, I wish to plead not guilty to their accusations, and, with submission, to offer these pages to the perusal of the few kind and partial friends who may condescend to read them, assured that their criticism will be tempered with mercy.

Happily it is not now, as it was in the days of Pope,[6] who was so early in actual danger of thinking himself "the greatest genius of the age." Now, even the female may drive her Pegasus through the realms of Parnassus,[7] without being saluted with the most equivocal of all appellations, a learned lady; without being celebrated by her friends as a Sappho,[8] or traduced by her enemies as a pedant; without being abused in the Review, or criticised in society; how justly then may a child hope to pass unheeded!

In these reading days there need be little vulgar anxiety among Poets for the fate of their works: the public taste is no longer so epicurean. As the press pours forth profusion, the literary multitude eagerly receive its lavish offerings, while the sublimity of Homer, and the majesty of Virgil, those grand and solitary specimens of ancient poetic excellence, so renowned through the lapse of ages, are by many read only as school books, and are justly estimated alone by the comparative few, whose hearts can be touched by the grandeur of their sentiments, or exalted by their kindred fire; by them this dereliction must be felt, but they can do no more than mourn over this semblance of decline in literary judgment and poetic taste. Yet, in contemplating the Poets of our own times—(for there are real Poets, though they be mingled with an inferior multitude of the common herd)—who, unsophisticated by prejudice, can peruse those inspired pages emitted from the soul of Byron,[9] or who can be dazzled by the gems sparkling from the rich mine of the imagination of Moore,[10] or captivated by scenes glowing in the descriptive powers of Scott,[11] without a proud consciousness that our day may boast the exuberance of true poetic genius? And if criticism be somewhat too general in its suffrage, may it not be attributed to an overwhelming abundance of contemporary Authors, which induces it to err in discrimination, and may cause its praises to be frequently ill-merited, and its censures ill-deserved; as the eye, wandering over a garden where flowers are mingled with weeds, harassed by exertion and dimmed by the brilliancy of colors, frequently mistakes the flower for the weed, and the weed for the flower.

It is worthy of remark, that when Poetry first burst from the mists of ignorance—when first she shone a bright star illumining the then narrow understanding of the Greeks—from that period when Homer, the sublime Poet of antiquity, awoke the first notes of poetic inspiration to the praise of valor, honor, patriotism, and, best of all, to a sense of the high attributes of the Deity, though darkly and mysteriously revealed; then it was, and not till then, that the seed of every virtue, of every great quality, which had so long lain dormant in the souls of the Greeks, burst into the germ; as when the sun disperses the mist cowering o'er the face of the Heavens, illumines with his resplendent rays the whole creation, and speaks to the verdant beauties of nature, joy, peace, and gladness. Then it was that Greece began to give those immortal examples of exalted feeling, and of patriotic virtue, which have since astonished the world; then it was that the unenlightened soul of the savage rose above the degradation which assimilated him to the brute creation, and discovered the first rays of social independence, and of limited freedom; not the freedom of barbarism, but that of a state enlightened by a wise jurisdiction, and restrained by civil laws. From that period man seems to have first proved his resemblance to his Creator, and his superiority to brutes, and the birth of Poetry was that of all the kindred arts; in the words of Cicero, "Quò minus ergo honoris erat poëtis eò minora studia fuerunt."[12]

*   *   *   *   *

He who writes an epic poem must transport himself to the scene of action; he must imagine himself possessed of the same opinions, manners, prejudices, and belief; he must suppose himself to be the hero he delineates, or his picture can no longer be nature, and what is not natural cannot please. It would be considered ridiculous in the historian or poet describing the ancient manners of Greece, to address himself to that Omnipotent Being who first called the world out of chaos, nor would it be considered less so if he were to be silent upon the whole subject; for in all nations, in all ages, religion must be the spur of every noble action, and the characteristic of every lofty soul.

Perhaps I have chosen the rhymes of Pope, and departed from the noble simplicity of the Miltonic verse, injudiciously. The immortal Poet of England,[13] in his apology for the verse of *Paradise Lost*, declares "rhymes to be, to all judicious ears, trivial, and of no true musical delight." In my opinion, humble as it is, the custom of rhyming would ere now have been abolished amongst Poets, had not Pope, the disciple of the immortal Dryden,[14] awakened the lyre to music, and proved that rhyme could equal blank verse in simplicity and gracefulness, and vie with it in elegance of composition, and in sonorous melody. No one who has read his translation of Homer, can refuse him the immortality which he merits so well, and for which he laboured so long. He it was who planted rhyme for ever in the regions of Parnassus, and uniting elegance with strength, and sublimity with beauty, raised the English language to the highest excellence of smoothness and purity.

I confess that I have chosen Homer for a model, and perhaps I have attempted to imitate his style too often and too closely; and yet some imitation is authorized by poets immortalized in the annals of Parnassus, whose memory will be revered as long as man has a soul to appreciate their merits. Virgil's magnificent description of the storm in the first book of the *Aeneid*, is almost literally translated from Homer, where Ulysses, quitting the Isle of Calypso for "Phaeacia's dusty shore," is overwhelmed by Neptune. That sublime picture, "Ponto nox incubat atra,"[15] and the beautiful apostrophe, "Oh terque quaterque beati,"[16] is a literal translation of the same incident in Homer. There are many other imitations, which it would be unnecessary and tedious here to enumerate. Even Milton, the pride and glory of English taste, has not disdained to replenish his imagination from the abundant fountains of the first and greatest of poets. It would have been both absurd and presumptuous, young and inexperienced as I am, to have attempted to strike out a path for myself, and to have wandered among the varied windings of Parnassus, without a guide to direct my steps, or to warn me from those fatal quicksands of literary blunders, in which, even with the best guide, I find myself so frequently immersed. There is no humility, but rather folly, in taking inferiority for a model, and there is no vanity, but rather wisdom, in following humbly the footsteps of perfection; for who would prefer quenching his thirst at the stagnant pool, when he may drink the pure waters of the fountain head? Thus, then, however unworthily, I have presumed to select, from all the poets of ancient or modern ages, Homer, the most perfect of the votaries of Apollo, whom every nation has contributed to immortalize, to celebrate, and to admire.

*   *   *   *   *

THE BATTLE OF MARATHON

Book I

The war of Greece with Persia's haughty King,[17]
No vulgar strain, eternal Goddess,[18] sing!
What dreary ghosts to glutted Pluto fled,
What nations suffered, and what heroes bled:
Sing Asia's powerful Prince, who envious saw
The fame of Athens, and her might in war;
And scorns her power, at Cytherea's[19] call
Her ruin plans, and meditates her fall;
How Athens, blinded to the approaching chains
By Vulcan's artful spouse,[20] unmoved remains;   10
Deceived by Venus thus, unconquered Greece
Forgot her glories in the lap of peace;
While Asia's realms, and Asia's lord prepare
T' ensnare her freedom, by the wiles of war:
Hippias[21] t' exalt upon th' Athenian throne,
Where once Pisistratus his father shone.
For yet her son Aeneas' wrongs impart
Revenge and grief to Cytherea's heart;
And still from smoking Troy's once sacred wall,
Does Priam's reeking shade [22] for vengeance call.   20
Minerva[23] saw, and Paphia's Queen defied,
A boon she begged, nor Jove the boon denied;
That Greece should rise, triumphant o'er her foe,
Disarm th' invaders, and their power o'erthrow.
Her prayer obtained, the blue-eyed Goddess flies
As the fierce eagle, thro' the radiant skies.
To Aristides[24] then she stood confessed,
Shews Persia's arts, and fires his warlike breast:
Then pours celestial ardour o'er his frame
And points the way to glory and to fame.   30
Awe struck the Chief, and swells his troubled soul,
In pride and wonder thoughts progressive roll.
He inly groaned and smote his labouring breast,
At once by Pallas, and by care opprest.
Inspired he moved, earth echoed where he trod,
All full of Heaven, all burning with the God.
Th' Athenians viewed with awe the mighty man,
To whom the Chief impassioned thus began:
"Hear, all ye Sons of Greece! Friends, Fathers, hear!

The Gods command it, and the Gods revere!   40
No madness mine, for mark, oh favoured Greeks!
That by my mouth the martial Goddess speaks!
This know, Athenians, that proud Persia now
Prepares to twine thy laurels on her brow;
Behold her princely Chiefs their weapons wield
By Venus fired, and shake the brazen shield.
I hear their shouts that echo to the skies,
I see their lances blaze, their banners rise,
I hear the clash of arms, the battle's roar,
And all the din and thunder of the war!   50
I know that Greeks shall purchase just renown,
And fame impartial, shall Athena crown.
Then Greeks, prepare your arms! award the yoke,
Thus Jove commands"—sublime the hero spoke;
The Greeks assent with shouts, and rend the skies
With martial clamour, and tumultuous cries.
So struggling winds with rage indignant sweep
The azure waters of the silent deep,
Sudden the seas rebellowing, frightful rise,
And dash their foaming surges to the skies;   60
Burst the firm sand, and boil with dreadful roar,
Lift their black waves, and combat with the shore.
So each brave Greek in thought aspires to fame,
Stung by his words, and dread of future shame;
Glory's own fires within their bosom rise
And shouts tumultuous thunder to the skies.

                    *   *   *   *   *

                        Book IV

The Persians spread the sail, nor dare delay,
And suppliant call upon the King of day,
But vainly to their Gods the cowards pray.
Some of the ships th' Athenian warriors stay
And fire their bulks; the flames destroying rise,
Rushing they swell, and mount into the skies.
Foremost Cynoegirus[25] with might divine,
While midst the waves his arms majestic shine;
With blood-stained hand a Persian ship he seized,
The vessel vainly strove to be released;   1440
With fear the crew the godlike man beheld,

And pride and shame their troubled bosoms swelled.
They lop his limb; then Pallas fires his frame
With scorn of death, and hope of future fame:
Then with the hand remaining seized the prize,
A glorious spirit kindling in his eyes.
Again the Persians wield the unmanly blow
And wreck their vengeance on a single foe.
The fainting Greek by loss of blood opprest
Still feels the patriot rise within his breast.   1450
Within his teeth the shattered ship he held,
Nor in his soul one wish for life rebelled.
But strength decaying, fate supprest his breath,
And o'er his brows expand the dews of death.
The Elysium plains[26] his generous spirit trod,
"He lived a Hero and he died a God."
By vengeance fired, the Grecians from the deep
With rage and shouting, scale the lofty ship,
Then in the briny bosom of the main
They hurl in heaps the living and the slain.   1460
Thro' the wide shores resound triumphant cries,
Fill all the seas, and thunder thro' the skies.

[A DAY AT HOPE END][27]

Ye Muses warbling in melodious spells
Near resting Helicons[28] immortal wells
And bending graceful o'er the sacred spring
Rouse all your powers and aid me as I sing
And thou Apollo patron of lost wits
The glaring sun and rise of verse by fits
But when that sun! alas thy votaries mourn
And call in vain deserted and forlorn
Their dull thoughts stop for want of custommed fire
And critics rage & talk in endless ire   10
In vain they call & critics rage about
Thou seldom reigns within scarce e'er without
Be merciful for once — for once agree
To lend thy succour and to pity *me*!
First e're the gentle moon desert her sway
Ere rosy morning blushes into day
Pillowed with pillows snug in bed reclined

With Nodkin wisdom I refresh my mind
Then swift Time in open daylight flies
I read a page from scripture ere I rise   20
Till the loud clock seven—fatal number tolls
And strikes all terror on our fainting souls
We rise and dress then thank the almighty power
For all his mercies and our God adore
In haste we fly to school and half asleep
On tiptoe up the creaking staircase creep
Arrived—one instinct all our souls inspire
At once we crowd around the ready fire
Till at the door we hear the fatal tread
And fancy sees the ruler near our head   30
Quick to our seats we run while open flies
The door! and Mr —[29] stands before our eyes
What we have learnt we say—the clock strikes nine
And all our thoughts to breakfast straight incline
Down stairs we clamourous rush to break our fast
On lasting bread & milk—no "rich repast"
To school again till twelve then glad we run
To seek the glories of a midday sun
Till dinner—then immerging from the air
At home again, to dine, we then repair—   40
Roast mutton smoking on the board we view
In a cracked dish theres mashed potatoes too
O'er joyed and hungry to our seats we haste
And bless the cook who served the rich "repast"
And then we guess what pudding shall arrive
Some hope tis tart & on that hope they live.
One says "Its bad I know"—another "nice"
One bread—one suet—lo! it comes—'tis rice!
Oh fatal pudding! At that hated sound
Fierce Discord spreads her jealous wings around   50
On every side despair & murmurs rise
And Nursery Hall resounds repeated cries
Not half such grief in Hectors[30] bosom sprung
When Troy in ruins jaws tremendous hung
Not half such cries nor such resounding ire
The Trojans uttered with their towers on fire
But midst such horrid woes to mortals due
Time does not flag the fatal clock strikes two
To school till five!—& then again we fly
To play & joy & mirth & pleasures ply   60

Some dance, some fight, some laugh, some play—
   some squall,
And the loud organs thunder circles all
And then at tea we snatch a short repast
As long as one large plate of toast doth last
At nine fatigued upon the grateful bed
We stretch our weary limbs & rest our head
A gentle night succeeds & silent peace
Infolds our bodies in the sweets of ease
So pass our days so pass our happy hours
Our time may well be said to glide in flowers.   70

(*LBGB*) 1958

AN ESSAY ON MIND, WITH OTHER POEMS[31]
1826

"Brama assai, poco spera, e nulla chiede."
    —Tasso

Preface

In offering this little Volume to the world, it is not my intention to trespass long on its indulgence, "with prefaces, and passages, and excusations."[32] As, however, preface-writing strangely reminds one of Bottom's prologuizing device,[33] which so ingeniously sheweth the 'disfiguration of moonshine,' and how lion was no lion after all, but plain "Snug the joiner," I will treat the subject according to my great prototype; declaring to those readers who "cannot abide lions," that their "parlous fear" is here unnecessary, and assuring the public that 'moonshine' shall be introduced as seldom as is consistent with modern composition.

But something more is necessary; and since writers commonly make use of their prefaces as opportunities for auricular confession to the absolving reader, I am prepared to acknowledge, with unfeigned humility, that the imputation of presumption is likely to be attached to me, on account of the form and title of this production. And yet, to imagine that a confidence in our powers is undeviatingly shewn by our selection of an extensive field for their exertion, is an error; for the subject supports the writer, as much as it is supported by him. It is not difficult to draw a succession of affecting images from objects intrinsically affecting; and ideas arising from an elevated subject are naturally elevated. As Tacitus hath it, "materiâ aluntur."[34] Thought catches the light reflected from the object of her contemplation, and, "expanded by

the genius of the spot," loses much of her material grossness; unless in-
deed, like Thales,[35] she fall into the water while looking at the stars.

"Ethical poetry," says that immortal writer[36] we have lost, "is the
highest of all poetry, as the highest of all earthly objects must be moral
truth." I am nevertheless aware how often it has been asserted that
poetry is not a proper vehicle for abstract ideas—how far the assertion
may be correct, is with me a matter of doubt. We do not deem the im-
aginative incompatible with the philosophic, for the name of Bacon[37] is
on our lips; then why should we expel the argumentative from the
limits of the poetic? If indeed we consider Poetry as Plato considered
her, when he banished her from his republic;[38] or as Newton, when he
termed her "a kind of ingenious nonsense;" or as Locke, when he pro-
nounced that "gaming and poetry went usually together;" or as Boileau,
when he boasted of being acquainted with two arts equally useful to
mankind—"writing verses, and playing at skittles,"—we shall find no
difficulty in assenting to this opinion.[39] But while we behold in poetry,
the inspiritings to political feeling, the "monumentum aere peren-
nius"[40] of buried nations, we are loth to believe her unequal to the
higher walks of intellect: when we behold the works of the great though
erring Lucretius,[41] the sublime Dante, the reasoning Pope—when we
hear Quintillian acknowledge the submission due from Philosophers to
Poets, and Gibbon[42] declare Homer to be "the law-giver, the
theologian, the historian, and the philosopher of the ancients," we are
unable to believe it. Poetry is the enthusiasm of the understanding; and,
as Milton finely expresses it, there is "a high reason in her fancies."[43]

*   *   *   *   *

Poetry is treated in as cursory a manner as Philosophy, though not
precisely for the same reasons. I have been deterred from a further
development of her nature and principles, by observing that no single
subject has employed the didactic pen with such frequent success, and
by a consequent unwillingness to incur a charge of tediousness, when
repeating what is well known, or one of presumption, when intruding
new-fangled maxims in the place of those deservedly established. The
act of white-washing an ancient Gothic edifice would be less indicative
of bad taste than the latter attempt. Since the time of Horace,[44] many
excellent didactic writers have formed poetic systems from detached
passages of that unsystematic work, his 'Ars Poetica.' Pope, and Boileau,
in their Essays on Poetry and Criticism, have with superior method
traced his footsteps. And yet, "haud passibus aequis"[45]—it is only
justice to observe, that though the poem has been excelled, the Poet re-
mains unequalled. For the merits of his imitators are, except in arrange-
ment, Horace's merits, while the merits of Horace are his own.[46]

I wish that the sublime circuit of intellect, embraced by the plan of my Poem, had fallen to the lot of a spirit more powerful than mine. I wish it had fallen to the lot of one familiar with the dwelling-place of Mind, who could search her secret chambers, and call forth those that sleep; or of one who could enter into her temples, and cast out the iniquitous who buy and sell, profaning the sanctuary of God; or of one who could try the golden links of that chain[47] which hangs from Heaven to earth, and shew that it is not placed there for man to covet for lucre's sake, or for him to weigh his puny strength at one end against Omnipotence at the other; but that it is placed there to join, in mysterious union, the natural and the spiritual, the mortal and the eternal, the creature and the Creator. I wish the subject of my Poem had fallen into such hands, that the powers of the execution might have equalled the vastness of the design—and the Public will wish so too. But as it is—though I desire this field to be more meritoriously occupied by others—I would mitigate the voice of censure for myself. I would endeavour to shew, that while I may have often erred, I have not clung willingly to error; and that while I may have failed in representing, I have never ceased to love Truth. If there be much to condemn in the following pages, let my narrow capacity, as opposed to the infinite object it would embrace, be generously considered; if there be any thing to approve, I am ready to acknowledge the assistance which my illustrations have received from the exalting nature of their subject—as the waters of Halys[48] acquire a peculiar taste from the soil over which they flow.

AN ESSAY ON MIND

"My narrow leaves cannot in them contayne
The large discourse."—Spenser[49]

Book I[50]

Since Spirit first inspir'd, pervaded all,
And Mind met Matter, at th' Eternal call—
Since dust weigh'd Genius down, or Genius gave
Th' immortal halo to the mortal's grave;
Th' ambitious soul her essence hath defin'd,
And Mind hath eulogiz'd the pow'rs of Mind.
Ere Revelation's holy light began
To strengthen Nature, and illumine Man—
When Genius, on Icarian pinions,[51] flew,
And Nature's pencil, Nature's portrait, drew;   10

When Reason shudder'd at her own wan beam,
And Hope turn'd pale beneath the sickly gleam—
Ev'n then hath Mind's triumphant influence spoke,
Dust own'd the spell, and Plato's spirit woke—
Spread her eternal wings, and rose sublime
Beyond th' expanse of circumstance and time:
Blinded, but free, with faith instinctive, soar'd,
And found her home, where prostrate saints ador'd!

Thou thing of light! that warm'st the breasts of men,
Breath'st from the lips, and tremblest from the pen!   20
Thou, form'd at once t' astonish, fire, beguile, —
With Bacon reason, and with Shakespeare smile!
The subtle cause, ethereal essence! say,
Why dust rules dust, and clay surpasses clay;
Why a like mass of atoms should combine
To form a Tully, and a Catiline?[52]
Or why, with flesh perchance of equal weight,
One cheers a prize-fight, and one frees a state?
Why do not I the muse of Homer call,
Or why, indeed, did Homer sing at all?   30
Why wrote not Blackstone[53] upon love's delusion,
Or Moore, a libel on the Constitution?
Why must the faithful page refuse to tell
That Dante, Laura sang, and Petrarch, Hell—
That Tom Paine argued in the throne's defence—
That Byron nonsense wrote, and Thurlow sense—
That Southey sigh'd with all a patriot's cares,
While Locke gave utterance to Hexameters?
Thou thing of light! instruct my pen to find
Th' unequal pow'rs, the various forms of Mind!   40

O'er Nature's changeful face direct your sight;
View light meet shade, and shade dissolve in light!
Mark, from the plain, the cloud-capp'd mountain soar;
The sullen ocean spurn the desert shore!
Behold, afar, the playmate of the storm,
Wild Niagara lifts his awful form—
Spits his black foam above the madd'ning floods,
Himself the savage of his native woods—
See him, in air, his smoking torrents wheel,
While the rocks totter, and the forests reel—   50
Then, giddy, turn! lo! Shakespeare's Avon flows,

Charm'd, by the green-sward's kiss, to soft repose;
With tranquil brow reflects the smile of fame,
And, 'midst her sedges, sighs her Poet's name.
Thus, in bright sunshine, and alternate storms,
Is various mind express'd in various forms.
In equal men, why burns not equal fire?
Why are not valleys hills,—or mountains higher?
Her destin'd way, hath destin'd Nature trod;
While Matter, Spirit rules, and Spirit, God.   60

*   *   *   *   *

Book II[54]

But now to higher themes! no more confin'd
To copy Nature, Mind returns to Mind.
We leave the throng, so nobly, and so well,
Tracing, in Wisdom's book, things visible,—
And turn to things unseen; where, greatly wrought,
Soul questions soul, and thought revolves on thought.
My spirit loves, my voice shall hail ye, now,
Sons of the patient eye, and passionless brow!
Students sublime! Earth, man, unmov'd, ye view,
Time, circumstance; for what are they to you?   610
What is the crash of worlds,—the fall of kings,—
When worlds and monarchs are such brittle things!
What the tost, shatter'd bark, that blindly dares
A sea of storm? Ye sketch the wave which bears!
The cause, and not th' effect, your thoughts exact;
The principle of action, not the act,—
The soul! the soul! and, 'midst so grand a task,
Ye call her rushing passions, and ye ask
Whence are ye? and each mystic thing responds!
I would be all *ye* are—except those bonds![55]   620
Except those bonds! ev'n here is oft descried
The love to parts, the poverty of pride!
Ev'n here, while Mind, in Mind's horizon, springs,
Her "native mud" is weighing on her wings!
Ev'n here, while Truth invites the ardent crowd,
Ixion-like,[56] they rush t' embrace a cloud!
Ev'n here, oh! foul reproach to human wit!
A Hobbes[57] hath reasoned, and Spinosa writ!

Rank pride does much! and yet we justly cry,
Our greatest errors in our weakness lie. 630
For thoughts uncloth'd by language are, at best,
Obscure; while grossness injures those exprest—
Through words,—in whose analysis, we find
Th' analogies of Matter, not of Mind:
Hence, when the use of words is graceful brought,
As physical dress to metaphysic thought,
The thought, howe'er sublime its pristine state,
Is by th' expression made degenerate;
Its spiritual essence changed, or cramp'd; and hence
Some hold by words, who cannot hold by sense; 640
And leave the thought behind, and take th' attire—
Elijah's mantle[58]—but without his fire!
Yet spurn not words! 'tis needful to confess
They give ideas, a body and a dress!
Behold them traverse Learning's region round,
The vehicles of thought on wheels of sound;
Mind's winged strength, wherewith the height is won,
Unless she trust their frailty to the sun.

*   *   *   *   *

The Seraphim,[1]
And Other Poems
1838

Preface[2]

The agents in this poem of imperfect form—a dramatic lyric, rather than a lyrical drama—are those mystic beings who are designated in Scripture the Seraphim. The subject has thus assumed a character of exaggerated difficulty, the full sense of which I have tried to express in my Epilogue. But my desire was, to gather some vision of the supreme spectacle under a less usual aspect,—to glance at it, as dilated in seraphic eyes, and darkened and deepened by the near association with blessedness and Heaven. Are we not too apt to measure the depth of the Saviour's humiliation from the common estate of man, instead of from His own peculiar and primaeval one? To avoid which error, I have endeavoured to count some steps of the ladder at Bethel,[3]—a very few steps, and as seen between the clouds.

And thus I have endeavoured to mark in my two Seraphic personages, distinctly and predominantly, that shrinking from, and repugnance to, evil, which in my weaker Seraph is expressed by *fear*, and in my stronger one by a more complex passion; in order to contrast with such, the voluntary debasement of Him who became lower than the angels, and touched in His own sinless being, sin and sorrow and death. In my attempted production of such a contrast, I have been true to at least my own idea of angelic excellence, as well as to that of His perfection. For one holiness differs from another holiness in glory. To recoil from evil, is according to the stature of an angel; to subdue it, is according to the infinitude of a God.

* * * * *

. . . For there is no greater fiction, than that poetry is fiction. Poetry is essentially truthfulness; and the very incoherences of poetic dreaming are but the struggle and the strife to reach the True in the Unknown.

* * * * *

Nothing more is left to me to explain in relation to any particular poem of this collection. I need not defend them for being religious in their general character. The generation of such as held the doctrine of that critic[4] who was *not* Longinus, and believed in the inadmissibility of religion into poetry, may have seen the end of vanity. That "contemplative piety, or the intercourse between God and the human soul, cannot be poetical," is true *if* it be true that the human soul having such intercourse is parted from its humanity, or *if* it be true that poetry is not expressive of that humanity's most exalted state. The first supposition is contradicted by man's own experience, and the latter by the testimony of Him who knoweth what is in man. For otherwise David's 'glory' would have awakened with no 'harp and lute;' and Isaiah's poetry of diction would have fallen in ashes from his lips, beneath the fire which cleansed them.

To any less reverent objection, I would not willingly reply. "An irreligious poet," said Burns,[5] meaning an undevotional one, "is a monster." An irreligious poet, he might have said, is no poet at all. The gravitation of poetry is upwards. The poetic wing, if it move, ascends. What did even the heathen Greeks—Homer, Aeschylus, Sophocles, Pindar? Sublimely, because born poets, darkly, because born of Adam and unrenewed in Christ, their spirits wandered like the rushing chariots and winged horses, black and white, of their brother-poet Plato,[6] through the universe of Deity, seeking if haply they might find Him: and as that universe closed around the seekers, not with the transparency in which it flowed first from His hand, but opaquely, as double-dyed with the transgression of its sons,—they felt though they could not discern the God beyond, and used the gesture though ignorant of the language of worshipping. The blind eagle missed the sun, but soared towards its sphere. Shall the blind eagle soar—and the seeing eagle peck chaff? Surely it should be the gladness and the gratitude of such as are poets among us, that in turning towards the beautiful, they may behold the true face of God.

                        *   *   *   *   *

I assume no power of art, except that power of love towards it, which has remained with me from my childhood until now. In the power of such a love, and in the event of my life being prolonged, I would fain hope to write hereafter better verses; but I never can feel more intensely than at this moment—nor can it be needful that any should—the sublime uses of poetry, and the solemn responsibilities of the poet.

THE ROMAUNT OF MARGRET[7]

"Can my affections find out nothing best,
But still and still remove?" — Quarles

I.

I plant a tree whose leaf
    The yew-tree leaf[8] will suit:
But when its shade is o'er you laid,
    Turn round and pluck the fruit.
Now reach my harp from off the wall
    Where shines the sun aslant;
The sun may shine and we be cold!
O hearken, loving hearts and bold,
    Unto my wild romaunt.
                Margret, Margret.   10

II.

Sitteth the fair ladye
    Close to the river side
Which runneth on with a merry tone
    Her merry thoughts to guide:
It runneth through the trees,
    It runneth by the hill,
Nathless the lady's thoughts have found
    A way more pleasant still.
                Margret, Margret.

III.

The night is in her hair   20
    And giveth shade to shade,
And the pale moonlight on her forehead white
    Like a spirit's hand is laid;
Her lips part with a smile
    Instead of speakings done:
I ween, she thinketh of a voice,
    Albeit uttering none.
                Margret, Margret.

IV.

All little birds do sit
          With heads beneath their wings: 30
Nature doth seem in a mystic dream,
          Absorbed from her living things:
That dream by that ladye
          Is certes⁹ unpartook,
For she looketh to the high cold stars
          With a tender human look.
                              Margret, Margret.

V.

The lady's shadow lies
          Upon the running river;
It lieth no less in its quietness,   40
          For that which resteth never:
Most like a trusting heart
          Upon a passing faith,
Or as upon the course of life
          The steadfast doom of death.
                              Margret, Margret.

VI.

The lady doth not move,
          The lady doth not dream,
Yet she seeth her shade no longer laid
          In rest upon the stream: 50
It shaketh without wind,
          It parteth from the tide,
It standeth upright in the cleft moonlight,
          It sitteth at her side.
                              Margret, Margret.

VII.

Look in its face, ladye,
          And keep thee from thy swound;
With a spirit bold thy pulses hold
          And hear its voice's sound:
For so will sound thy voice   60
          When thy face is to the wall,
And such will be thy face, ladye,
          When the maidens work thy pall.
                              Margret, Margret.

VIII.

"Am I not like to thee?"
The voice was calm and low,
And between each word you might have heard
The silent forests grow;
"The like may sway the like;"
By which mysterious law   70
Mine eyes from thine and my lips from thine
The light and breath may draw.
Margret, Margret.

IX.

"My lips do need thy breath,
My lips do need thy smile,
And my pallid eyne, that light in thine
Which met the stars erewhile:
Yet go with light and life
If that thou lovest one
In all the earth who loveth thee   80
As truly as the sun.
Margret, Margret."

X.

Her cheek had waxèd white
Like cloud at fall of snow;
Then like to one at set of sun,
It waxèd red alsò;
For love's name maketh bold
As if the loved were near:
And then she sighed the deep long sigh
Which cometh after fear.   90
Margret, Margret.

XI.

"Now, sooth, I fear thee not—
Shall never fear thee now!"
(And a noble sight was the sudden light
Which lit her lifted brow.)
"Can earth be dry of streams,
Or hearts of love?" she said;
"Who doubteth love, can know not love:
He is already dead."
Margret, Margret.   100

XII.

"I have" . . . and here her lips
    Some words in pause did keep,
And gave the while a quiet smile
    As if they paused in sleep,—
"I have . . . a brother dear,
    A knight of knightly fame!
I broidered him a knightly scarf
    With letters of my name
            Margret, Margret.

XIII.

"I fed his grey goshawk,   110
    I kissed his fierce bloodhoùnd,
I sate at home when he might come
    And caught his horn's far sound:
I sang him hunter's songs,
    I poured him the red wine,
He looked across the cup and said,
    I love thee, sister mine."
            Margret, Margret.

XIV.

IT trembled on the grass
    With a low, shadowy laughter;   120
The sounding river which rolled, for ever
    Stood dumb and stagnant after:
"Brave knight thy brother is!
    But better loveth he
Thy chaliced wine than thy chaunted song,
    And better both than thee,
            Margret, Margret."

XV.

The lady did not heed
    The river's silence while
Her own thoughts still ran at their will,   130
    And calm was still her smile.
"My little sister wears
    The look our mother wore:
I smooth her locks with a golden comb,
    I bless her evermore."
            Margret, Margret.

XVI.

"I gave her my first bird
        When first my voice it knew;
I made her share my posies rare
        And told her where they grew: 140
    I taught her God's dear name
        With prayer and praise to tell,
She looked from heaven into my face
        And said, *I love thee well.*"
                    Margret, Margret.

XVII.

IT trembled on the grass
        With a low, shadowy laughter;
You could see each bird as it woke and stared
        Through the shrivelled foliage after.
    "Fair child thy sister is!   150
        But better loveth she
Thy golden comb than thy gathered flowers,
        And better both than thee,
                    Margret, Margret."

XVIII.

The lady did not heed
        The withering on the bough;
Still calm her smile, albeit the while
        A little pale her brow:
    "I have a father old,
        The lord of ancient halls;   160
An hundred friends are in his court
        Yet only me he calls.
                    Margret, Margret.

XIX.

"An hundred knights are in his court
        Yet read I by his knee;
And when forth they go to the tourney-show[10]
        I rise not up to see:
    'Tis a weary book to read,
        My tryst's at set of sun,
But loving and dear beneath the stars   170
        Is his blessing when I've done."
                    Margret, Margret.

XX.

IT trembled on the grass
With a low, shadowy laughter;
And moon and stars though bright and far
Did shrink and darken after.
"High lord thy father is!
But better loveth he
His ancient halls than his hundred friends,
His ancient halls, than thee,   180
Margret, Margret."

XXI.

The lady did not heed
That the far stars did fail;
Still calm her smile, albeit the while . . .
Nay, but she is not pale!
"I have more than a friend
Across the mountains dim:
No other's voice is soft to me,
Unless it nameth *him*."
Margret, Margret.   190

XXII.

"Though louder beats my heart,
I know his tread again,
And his fair plume aye, unless turned away,
For the tears do blind me then:
We brake no gold, a sign
Of stronger faith to be,
But I wear his last look in my soul,
Which said, *I love but thee!*"
Margret, Margret.

XXIII.

IT trembled on the grass   200
With a low, shadowy laughter;
And the wind did toll, as a passing soul
Were sped by church-bell after;
And shadows, 'stead of light,
Fell from the stars above,
In flakes of darkness on her face
Still bright with trusting love.
Margret, Margret.

XXIV.

"He *loved* but only thee!
　　That love is transient too.
The wild hawk's bill doth dabble still
　　I' the mouth that vowed thee true:
Will he open his dull eyes
　　When tears fall on his brow?
Behold, the death-worm to his heart
　　Is a nearer thing than *thou*,
　　　　　　Margret, Margret."

XXV.

Her face was on the ground—
　　None saw the agony;
But the men at sea did that night agree
　　They heard a drowning cry:
And when the morning brake,
　　Fast rolled the river's tide,
With the green trees waving overhead
　　And a white corse laid beside.
　　　　　　Margret, Margret.

XXVI.

A knight's bloodhound and he
　　The funeral watch did keep;
With a thought o' the chase he stroked its face
　　As it howled to see him weep.
A fair child kissed the dead,
　　But shrank before its cold.
And alone yet proudly in his hall
　　Did stand a baron old.
　　　　　　Margret, Margret.

XXVII.

Hang up my harp again!
　　I have no voice for song.
Not song but wail, and mourners pale,
　　Not bards, to love belong.
O failing human love!
　　O light, by darkness known!
O false, the while thou treadest earth!
　　O deaf beneath the stone!
　　　　　　Margret, Margret.

A SEA-SIDE WALK[11]

I.

We walked beside the sea
After a day which perished silently
Of its own glory—like the princess weird
Who, combating the Genius, scorched and seared,
Uttered with burning breath, "Ho! victory!"
And sank adown, a heap of ashes pale:
        So runs the Arab tale.[12]

II.

The sky above us showed
A universal and unmoving cloud
On which the cliffs permitted us to see   10
Only the outline of their majesty,
As master-minds when gazed at by the crowd:
And shining with a gloom, the water grey
        Swang in its moon-taught way.

III.

Nor moon, nor stars were out;
They did not dare to tread so soon about,
Though trembling, in the footsteps of the sun:
The light was neither night's nor day's, but one
Which, life-like, had a beauty in its doubt,
And silence's impassioned breathings round   20
        Seemed wandering into sound.[13]

IV.

O solemn-beating heart
Of nature! I have knowledge that thou art
Bound unto man's by cords he cannot sever;
And, what time they are slackened by him ever,
So to attest his own supernal part,
Still runneth thy vibration fast and strong
        The slackened cord along:

V.

For though we never spoke
Of the grey water and the shaded rock,   30
Dark wave and stone unconsciously were fused
Into the plaintive speaking that we used

Of absent friends and memories unforsook;
And, had we seen each other's face, we had
    Seen haply each was sad.

THE DESERTED GARDEN[14]

I mind me in the days departed,
How often underneath the sun
With childish bounds I used to run
    To a garden long deserted.

The beds and walks were vanished quite;
And wheresoe'er had struck the spade,
The greenest grasses Nature laid
    To sanctify her right.

I called the place my wilderness,
For no one entered there but I;   10
The sheep looked in, the grass to espy,
    And passed it ne'ertheless.

The trees were interwoven wild,
And spread their boughs enough about
To keep both sheep and shepherd out,
    But not a happy child.

Adventurous joy it was for me!
I crept beneath the boughs, and found
A circle smooth of mossy ground
    Beneath a poplar tree.   20

Old garden rose-trees hedged it in,
Bedropt with roses waxen-white
Well satisfied with dew and light
    And careless to be seen.

Long years ago it might befall,
When all the garden flowers were trim,
The grave old gardener prided him
    On these the most of all.

Some lady, stately overmuch,
Here moving with a silken noise,   30
Has blushed beside them at the voice
    That likened her to such.

And these, to make a diadem,
She often may have plucked and twined,
Half-smiling as it came to mind
    That few would look at *them*.

Oh, little thought that lady proud,
A child would watch her fair white rose,
When buried lay her whiter brows,
    And silk was changed for shroud!   40

Nor thought that gardener, (full of scorns
For men unlearned and simple phrase,)
A child would bring it all its praise
    By creeping through the thorns!

To me upon my low moss seat,
Though never a dream the roses sent
Of science or love's compliment,
    I ween they smelt as sweet.

It did not move my grief to see
The trace of human step departed: 50
Because the garden was deserted,
    The blither place for me!

Friends, blame me not! a narrow ken
Has childhood 'twixt the sun and sward;
We draw the moral afterward,
    We feel the gladness then.

And gladdest hours for me did glide
In silence at the rose-tree wall:
A thrush made gladness musical
    Upon the other side.   60

Nor he nor I did e'er incline
To peck or pluck the blossoms white;
How should I know but roses might
    Lead lives as glad as mine?

To make my hermit-home complete,
I brought clear water from the spring
Praised in its own low murmuring,
    And cresses glossy wet.

And so, I thought, my likeness grew
(Without the melancholy tale)   70
To "gentle hermit of the dale,"[15]
    And Angelina too.

For oft I read within my nook
Such minstrel stories; till the breeze
Made sounds poetic in the trees,
    And then I shut the book.

If I shut this wherein I write
I hear no more the wind athwart
Those trees, nor feel that childish heart
    Delighting in delight.   80

My childhood from my life is parted,
My footstep from the moss which drew
Its fairy circle round: anew
    The garden is deserted.

Another thrush may there rehearse
The madrigals which sweetest are;
No more for me! myself afar
    Do sing a sadder verse.

Ah me, ah me! when erst I lay
In that child's-nest so greenly wrought,   90
I laughed unto myself and thought
    "The time will pass away."

And still I laughed, and did not fear
But that, whene'er was past away
The childish time, some happier play
    My womanhood would cheer.

I knew the time would pass away,
And yet, beside the rose-tree wall,
Dear God, how seldom, if at all,
    Did I look up to pray!   100

The time is past; and now that grows
The cypress high among the trees,
And I behold white sepulchres
    As well as the white rose,—

When graver, meeker thoughts are given,
And I have learnt to lift my face,
Reminded how earth's greenest place
    The colour draws from heaven,—

It something saith for earthly pain,
But more for Heavenly promise free,   110
That I who was, would shrink to be
    That happy child again.

Poems
1844[1]

"De patrie, et de Dieu, des poëtes, de l'âme
Qui s'élève en priant."[2] – Victor Hugo

DEDICATION

To My Father

When your eyes fall upon this page of dedication, and you start to see to whom it is inscribed, your first thought will be of the time far off when I was a child and wrote verses, and when I dedicated them to you who were my public and my critic. Of all that such a recollection implies of saddest and sweetest to both of us, it would become neither of us to speak before the world; nor would it be possible for us to speak of it to one another, with voices that did not falter. Enough, that what is in my heart when I write thus, will be fully known to yours.

And my desire is that you, who are a witness how if this art of poetry had been a less earnest object to me, it must have fallen from exhausted hands before this day,—that you, who have shared with me in things bitter and sweet, softening or enhancing them, every day,—that you, who hold with me, over all sense of loss and transiency, one hope by one Name,—may accept from me the inscription of these volumes, the exponents of a few years of an existence which has been sustained and comforted by you as well as given. Somewhat more faint-hearted than I used to be, it is my fancy thus to seem to return to a visible personal dependence on you, as if indeed I were a child again; to conjure your beloved image between myself and the public, so as to be sure of one smile,—and to satisfy my heart while I sanctify my ambition, by associating with the great pursuit of my life its tenderest and holiest affection.—Your

E. B. B.

London: 50 Wimpole Street,
1844

PREFACE

The collection here offered to the public consists of Poems which have been written in the interim between the period of the publication of my "Seraphim" and the present; variously coloured, or perhaps shadowed, by the life of which they are the natural expression,—and, with the exception of a few contributions to English or American periodicals, are printed now for the first time.

As the first poem of this collection, the "Drama of Exile," is the longest and most important work (to *me!*) which I ever trusted into the current of publication, I may be pardoned for entreating the reader's attention to the fact, that I decided on publishing it after considerable hesitation and doubt. The subject of the Drama rather fastened on me than was chosen; and the form, approaching the model of the Greek tragedy, shaped itself under my hand, rather by force of pleasure than of design. But when the excitement of composition had subsided, I felt afraid of my position. My subject was the new and strange experience of the fallen humanity, as it went forth from Paradise into the wilderness; with a peculiar reference to Eve's alloted grief, which, considering that self-sacrifice belonged to her womanhood, and the consciousness of originating the Fall to her offence,—appeared to me imperfectly apprehended hitherto, and more expressible by a woman than a man.

*   *   *   *   *

. . . When the old mysteries represented the Holiest Being in a rude familiar fashion, and the people gazed on, with the faith of children in their earnest eyes, the critics of a succeeding age, who rejoiced in Congreve,[3] cried out "Profane." Yet Andreini's[4] mystery suggested Milton's epic; and Milton, the most reverent of poets, doubting whether to throw his work into the epic form or the dramatic, left, on the latter basis, a rough ground-plan, in which his intention of introducing the "Heavenly Love" among the persons of his drama is extant to the present day. But the tendency of the present day is to sunder the daily life from the spiritual creed,—to separate the worshipping from the acting man,—and by no means to "live by faith." There is a feeling abroad which appears to me (I say it with deference) nearer to superstition than to religion, that there should be no touching of holy vessels except by consecrated fingers, nor any naming of holy names except in consecrated places. As if life were not a continual sacrament to man, since Christ brake the daily bread of it in His hands! As if the name of God did not build a church, by the very naming of it! As if the word God were not, everywhere in His creation, and at every moment in His eternity, an appropriate word! As if it could be uttered unfitly, if devoutly! I appeal on these points, which I will not argue, from the conventions of the Christian to his devout heart; and I beseech him generously to believe of me that I have done that in reverence from which, through reverence, he might have abstained; and that where he might have been driven to silence by the principle of adoration, I, by the very same principle, have been hurried into speech.

*   *   *   *   *

The next longest poem to the "Drama of Exile," in the collection, is the "Vision of Poets," in which I have endeavoured to indicate the necessary relations of genius to suffering and self-sacrifice. In the eyes of the living generation, the poet is at once a richer and poorer man than he used to be; he wears better broadcloth, but speaks no more oracles: and the evil of this social incrustation over a great idea is eating deeper and more fatally into our literature than either readers or writers may apprehend fully. I have attempted to express in this poem my view of the mission of the poet, of the self-abnegation implied in it, of the great work involved in it, of the duty and glory of what Balzac[5] has beautifully and truly called "la patience angélique du génie"[6]; and of the obvious truth, above all, that if knowledge is power, suffering should be acceptable as a part of knowledge. It is enough to say of the other poems, that scarcely one of them is unambitious of an object and a significance.

*   *   *   *   *

A DRAMA OF EXILE[7]

Flower Spirits.
We linger, we linger,
    The last of the throng,
Like the tones of a singer
    Who loves his own song.
We are spirit-aromas
    Of blossom and bloom.   360
We call your thoughts home,—as
    Ye breathe our perfume,—
To the amaranth's[8] splendour
    Afire on the slopes;
To the lily-bells tender,
    And grey heliotropes;
To the poppy-plains keeping
    Such dream-breath and blee[9]
That the angels there stepping
    Grew whiter to see: 370

To the nook, set with moly,[10]
    Ye jested one day in,
Till your smile waxed too holy
    And left your lips praying:
To the rose in the bower-place,
    That dripped o'er you sleeping;
To the asphodel[11] flower-place,
    Ye walked ankle-deep in.
We pluck at your raiment,
    We stroke down your hair,   380
We faint in our lament
    And pine into air.
Fare ye well, farewell!
The Eden scents, no longer sensible,
    Expire at Eden's door.
Each footstep of your treading
Treads out some fragrance which ye knew before.
Farewell! the flowers of Eden,
    Ye shall smell nevermore.
    [*There is silence.* Adam *and* Eve *fly on, and*
       never look back. Only a colossal shadow,
       as of the dark Angel *passing quickly, is cast*
       upon the Sword-glare.

        *   *   *   *   *[12]

    [*A vision of* CHRIST *appears in the midst of the*
    Zodiac, *which pales before the heavenly light.*
    The Earth Spirits grow greyer and fainter.

CHRIST.   I AM HERE!
Adam. This is God!—Curse us not, God, any more!
Eve. But gazing so—so—with omnific eyes,   1760
Lift my soul upward till it touch thy feet!
Or lift it only,—not to seem too proud,—
To the low height of some good angel's feet,
For such to tread on when he walketh straight
And thy lips praise him!
    CHRIST.   Spirits of the earth,
I meet you with rebuke for the reproach
And cruel and unmitigated blame
Ye cast upon your masters. True, they have sinned;
And true their sin is reckoned into loss
For you the sinless. Yet, your innocence   1770

Which of you praises? since God made your acts
Inherent in your lives, and bound your hands
With instincts and imperious sanctities
From self-defacement. Which of you disdains
These sinners who in falling proved their height
Above you by their liberty to fall?[13]
And which of you complains of loss by them,
For whose delight and use ye have your life
And honour in creation? Ponder it!
This regent and sublime Humanity,   1780
Though fallen, exceeds you! this shall film your sun,
Shall hunt your lightning to its lair of cloud,
Turn back your rivers, footpath all your seas,
Lay flat your forests, master with a look
Your lion at his fasting, and fetch down
Your eagle flying. Nay, without this law
Of mandom, ye would perish,—beast by beast
Devouring,—tree by tree, with strangling roots
And trunks set tuskwise. Ye would gaze on God
With imperceptive blankness up the stars,   1790
And mutter, "Why, God, hast thou made us thus?"
And pining to a sallow idiocy
Stagger up blindly against the ends of life,
Then stagnate into rottenness and drop
Heavily—poor, dead matter—piecemeal down
The absymal spaces—like a little stone
Let fall to chaos. Therefore over you
Receive man's sceptre!—therefore be content
To minister with voluntary grace
And melancholy pardon, every rite   1800
And function in you, to the human hand!
Be ye to man as angels are to God,
Servants in pleasure, singers of delight,
Suggesters to his soul of higher things
Than any of your highest! So at last,
He shall look round on you with lids too straight
To hold the grateful tears, and thank you well,
And bless you when he prays his secret prayers,
And praise you when he sings his open songs
For the clear song-note he has learnt in you   1810
Of purifying sweetness, and extend
Across your head his golden fantasies
Which glorify you into soul from sense.

Go, serve him for such price! That not in vain
Nor yet ignobly ye shall serve, I place
My word here for an oath, mine oath for act
To be hereafter. In the name of which
Perfect redemption and perpetual grace,
I bless you through the hope and through the peace
Which are mine,—to the Love, which is myself.   1820
  Eve. Speak on still, Christ! Albeit thou bless me not
In set words, I am blessed in hearkening thee—
Speak, Christ!
  CHRIST. Speak, Adam! Bless the woman, man!
It is thine office.
  Adam.   Mother of the world,
Take heart before this Presence! Lo, my voice,
Which, naming erst the creatures, did express
(God breathing through my breath) the attributes
And instincts of each creature in its name,
Floats to the same afflatus,—floats and heaves
Like a water-weed that opens to a wave,—   1830
A full-leaved prophecy affecting thee,
Out fairly and wide. Henceforward, arise, aspire
To all the calms and magnanimities,
The lofty uses and the noble ends,
The sanctified devotion and full work,
To which thou art elect for evermore,
First woman, wife, and mother!
  Eve.   And first in sin.
  Adam. And also the sole bearer of the Seed[14]
Whereby sin dieth. Raise the majesties
Of thy disconsolate brows, O well-beloved,   1840
And front with level eyelids the To-come,
And all the dark o' the world! Rise, woman, rise
To thy peculiar and best altitudes
Of doing good and of enduring ill,
Of comforting for ill, and teaching good,
And reconciling all that ill and good
Unto the patience of a constant hope,—
Rise with thy daughters! If sin came by thee,
And by sin, death,—the ransom-righteousness,
The heavenly life and compensative rest   1850
Shall come by means of thee. If woe by thee
Had issue to the world, thou shalt go forth
An angel of the woe thou didst achieve,

Found acceptable to the world instead
Of others of that name, of whose bright steps
Thy deed stripped bare the hills. Be satisfied;
Something thou hast to bear through womanhood,
Peculiar suffering answering to the sin,—
Some pang paid down for each new human life,
Some weariness in guarding such a life,   1860
Some coldness from the guarded, some mistrust
From those thou hast too well served, from those
      beloved
Too loyally some treason; feebleness
Within thy heart, and cruelty without,
And pressures of an alien tyranny
With its dynastic reasons of larger bones
And stronger sinews. But, go to! thy love
Shall chant itself its own beatitudes
After its own life-working. A child's kiss
Set on thy sighing lips shall make thee glad;   1870
A poor man served by thee shall make thee rich;
A sick man helped by thee shall make thee strong;
Thou shalt be served thyself by every sense
Of service which thou renderest. Such a crown
I set upon thy head,—Christ witnessing
With looks of prompting love—to keep thee clear
Of all reproach against the sin forgone,
From all the generations which succeed.
Thy hand which plucked the apple I clasp close,
Thy lips which spake wrong counsel I kiss close,   1880
I bless thee in the name of Paradise
And by the memory of Edenic joys
Forfeit and lost,—by that last cypress tree,
Green at the gate, which thrilled as we came out,
And by the blessèd nightingale which threw
Its melancholy music after us,—
And by the flowers, whose spirits full of smells
Did follow softly, plucking us behind
Back to the gradual banks and vernal bowers
And fourfold river-courses.[15]—By all these,   1890
I bless thee to the contraries of these,
I bless thee to the desert and the thorns,
To the elemental change and turbulence,
And to the roar of the estrangèd beasts,
And to the solemn dignities of grief,—

To each one of these ends,—and to their END
Of Death and the hereafter.
    Eve.   I accept
For me and for my daughters this high part
Which lowly shall be counted. Noble work
Shall hold me in the place of garden-rest,   1900
And in the place of Eden's lost delight
Worthy endurance of permitted pain;
While on my longest patience there shall wait
Death's speechless angel, smiling in the east,
Whence cometh the cold wind. I bow myself
Humbly henceforward on the ill I did,
That humbleness may keep it in the shade.
Shall it be so? shall I smile, saying so?
O Seed! O King! O God, who *shalt* be seed,—
What shall I say? As Eden's fountains swelled   1910
Brightly betwixt their banks, so swells my soul
Betwixt thy love and power!
                          And, sweetest thoughts
Of forgone Eden! now, for the first time
Since God said "Adam," walking through the trees,
I dare to pluck you as I plucked erewhile
The lily or pink, the rose or heliotrope.
So pluck I you—so largely—with both hands,
And throw you forward on the outer earth,
Wherein we are cast out, to sweeten it.
    Adam. As thou, Christ, to illume it, holdest
              Heaven   1920
Broadly over our heads.

         *   *   *   *   *[16]

THE SOUL'S EXPRESSION[17]

With stammering lips and insufficient sound
I strive and struggle to deliver right
That music of my nature, day and night
With dream and thought and feeling interwound,
And inly answering all the senses round
With octaves of a mystic depth and height
Which step out grandly to the infinite
From the dark edges of the sensual ground.
This song of soul I struggle to outbear
Through portals of the sense, sublime and whole,   10
And utter all myself into the air:
But if I did it,—as the thunder-roll
Breaks its own cloud, my flesh would perish there,
Before that dread apocalypse of soul.

THE SERAPH AND POET[18]

The seraph sings before the manifest
God-One, and in the burning of the Seven,[19]
And with the full life of consummate Heaven
Heaving beneath him like a mother's breast
Warm with her first-born's slumber in that nest.
The poet sings upon the earth grave-riven,
Before the naughty world, soon self-forgiven
For wronging him,—and in the darkness prest
From his own soul by worldly weights. Even so,
Sing, seraph with the glory! heaven is high;   10
Sing, poet with the sorrow! earth is low:
The universe's inward voices cry
"Amen" to either song of joy and woe:
Sing, seraph,—poet,—sing on equally!

ON A PORTRAIT OF WORDSWORTH BY B. R. HAYDON[20]

Wordsworth upon Helvellyn![21] Let the cloud
Ebb audibly along the mountain-wind
Then break against the rock, and show behind
The lowland valleys floating up to crowd
The sense with beauty. He with forehead bowed
And humble-lidded eyes, as one inclined
Before the sovran thought of his own mind,
And very meek with inspirations proud,
Takes here his rightful place as poet-priest
By the high altar, singing prayer and prayer   10
To the higher Heavens. A noble vision free
Our Haydon's hand has flung out from the mist:
No portrait this, with Academic[22] air!
This is the poet and his poetry.

GRIEF[23]

I tell you, hopeless grief is passionless;
That only men incredulous of despair,
Half-taught in anguish, through the midnight air
Beat upward to God's throne in loud access
Of shrieking and reproach. Full desertness,
In souls as countries, lieth silent-bare
Under the blanching, vertical eye-glare
Of the absolute Heavens. Deep-hearted man, express
Grief for thy Dead in silence like to death —
Most like a monumental statue set   10
In everlasting watch and moveless woe
Till itself crumble to the dust beneath.
Touch it; the marble eyelids are not wet:
If it could weep, it could arise and go.

WORK AND CONTEMPLATION

The woman singeth at her spinning-wheel
A pleasant chant, ballad or barcarole;[24]
She thinketh of her song, upon the whole,
Far more than of her flax; and yet the reel
Is full, and artfully her fingers feel
With quick adjustment, provident control,
The lines—too subtly twisted to unroll—
Out to a perfect thread. I hence appeal
To the dear Christian Church—that we may do
Our Father's business[25] in these temples mirk,   10
Thus swift and steadfast, thus intent and strong;
While thus, apart from toil, our souls pursue
Some high calm spheric tune, and prove our work
The better for the sweetness of our song.

PAIN IN PLEASURE[26]

A thought lay like a flower upon mine heart,
And drew around it other thoughts like bees
For multitude and thirst of sweetnesses;
Whereat rejoicing, I desired the art
Of the Greek whistler,[27] who to wharf and mart
Could lure those insect swarms from orange-trees,
That I might hive with me such thoughts and please
My soul so, always. Foolish counterpart
Of a weak man's vain wishes! While I spoke,
The thought I called a flower grew nettle-rough,   10
The thoughts, called bees, stung me to festering:
Oh, entertain (cried Reason as she woke)
Your best and gladdest thoughts but long enough,
And they will all prove sad enough to sting!

TO GEORGE SAND. A DESIRE

Thou large-brained woman and large-hearted man,
Self-called George Sand![28] whose soul, amid the lions
Of thy tumultuous senses, moans defiance
And answers roar for roar, as spirits can:
I would some mild miraculous thunder ran
Above the applauded circus, in appliance
Of thine own nobler nature's strength and science,
Drawing two pinions, white as wings of swan,
From thy strong shoulders, to amaze the place
With holier light! that thou to woman's claim   10
And man's, mightst join beside the angel's grace
Of a pure genius sanctified from blame,
Till child and maiden pressed to thine embrace
To kiss upon thy lips a stainless fame.

TO GEORGE SAND. A RECOGNITION

True genius, but true woman! dost deny
The woman's nature with a manly scorn,
And break away the gauds and armlets worn
By weaker women in captivity?
Ah, vain denial! that revolted cry
Is sobbed in by a woman's voice forlorn, —
Thy woman's hair, my sister, all unshorn
Floats back dishevelled strength in agony,
Disproving thy man's name: and while before
The world thou burnest in a poet-fire,   10
We see thy woman-heart beat evermore
Through the large flame. Beat purer, heart, and higher,
Till God unsex thee on the heavenly shore
Where unincarnate spirits purely aspire!

LADY GERALDINE'S COURTSHIP: A Romance of the Age[29]

*A Poet writes to his Friend. Place — A Room in
Wycombe Hall. Time — Late in the evening.*

I.

Dear my friend and fellow-student, I would lean my
    spirit o'er you!
Down the purple of this chamber tears should scarcely
    run at will.[30]
I am humbled who was humble. Friend, I bow my
    head before you:
You should lead me to my peasants, but their faces
    are too still.

II.

There's a lady, an earl's daughter, — she is proud
    and she is noble,
And she treads the crimson carpet and she breathes
    the perfumed air,
And a kingly blood sends glances up, her princely eye
    to trouble,
And the shadow of a monarch's crown is softened in
    her hair.

III.

She has halls among the woodlands, she has castles by
    the breakers,
She has farms and she has manors, she can threaten
    and command: 10
And the palpitating engines[31] snort in steam across her
    acres,
As they mark upon the blasted heaven the measure of
    the land.

IV.

There are none of England's daughters who can show
    a prouder presence;
Upon princely suitors' praying she has looked in her
    disdain.
She was sprung of English nobles, I was born of
    English peasants;
What was *I* that I should love her, save for competence
    to pain?

V.

I was only a poor poet, made for singing at her case-
        ment,
As the finches or the thrushes, while she thought of
        other things.
Oh, she walked so high above me, she appeared to
        my abasement,
In her lovely silken murmur, like an angel clad in
        wings!   20

VI.

Many vassals bow before her as her carriage sweeps
        their doorways;
She has blest their little children, as a priest or queen
        were she:
Far too tender, or too cruel far, her smile upon
        the poor was,
For I thought it was the same smile which she used
        to smile on *me*.

VII.

She has voters in the Commons,[32] she has lovers in the
        palace,
And, of all the fair court-ladies, few have jewels half
        as fine;
Oft the Prince has named her beauty 'twixt the red
        wine and the chalice:
Oh, and what was *I* to love her? my beloved,
        my Geraldine!

VIII.

Yet I could not choose but love her: I was born to
        poet-uses,
To love all things set above me, all of good and all of
        fair.   30
Nymphs of mountain, not of valley, we are wont to
        call the Muses;
And in nympholeptic[33] climbing, poets pass from
        mount to star.

IX.

And because I was a poet, and because the public
    praised me,
With a critical deduction for the modern writer's
    fault,
I could sit at rich men's tables,—though the courte-
    sies that raised me,
Still suggested clear between us the pale spectrum
    of the salt.[34]

X.

And they praised me in her presence—"Will your
    book appear this summer?"
Then returning to each other—"Yes, our plans are
    for the moors."
Then with whisper dropped behind me—"There
    he is! the latest comer.
Oh, she only likes his verses! what is over, she
    endures.   40

XI.

"Quite low-born, self-educated! somewhat gifted
    though by nature,
And we make a point of asking him,—of being very
    kind.
You may speak, he does not hear you! and, besides,
    he writes no satire,—
All these serpents kept by charmers leave the natural
    sting behind."

XII.

I grew scornfuller, grew colder, as I stood up there
    among them,
Till as frost intense will burn you, the cold scorning
    scorched my brow;
When a sudden silver speaking, gravely cadenced,
    over-rung them,
And a sudden silken stirring touched my inner nature
    through.

XIII.

I looked upward and beheld her: with a calm and
      regnant spirit,
Slowly round she swept her eyelids, and said clear
      before them all—   50
"Have you such superfluous honour, sir, that able to
      confer it
You will come down, Mister Bertram, as my guest
      to Wycombe Hall?"

XIV.

Here she paused; she had been paler at the first word
      of her speaking,
But, because a silence followed it, blushed somewhat,
      as for shame:
Then, as scorning her own feeling, resumed calmly—
      "I am seeking
More distinction than these gentlemen think worthy
      of my claim.

XV.

"Ne'ertheless, you see, I seek it—not because I am
      a woman,"
(Here her smile sprang like a fountain and, so, over-
      flowed her mouth)
"But because my woods in Sussex have some purple
      shades at gloaming
Which are worthy of a king in state, or poet in his
      youth.   60

XVI.

"I invite you, Mister Bertram, to no scene for
      worldly speeches—
Sir, I scarce should dare—but only where God
      asked the thrushes first:
And if *you* will sing beside them, in the covert of my
      beeches,
I will thank you for the woodlands,—for the human
      world, at worst."

XVII.

Then she smiled around right childly, then she gazed
    around right queenly,
And I bowed—I could not answer; alternated light
    and gloom—
While as one who quells the lions, with a steady eye
    serenely,
She, with level fronting eyelids, passed out stately
    from the room.

XVIII.

Oh, the blessèd woods of Sussex, I can hear them
    still around me,
With their leafy tide of greenery still rippling up the wind! 70
Oh, the cursèd woods of Sussex! where the hunter's
    arrow found me,
When a fair face and a tender voice had made me
    mad and blind!

XIX.

In that ancient hall of Wycombe thronged the numer-
    ous guests invited,
And the lovely London ladies trod the floors with
    gliding feet;
And their voices low with fashion, not with feeling,
    softly freighted
All the air about the windows with elastic laughters
    sweet.

XX.

For at eve the open windows flung their light out on
    the terrace
Which the floating orbs of curtains did with gradual
    shadow sweep,
While the swans upon the river, fed at morning by the
    heiress,
Trembled downward through their snowy wings at
    music in their sleep.   80

XXI.

And there evermore was music, both of instrument
    and singing,
Till the finches of the shrubberies grew restless in the
    dark;
But the cedars stood up motionless, each in a moon-
    light's ringing,
And the deer, half in the glimmer, strewed the
    hollows of the park.

XXII.

And though sometimes she would bind me with her
    silver-corded speeches
To commix my words and laughter with the converse
    and the jest,
Oft I sat apart and, gazing on the river through the
    beeches,
Heard, as pure the swans swam down it, her pure
    voice o'erfloat the rest.

XXIII.

In the morning, horn of huntsman, hoof of steed and
    laugh of rider,
Spread out cheery from the courtyard till we lost them
    in the hills,   90
While herself and other ladies, and her suitors left
    beside her,
Went a-wandering up the gardens through the laurels
    and abeles.[35]

XXIV.

Thus, her foot upon the new-mown grass, bareheaded,
    with the flowing
Of the virginal white vesture gathered closely to her
    throat,
And the golden ringlets in her neck just quickened by
    her going,
And appearing to breathe sun for air, and doubting if
    to float,—

XXV.

With a bunch of dewy maple, which her right hand
    held above her,
And which trembled a green shadow in betwixt her
    and the skies,
As she turned her face in going, thus, she drew me on
    to love her,
And to worship the divineness of the smile hid in her
    eyes.   100

XXVI.

For her eyes alone smile constantly; her lips have
    serious sweetness,
And her front is calm, the dimple rarely ripples on the
    cheek;
But her deep blue eyes smile constantly, as if they in
    discreetness
Kept the secret of a happy dream she did not care to
    speak.

XXVII.

Thus she drew me the first morning, out across into
    the garden,
And I walked among her noble friends and could not
    keep behind.
Spake she unto all and unto me—"Behold, I am the
    warden
Of the song-birds in these lindens, which are cages to
    their mind.

XXVIII.

"But within this swarded[36] circle into which the lime-
    walk brings us,
Whence the beeches, rounded greenly, stand away in
    reverent fear,   110
I will let no music enter, saving what the fountain
    sings us
Which the lilies round the basin may seem pure enough
    to hear.

XXIX.

"The live air that waves the lilies waves the slender
          jet of water
Like a holy thought sent feebly up from soul of fasting
          saint:
Whereby lies a marble Silence, sleeping (Lough[37] the
          sculptor wrought her),
So asleep she is forgetting to say Hush!—a fancy
          quaint.

XXX.

"Mark how heavy white her eyelids! not a dream
          between them lingers;
And the left hand's index droppeth from the lips upon
          the cheek:
While the right hand,—with the symbol-rose[38] held
          slack within the fingers,—
Has fallen backward in the basin—yet this Silence
          will not speak!   120

XXXI.

"That the essential meaning growing may exceed the
          special symbol,
Is the thought as I conceive it: it applies more high
          and low.
Our true noblemen will often through right nobleness
          grow humble,
And assert an inward honour by denying outward show."

XXXII.

"Nay, your Silence," said I, "truly, holds her
          symbol-rose but slackly,
Yet *she holds it*, or would scarcely be a Silence to our
          ken:
And your nobles wear their ermine on the outside, or
          walk blackly
In the presence of the social law as mere ignoble men.

XXXIII.

"Let the poets dream such dreaming! madam, in
          these British islands
'Tis the substance that wanes ever, 'tis the symbol
          that exceeds.   130

Soon we shall have nought but symbol: and, for statues
    like this Silence,
Shall accept the rose's image—in another case, the
    weed's."

XXXIV.

"Not so quickly," she retorted,—"I confess,
    where'er you go, you
Find for things, names—shows for actions, and pure
    gold for honour clear:
But when all is run to symbol in the Social, I will
    throw you
The world's book which now reads dryly, and sit
    down with Silence here."

XXXV.

Half in playfulness she spoke, I thought, and half in
    indignation;
Friends, who listened, laughed her words off, while
    her lovers deemed her fair:
A fair woman, flushed with feeling, in her noble-
    lighted station
Near the statue's white reposing—and both bathed in
    sunny air!   140

XXXVI.

With the trees round, not so distant but you heard
    their vernal murmur,
And beheld in light and shadow the leaves in and out-
    ward move,
And the little fountain leaping toward the sun-heart to be
    warmer,
Then recoiling in a tremble from the too much light
    above.

XXXVII.

'Tis a picture for remembrance. And thus, morning
    after morning,
Did I follow as she drew me by the spirit to her feet.
Why, her greyhound followed also! dogs—we both
    were dogs for scorning—
To be sent back when she pleased it and her path lay
    through the wheat.

XXXVIII.

And thus, morning after morning, spite of vows and
    spite of sorrow,
Did I follow at her drawing, while the week-days
    passed along, —   150
Just to feed the swans this noontide, or to see the
    fawns to-morrow,
Or to teach the hill-side echo some sweet Tuscan in a
    song.

XXXIX.

Ay, for sometimes on the hill-side, while we sate down
    in the gowans,[39]
With the forest green behind us and its shadow cast
    before,
And the river running under, and across it from the
    rowans[40]
A brown partridge whirring near us till we felt the air
    it bore, —

XL.

There, obedient to her praying, did I read aloud the
    poems
Made to Tuscan flutes, or instruments more various of
    our own;
Read the pastoral parts of Spenser,[41] or the subtle inter-
    flowings
Found in Petrarch's sonnets—here's the book, the
    leaf is folded down!   160

XLI.

Or at times a modern volume, Wordsworth's solemn-
    thoughted idyl,
Howitt's[42] ballad-verse, or Tennyson's enchanted
    reverie, —
Or from Browning some "Pomegranate,"[43] which, if
    cut deep down the middle,
Shows a heart within blood-tinctured, of a veined hu-
    manity.

XLII.

Or at times I read there, hoarsely, some new poem of
    my making:
Poets ever fail in reading their own verses to their
    worth,
For the echo in you breaks upon the words which you
    are speaking,
And the chariot wheels jar in the gate through which
    you drive them forth.

XLIII.

After, when we were grown tired of books, the si-
    lence round us flinging
A slow arm of sweet compression, felt with beatings
    at the breast,   170
She would break out on a sudden in a gush of wood-
    land singing,
Like a child's emotion in a god—a naiad tired of
    rest.

XLIV.

Oh, to see or hear her singing! scarce I know which
    is divinest,
For her looks sing too—she modulates her gestures
    on the tune,
And her mouth stirs with the song, like song; and
    when the notes are finest,
'Tis the eyes that shoot out vocal light and seem to
    swell them on.

XLV.

Then we talked—oh, how we talked! her voice, so
    cadenced in the talking,
Made another singing—of the soul! a music without
    bars:
While the leafy sounds of woodlands, humming round
    where we were walking,
Brought interposition worthy-sweet,—as skies about
    the stars.   180

XLVI.

And she spake such good thoughts natural, as if she
    always thought them;
She had sympathies so rapid, open, free as bird on
    branch,
Just as ready to fly east as west, whichever way be-
    sought them,
In the birchen-wood a chirrup, or a cock-crow in the
    grange.

XLVII.

In her utmost lightness there is truth—and often she
    speaks lightly,
Has a grace in being gay which even mournful souls
    approve,
For the root of some grave earnest thought is under-
    struck so rightly
As to justify the foliage and the waving flowers above.

XLVIII.

And she talked on—*we* talked, rather! upon all
    things, substance, shadow,
Of the sheep that browsed the grasses, of the reapers
    in the corn,   190
Of the little children from the schools, seen winding
    through the meadow,
Of the poor rich world beyond them, still kept poorer
    by its scorn.

XLIX.

So, of men, and so, of letters—books are men of
    higher stature,
And the only men that speak aloud for future times to
    hear;
So, of mankind in the abstract, which grows slowly
    into nature,
Yet will lift the cry of "progress," as it trod from
    sphere to sphere.

L.

And her custom was to praise me when I said,—
    "The Age culls simples,
With a broad clown's back turned broadly to the glory
    of the stars.

We are gods by our own reck'ning, and may well
       shut up the temples,
And wield on, amid the incense-steam, the thunder of
       our cars.   200

LI.

"For we throw out acclamations of self-thanking, self-
       admiring,
With, at every mile run faster, –'O the wondrous
       wondrous age!'
Little thinking if we work our SOULS as nobly as our
       iron,
Or if angels will commend us at the goal of pilgrimage.

LII.

"Why, what *is* this patient entrance into nature's deep
       resources
But the child's most gradual learning to walk upright
       without bane!
When we drive out, from the cloud of steam, majes-
       tical white horses,
Are we greater than the first men who led black ones
       by the mane?

LIII.

"If we trod the deeps of ocean, if we struck the stars
       in rising,
If we wrapped the globe intensely with one hot elec-
       tric breath,[44]   210
'Twere but power within our tether, no new spirit-
       power comprising,
And in life we were not greater men, nor bolder men
       in death."

LIV.

She was patient with my talking; and I loved her,
       loved her certes
As I loved all heavenly objects, with uplifted eyes and
       hands;
As I loved pure inspirations, loved the graces, loved
       the virtues,
In a Love content with writing his own name on des-
       ert sands.

LV.
Or at least I thought so, purely; thought no idiot
    Hope was raising
Any crown to crown Love's silence, silent Love that
    sate alone:
Out, alas! the stag is like me, he that tries to go on
    grazing
With the great deep gun-wound in his neck, then
    reels with sudden moan.   220

LVI.
It was thus I reeled. I told you that her hand had
    many suitors;
But she smiles them down imperially as Venus did the
    waves,
And with such a gracious coldness that they cannot
    press their futures
On the present of her courtesy, which yieldingly
    enslaves.

LVII.
And this morning as I sat alone within the inner
    chamber
With the great saloon beyond it, lost in pleasant
    thought serene,
For I had been reading Camoëns,[45] that poem you
    remember,
Which his lady's eyes are praised in as the sweetest
    ever seen.

LVIII.
And the book lay open, and my thought flew from it,
    taking from it
A vibration and impulsion to an end beyond its own,   230
As the branch of a green osier,[46] when a child would
    overcome it,
Springs up freely from his claspings and goes swinging
    in the sun.

LIX.
As I mused I heard a murmur; it grew deep as it
    grew longer,
Speakers using earnest language—"Lady Geraldine,
    you *would!*"

And I heard a voice that pleaded, ever on in accents
      stronger,
As a sense of reason gave it power to make its rhetoric
      good.

LX.

Well I knew that voice; it was an earl's, of soul that
      matched his station,
Soul completed into lordship, might and right read on
      his brow;
Very finely courteous; far too proud to doubt his
      domination
Of the common people, he atones for grandeur by a
      bow.   240

LXI.

High straight forehead, nose of eagle, cold blue eyes
      of less expression
Than resistance, coldly casting off the looks of other
      men,
As steel, arrows; unelastic lips which seem to taste
      possession
And be cautious lest the common air should injure or
      distrain.

LXII.

For the rest, accomplished, upright,—ay, and stand-
      ing by his order
With a bearing not ungraceful; fond of art and letters
      too;
Just a good man made a proud man,—as the sandy
      rocks that border
A wild coast, by circumstances, in a regnant ebb and
      flow.

LXIII.

Thus, I knew that voice, I heard it, and I could not
      help the hearkening:
In the room I stood up blindly, and my burning
      heart within   250
Seemed to seethe and fuse my senses till they ran on
      all sides darkening,
And scorched, weighed like melted metal round my
      feet that stood therein.

LXIV.

And that voice, I heard it pleading, for love's sake,
    for wealth, position,
For the sake of liberal uses and great actions to be
    done:
And she interrupted gently, "Nay, my lord, the old
    tradition
Of your Normans, by some worthier hand than mine
    is, should be won."

LXV.

"Ah, that white hand!" he said quickly,—and in
    his he either drew it
Or attempted—for with gravity and instance she
    replied,
"Nay, indeed, my lord, this talk is vain, and we had
    best eschew it
And pass on, like friends, to other points less easy to
    decide."   260

LXVI.

What he said again, I know not: it is likely that his
    trouble
Worked his pride up to the surface, for she answered
    in slow scorn,
"And your lordship judges rightly. Whom I marry
    shall be noble,
Ay, and wealthy. I shall never blush to think how
    he was born."

LXVII.

There, I maddened! her words stung me. Life
    swept through me into fever,
And my soul sprang up astonished, sprang full-statured
    in an hour.
Know you what it is when anguish, with apocalyptic
    NEVER,
To a Pythian[47] height dilates you, and despair sublimes
    to power?

LXVIII.

From my brain the soul-wings budded, waved a flame
    about my body,
Whence conventions coiled to ashes. I felt self-drawn
    out, as man,   270
From amalgamate false natures, and I saw the skies
    grow ruddy
With the deepening feet of angels, and I knew what
    spirits can.

LXIX.

I was mad, inspired—say either (anguish worketh
    inspiration)
Was a man or beast—perhaps so, for the tiger roars
    when speared;
And I walked on, step by step along the level of my
    passion—
Oh my soul! and passed the doorway to her face, and
    never feared.

LXX.

He had left her, peradventure, when my footstep
    proved my coming,
But for *her*—she half arose, then sate, grew scarlet
    and grew pale.
Oh, she trembled! 'tis so always with a worldly man
    or woman
In the presence of true spirits; what else *can* they do
    but quail?   280

LXXI.

Oh, she fluttered like a tame bird, in among its forest
    brothers
Far too strong for it; then drooping, bowed her face
    upon her hands;
And I spake out wildly, fiercely, brutal truths of her
    and others:
I, she planted in the desert, swathed her, windlike,
    with my sands.

LXXII.

I plucked up her social fictions, bloody-rooted though
    leaf-verdant,
Trod them down with words of shaming,—all the
    purple and the gold,
All the "landed stakes" and lordships, all that spirits
    pure and ardent
Are cast out of love and honour because chancing not
    to hold.

LXXIII.

"For myself I do not argue," said I, "though I love
    you, madam.
But for better souls that nearer to the height of yours
    have trod: 290
And this age shows, to my thinking, still more infidels
    to Adam
Than directly, by profession, simple infidels to God.

LXXIV.

"Yet, O God," I said, "O grave," I said, "O
    mother's heart and bosom,
With whom first and last are equal, saint and corpse
    and little child!
We are fools to your deductions, in these figments of
    heart-closing;
We are traitors to your causes, in these sympathies
    defiled.

LXXV.

"Learn more reverence, madam, not for rank or
    wealth—*that* needs no learning:
That comes quickly, quick as sin does, ay, and cul-
    minates to sin;
But for Adam's seed, MAN! Trust me, 'tis a clay
    above your scorning,
With God's image stamped upon it, and God's kin-
    dling breath within.   300

LXXVI.

"What right have you, madam, gazing in your palace
    mirror daily,
Getting so by heart your beauty which all others must
    adore,

While you draw the golden ringlets down your fingers,
    to vow gaily
You will wed no man that's only good to God, and
    nothing more?

LXXVII.

"Why, what right have you, made fair by that same
    God, the sweetest woman
Of all women He has fashioned, with your lovely
    spirit face
Which would seem so near to vanish if its smile were
    not so human,
And your voice of holy sweetness, turning common
    words to grace,—

LXXVIII.

"What right *can* you have, God's other works to
    scorn, despise, revile them
In the gross, as mere men, broadly—not as *noble*
    men, forsooth,—   310
As mere Pariahs of the outer world, forbidden to assoil
    them
In the hope of living, dying, near that sweetness of
    your mouth?

LXXIX.

"Have you any answer, madam? If my spirit were
    less earthly,
If its instrument were gifted with a better silver string,
I would kneel down where I stand, and say—Behold
    me! I am worthy
Of thy loving, for I love thee. I am worthy as a
    king.

LXXX.

"As it is—your ermined pride, I swear, shall feel
    this stain upon her,
That *I*, poor, weak, tost with passion, scorned by me
    and you again,
Love you, madam, dare to love you, to my grief and
    your dishonour,
To my endless desolation, and your impotent dis-
    dain!"   320

LXXXI.

More mad words like these—mere madness! friend,
          I need not write them fuller,
For I hear my hot soul dropping on the lines in
          showers of tears.
Oh, a woman! friend, a woman! why, a beast had
          scarce been duller
Than roar bestial loud complaints against the shining
          of the spheres.

LXXXII.

But at last there came a pause. I stood all vibrating
          with thunder
Which my soul had used. The silence drew her face
          up like a call.
Could you guess what word she uttered? She looked
          up, as if in wonder,
With tears beaded on her lashes, and said—"Ber-
          tram!"—It was all.

LXXXIII.

If she had cursed me, and she might have, or if even,
          with queenly bearing
Which at need is used by women, she had risen up
          and said,   330
"Sir, you are my guest, and therefore I have given
          you a full hearing:
Now, beseech you, choose a name exacting somewhat
          less, instead!"—

LXXXIV.

I had borne it: but that "Bertram"—why, it lies
          there on the paper
A mere word, without her accent, and you cannot
          judge the weight
Of the calm which crushed my passion: I seemed
          drowning in a vapour;
And her gentleness destroyed me whom her scorn
          made desolate.

LXXXV.

So, struck backward and exhausted by that inward
      flow of passion
Which had rushed on, sparing nothing, into forms of
      abstract truth,
By a logic agonising through unseemly demonstration,
And by youth's own anguish turning grimly grey the
      hairs of youth,—   340

LXXXVI.

By the sense accursed and instant, that if even I spake
      wisely
I spake basely—using truth, if what I spake indeed
      was true,
To avenge wrong on a woman—*her*, who sate there
      weighing nicely
A poor manhood's worth, found guilty of such deeds
      as I could do!—

LXXXVII.

By such wrong and woe exhausted—what I suffered
      and occasioned,—
As a wild horse through a city runs with lightning
      in his eyes,
And then dashing at a church's cold and passive wall,
      impassioned,
Strikes the death into his burning brain, and blindly
      drops and dies—

LXXXVIII.

So I fell, struck down before her—do you blame me,
      friend, for weakness?
'Twas my strength of passion slew me!—fell before
      her like a stone;   350
Fast the dreadful world rolled from me on its roaring
      wheels of blackness:
When the light came I was lying in this chamber and
      alone.

LXXXIX.

Oh, of course she charged her lacqueys to bear out
      the sickly burden,
And to cast it from her scornful sight, but not *beyond*
      the gate;

She is too kind to be cruel, and too haughty not to
    pardon
Such a man as I; 'twere something to be level to her
    hate.

                            XC.
But for me—you now are conscious why, my friend,
    I write this letter,
How my life is read all backward, and the charm of
    life undone.
I shall leave her house at dawn; I would to-night, if
    I were better—
And I charge my soul to hold my body strengthened
    for the sun.   360

                            XCI.
When the sun has dyed the oriel,[48] I depart, with no
    last gazes,
No weak moanings (one word only, left in writing
    for her hands),
Out of reach of all derision, and some unavailing
    praises,
To make front against this anguish in the far and
    foreign lands.

                            XCII.
Blame me not. I would not squander life in grief—
    I am abstemious.
I but nurse my spirit's falcon that its wing may soar
    again.
There's no room for tears of weakness in the blind
    eyes of a Phemius:[49]
Into work the poet kneads them, and he does not die
    till then.

                        Conclusion

                            I.
Bertram finished the last pages, while along the silence
    ever
Still in hot and heavy splashes fell the tears on every
    leaf.   370

Having ended, he leans backward in his chair, with
    lips that quiver
From the deep unspoken, ay, and deep unwritten
    thoughts of grief.

II.

Soh! how still the lady standeth! 'Tis a dream—a
    dream of mercies!
'Twixt the purple lattice-curtains how she standeth
    still and pale!
'Tis a vision, sure, of mercies, sent to soften his self-
    curses,
Sent to sweep a patient quiet o'er the tossing of his
    wail.

III.

"Eyes," he said, "now throbbing through me! are
    ye eyes that did undo me?
Shining eyes, like antique jewels set in Parian[50] statue-
    stone!
Underneath that calm white forehead are ye ever
    burning torrid
O'er the desolate sand-desert of my heart and life
    undone?"   380

IV.

With a murmurous stir uncertain, in the air the purple
    curtain
Swelleth in and swelleth out around her motionless
    pale brows,
While the gliding of the river sends a rippling noise
    for ever
Through the open casement whitened by the moon-
    light's slant repose.

V.

Said he—"Vision of a lady! stand there silent,
    stand there steady!
Now I see it plainly, plainly now I cannot hope or
    doubt—
There, the brows of mild repression—there, the lips
    of silent passion,
Curvèd like an archer's bow to send the bitter arrows
    out."

VI.

Ever, evermore the while in a slow silence she kept
    smiling,
And approached him slowly, slowly, in a gliding
    measured pace;   390
With her two white hands extended as if praying one
    offended,
And a look of supplication gazing earnest in his face.

VII.

Said he—"Wake me by no gesture,—sound of
    breath, or stir of vesture!
Let the blessèd apparition melt not yet to its divine!
No approaching—hush, no breathing! or my heart
    must swoon to death in
The too utter life thou bringest, O thou dream of
    Geraldine!"

VIII.

Ever, evermore the while in a slow silence she kept
    smiling,
But the tears ran over lightly from her eyes and
    tenderly:—
"Dost thou, Bertram, truly love me? Is no woman
    far above me
Found more worthy of thy poet-heart than such a one
    as I?"   400

IX.

Said he—"I would dream so ever, like the flowing
    of that river,
Flowing ever in a shadow greenly onward to the sea!
So, thou vision of all sweetness, princely to a full
    completeness
Would my heart and life flow onward, deathward,
    through this dream of THEE!"

X.

Ever, evermore the while in a slow silence she kept
    smiling,
While the silver tears ran faster down the blushing of
    her cheeks;

Then with both her hands enfolding both of his, she
    softly told him,
"Bertram, if I say I love thee, . . . 'tis the
    vision only speaks."

XI.

Softened, quickened to adore her, on his knee he fell
    before her,
And she whispered low in triumph, "It shall be as I
    have sworn.   410
Very rich he is in virtues, very noble — noble, certes;
And I shall not blush in knowing that men call him
    lowly born."

A VISION OF POETS

"O Sacred Essence, lighting me this hour,
How may I lightly stile thy great power?
Echo.   Power.
   Power! but of whence? under the greenwood spraye?
   Or liv'st in Heaven? saye.
Echo.   In Heavens aye
   In Heavens aye! tell, may I it obtayne
   By alms, by fasting, prayer, — by paine?
Echo.   By paine.
   Show my the paine, it shall be undergone:
   I to mine end will still go on.
Echo.   Go on."
                           — *Britannia's Pastorals*[51]

A POET could not sleep aright,
For his soul kept up too much light
Under his eyelids for the night.

And thus he rose disquieted
With sweet rhymes ringing through his head,
And in the forest wanderèd

Where, sloping up the darkest glades,
The moon had drawn long colonnades
Upon whose floor the verdure fades

To a faint silver: pavement fair,　　　　　　　10
The antique wood-nymphs scarce would dare
To foot-print o'er, had such been there,

And rather sit by breathlessly,
With fear in their large eyes, to see
The consecrated sight. But HE—

The poet who, with spirit-kiss
Familiar, had long claimed for his
Whatever earthly beauty is,

Who also in his spirit bore
A beauty passing the earth's store,—　　　　　20
Walked calmly onward evermore.

His aimless thoughts in metre went,
Like a babe's hand without intent
Drawn down a seven-stringed instrument:

Nor jarred it with his humour as,
With a faint stirring of the grass,
An apparition fair did pass.

He might have feared another time,
But all things fair and strange did chime
With his thoughts then, as rhyme to rhyme.　　30

An angel had not startled him,
Alighted from heaven's burning rim
To breathe from glory in the Dim;

Much less a lady riding slow
Upon a palfrey white as snow,
And smooth as a snow-cloud could go.

Full upon his she turned her face,
"What ho, sir poet! dost thou pace
Our woods at night in ghostly chase

"Of some fair Dryad[52] of old tales　　　　　40
Who chants between the nightingales
And over sleep by song prevails?"

She smiled; but he could see arise
Her soul from far adown her eyes,
Prepared as if for sacrifice.

She looked a queen who seemeth gay
From royal grace alone. "Now, nay,"
He answered, "slumber passed away,

"Compelled by instincts in my head
That I should see to-night, instead   50
Of a fair nymph, some fairer Dread."

She looked up quickly to the sky
And spake: "The moon's regality
Will hear no praise; She is as I.

"She is in heaven, and I on earth;
This is my kingdom: I come forth
To crown all poets to their worth."

He brake in with a voice that mourned;
"To their worth, lady? They are scorned
By men they sing for, till inurned.   60

"To their worth? Beauty in the mind
Leaves the hearth cold, and love-refined
Ambitions make the world unkind.

"The boor who ploughs the daisy down,
The chief whose mortgage of renown,
Fixed upon graves, has bought a crown—

"Both these are happier, more approved
Than poets!—why should I be moved
In saying, both are more beloved?"

"The south can judge not of the north,"   70
She resumed calmly; "I come forth
To crown all poets to their worth.

"Yea, verily, to anoint them all
With blessèd oils which surely shall
Smell sweeter as the ages fall."

"As sweet," the poet said, and rung
A low sad laugh, "as flowers are, sprung
Out of their graves when they die young;

"As sweet as window-eglantine,
Some bough of which, as they decline,   80
The hired nurse gathers at their sign:

"As sweet, in short, as perfumed shroud
Which the gay Roman maidens sewed
For English Keats,[53] singing aloud."

The lady answered, "Yea, as sweet!
The things thou namest being complete
In fragrance, as I measure it.

"Since sweet the death-clothes and the knell
Of him who having lived, dies well;
And wholly sweet the asphodel   90

"Stirred softly by that foot of his,
When he treads brave on all that is,
Into the world of souls, from this.

"Since sweet the tears, dropped at the door
Of tearless Death, and even before:
Sweet, consecrated evermore.

"What, dost thou judge it a strange thing
That poets, crowned for vanquishing,
Should bear some dust from out the ring?

"Come on with me, come on with me,   100
And learn in coming: let me free
Thy spirit into verity."

She ceased: her palfrey's paces sent
No separate noises as she went;
'Twas a bee's hum, a little spent.

And while the poet seemed to tread
Along the drowsy noise so made,
The forest heaved up overhead

Its billowy foliage through the air,
And the calm stars did far and spare   110
O'erswim the masses everywhere;

Save when the overtopping pines
Did bar their tremulous light with lines
All fixed and black. Now the moon shines

A broader glory. You may see
The trees grow rarer presently;
The air blows up more fresh and free:

Until they come from dark to light,
And from the forest to the sight
Of the large heaven-heart, bare with night,   120

A fiery throb in every star,
Those burning arteries that are
The conduits of God's life afar,—

A wild brown moorland underneath,
And four pools breaking up the heath
With white low gleamings, blank as death.

Beside the first pool, near the wood,
A dead tree in set horror stood,
Peeled and disjointed, stark as rood;

Since thunder-stricken, years ago,   130
Fixed in the spectral strain and throe
Wherewith it struggled from the blow:

A monumental tree, alone,
That will not bend in storms, nor groan,
But break off sudden like a stone.

Its lifeless shadow lies oblique
Upon the pool where, javelin-like,
The star-rays quiver while they strike.

"Drink," said the lady, very still—
"Be holy and cold." He did her will   140
And drank the starry water chill.

The next pool they came near unto
Was bare of trees; there, only grew
Straight flags, and lilies just a few

Which sullen on the water sate
And leant their faces on the flat,
As weary of the starlight-state.

"Drink," said the lady, grave and slow—
"*World's use* behoveth thee to know."
He drank the bitter wave below.   150

The third pool, girt with thorny bushes
And flaunting weeds and reeds and rushes
That winds sang through in mournful gushes,

Was whitely smeared in many a round
By a slow slime; the starlight swound
Over the ghastly light it found.

"Drink," said the lady, sad and slow—
"*World's love* behoveth thee to know."
He looked to her commanding so;

Her brow was troubled, but her eye   160
Struck clear to his soul. For all reply
He drank the water suddenly,—

Then, with a deathly sickness, passed
Beside the fourth pool and the last,
Where weights of shadow were downcast

From yew and alder and rank trails
Of nightshade clasping the trunk-scales
And flung across the intervals

From yew to yew: who dares to stoop
Where those dank branches overdroop,   170
Into his heart the chill strikes up.

He hears a silent gliding coil,
The snakes strain hard against the soil,
His foot slips in their slimy oil,

And toads seem crawling on his hand,
And clinging bats but dimly scanned
Full in his face their wings expand.

A paleness took the poet's cheek:
"Must I drink *here*?" he seemed to seek
The lady's will with utterance meek: 180

"Ay, ay," she said, "it so must be;"
(And this time she spake cheerfully)
"Behoves thee know *World's cruelty.*"

        *   *   *   *   *[54]

And Burns, with pungent passionings
Set in his eyes: deep lyric springs
Are of the fire-mount's issuings.

And Shelley, in his white ideal,
All statue-blind.[55] And Keats the real
Adonis[56] with the hymeneal

Fresh vernal buds half sunk between
His youthful curls, kissed straight and sheen   410
In his Rome-grave, by Venus queen.

And poor, proud Byron, sad as grave
And salt as life; forlornly brave,
And quivering with the dart he drave.

And visionary Coleridge, who
Did sweep his thoughts as angels do
Their wings with cadence up the Blue.

These poets faced (and many more)
The lighted altar looming o'er
The clouds of incense dim and hoar: 420

And all their faces, in the lull
Of natural things, looked wonderful
With life and death and deathless rule.

All, still as stone and yet intense;
As if by spirit's vehemence
That stone were carved and not by sense.

But where the heart of each should beat,
There seemed a wound instead of it,
From whence the blood dropped to their feet

Drop after drop—dropped heavily   430
As century follows century
Into the deep eternity.

Then said the lady—and her word
Came distant, as wide waves were stirred
Between her and the ear that heard,—

"World's use is cold, *world's love* is vain,
World's cruelty is bitter bane,
But pain is not the fruit of pain.

"Hearken, O poet, whom I led
From the dark wood: dismissing dread,   440
Now hear this angel in my stead.

"His organ's clavier strikes along
These poets' hearts, sonorous, strong,
They gave him without count of wrong,—

"A diapason whence to guide
Up to God's feet, from these who died,
An anthem fully glorified—

"Whereat God's blessing, IBARAK (יברך) [57]

Breathes back this music, folds it back
About the earth in vapoury rack,   450

"And men walk in it, crying 'Lo
The world is wider, and we know
The very heavens look brighter so:

"'The stars move statelier round the edge
Of the silver spheres, and give in pledge
Their light for nobler privilege:

"'No little flower but joys or grieves,
Full life is rustling in the sheaves,
Full spirit sweeps the forest-leaves.'

"So works this music on the earth,   460
God so admits it, sends it forth
To add another worth to worth—

"A new creation-bloom that rounds
The old creation and expounds
His Beautiful in tuneful sounds.

"Now hearken!" Then the poet gazed
Upon the angel glorious-faced
Whose hand, majestically raised,

Floated across the organ-keys,
Like a pale moon o'er murmuring seas,   470
With no touch but with influences:

Then rose and fell (with swell and swound
Of shapeless noises wandering round
A concord which at last they found)

Those mystic keys: the tones were mixed,
Dim, faint, and thrilled and throbbed betwixt
The incomplete and the unfixed:

And therein mighty minds were heard
In mighty musings, inly stirred,
And struggling outward for a word: 480

Until these surges, having run
This way and that, gave out as one
An Aphroditè of sweet tune,

A Harmony that, finding vent,
Upward in grand ascension went,
Winged to a heavenly argument,

Up, upward like a saint who strips
The shroud back from his eyes and lips,
And rises in apocalypse:

A Harmony sublime and plain,   490
Which cleft (as flying swan, the rain,—
Throwing the drops off with a strain

Of her white wing) those undertones
Of perplext chords, and soared at once
And struck out from the starry thrones

Their several silver octaves as
It passed to God. The music was
Of divine stature; strong to pass:

And those who heard it understood
Something of life in spirit and blood,   500
Something of nature's fair and good:

And while it sounded, those great souls
Did thrill as racers at the goals
And burn in all their aureoles;

But she the lady, as vapour-bound,
Stood calmly in the joy of sound,
Like Nature with the showers around:

And when it ceased, the blood which fell
Again, alone grew audible,
Tolling the silence as a bell.   510

                    *   *   *   *   *[58]

THE CRY OF THE CHILDREN[59]

" Φεῖ, φεῦ, τί προσδέρκεσθέ μ' ὄμμασιν, τέκνα ; "—Medea[60]

I.

Do ye hear the children weeping, O my brothers,
    Ere the sorrow comes with years?
They are leaning their young heads against their
    mothers,
    And *that* cannot stop their tears.
The young lambs are bleating in the meadows,
    The young birds are chirping in the nest,
The young fawns are playing with the shadows,
    The young flowers are blowing toward the west—
But the young, young children, O my brothers,
    They are weeping bitterly!   10
They are weeping in the playtime of the others,
    In the country of the free.

II.

Do you question the young children in the sorrow
    Why their tears are falling so?
The old man may weep for his to-morrow
    Which is lost in Long Ago;
The old tree is leafless in the forest,
    The old year is ending in the frost,
The old wound, if stricken, is the sorest,
    The old hope is hardest to be lost: 20
But the young, young children, O my brothers,
    Do you ask them why they stand
Weeping sore before the bosoms of their mothers,
    In our happy Fatherland?

III.

They look up with their pale and sunken faces,
    And their looks are sad to see,
For the man's hoary anguish draws and presses
    Down the cheeks of infancy;
"Your old earth," they say, "is very dreary,
    Our young feet," they say, "are very weak;   30
Few paces have we taken, yet are weary—
    Our grave-rest is very far to seek:

Ask the aged why they weep, and not the children,
    For the outside earth is cold,
And we young ones stand without, in our bewildering,
    And the graves are for the old.

IV.
"True," say the children, "it may happen
    That we die before our time:
Little Alice died last year, her grave is shapen
    Like a snowball, in the rime.   40
We looked into the pit prepared to take her:
    Was no room for any work in the close clay!
From the sleep wherein she lieth none will wake her,
    Crying, 'Get up, little Alice! it is day.'
If you listen by that grave, in sun and shower,
    With your ear down, little Alice never cries;
Could we see her face, be sure we should not know
      her,
    For the smile has time for growing in her eyes:
And merry go her moments, lulled and stilled in
    The shroud by the kirk-chime.   50
It is good when it happens," say the children,
    "That we die before our time."

V.
Alas, alas, the children! they are seeking
    Death in life, as best to have:
They are binding up their hearts away from breaking,
    With a cerement from the grave.
Go out, children, from the mine and from the city,
    Sing out, children, as the little thrushes do;
Pluck your handfuls of the meadow-cowslips pretty,
    Laugh aloud, to feel your fingers let them through!   60
But they answer, "Are your cowslips of the meadows
    Like our weeds anear the mine?
Leave us quiet in the dark of the coal-shadows,
    From your pleasures fair and fine!

VI.
"For oh," say the children, "we are weary,
    And we cannot run or leap;
If we cared for any meadows, it were merely
    To drop down in them and sleep.

Our knees tremble sorely in the stooping,
    We fall upon our faces, trying to go;   70
And, underneath our heavy eyelids drooping
    The reddest flower would look as pale as snow.
For, all day, we drag our burden tiring
    Through the coal-dark, underground;
Or, all day, we drive the wheels of iron
    In the factories, round and round.

VII.

"For all day the wheels are droning, turning;
    Their wind comes in our faces,
Till our hearts turn, our heads with pulses burning,
    And the walls turn in their places: 80
Turns the sky in the high window, blank and reeling,
    Turns the long light that drops adown the wall,
Turn the black flies that crawl along the ceiling:
    All are turning, all the day, and we with all.
And all day the iron wheels are droning,
    And sometimes we could pray,
'O ye wheels' (breaking out in a mad moaning),
    'Stop! be silent for to-day!'"

VIII.

Ay, be silent! Let them hear each other breathing
    For a moment, mouth to mouth!   90
Let them touch each other's hands, in a fresh wreathing
    Of their tender human youth!
Let them feel that this cold metallic motion
    Is not all the life God fashions or reveals:
Let them prove their living souls against the notion
    That they live in you, or under you, O wheels!
Still, all day, the iron wheels go onward,
    Grinding life down from its mark;
And the children's souls which God is calling sunward,
    Spin on blindly in the dark.   100

IX.

Now tell the poor young children, O my brothers,
    To look up to Him and pray;
So the blessed One who blesseth all the others,
    Will bless them another day.

They answer, "Who is God that He should hear us,
      While the rushing of the iron wheels is stirred?
When we sob aloud, the human creatures near us
      Pass by, hearing not, or answer not a word.
And *we* hear not (for the wheels in their resounding)
      Strangers speaking at the door: 110
Is it likely God, with angels singing round Him,
      Hears our weeping any more?

                              X.

"Two words, indeed, of praying we remember,
      And at midnight's hour of harm,
'Our Father,' looking upward in the chamber,
      We say softly for a charm.
We know no other words except 'Our Father,'
      And we think that, in some pause of angels' song,
God may pluck them with the silence sweet to gather,
      And hold both within His right hand which is
            strong.   120
'Our Father!' If He heard us, He would surely
      (For they call Him good and mild)
Answer, smiling down the steep world very purely,
      'Come and rest with me, my child.'

                              XI.
"But, no!" say the children, weeping faster,
      "He is speechless as a stone:
And they tell us, of His image is the master
      Who commands us to work on.
Go to!" say the children,— "up in Heaven,
      Dark, wheel-like, turning clouds are all we find.   130
Do not mock us; grief has made us unbelieving:
      We look up for God, but tears have made us blind."
Do you hear the children weeping and disproving,
      O my brothers, what ye preach?
For God's possible is taught by His world's loving,
      And the children doubt of each.

                              XII.
And well may the children weep before you!
      They are weary ere they run;
They have never seen the sunshine, nor the glory
      Which is brighter than the sun.   140

They know the grief of man, without its wisdom;
    They sink in man's despair, without its calm;
Are slaves, without the liberty in Christdom,
    Are martyrs, by the pang without the palm:
Are worn as if with age, yet unretrievingly
    The harvest of its memories cannot reap,—
Are orphans of the earthly love and heavenly.
    Let them weep! let them weep!

XIII.

They look up with their pale and sunken faces,
    And their look is dread to see,   150
For they mind you of their angels in high places,
    With eyes turned on Deity.
"How long," they say, "how long, O cruel nation,
    Will you stand, to move the world, on a child's heart,—
Stifle down with a mailed heel its palpitation,
    And tread onward to your throne amid the mart?
Our blood splashes upward, O gold-heaper,
    And your purple shows your path!
But the child's sob in the silence curses deeper
    Than the strong man in his wrath."   160

CATARINA TO CAMOËNS[61]

(Dying in his absence abroad, and referring to the poem
in which he recorded the sweetness of her eyes).

I.

On the door you will not enter,
    I have gazed too long: adieu!
Hope withdraws her peradventure;
    Death is near me,—and not *you*.
      Come, O lover,
      Close and cover
These poor eyes, you called, I ween,
"Sweetest eyes were ever seen!"

II.

When I heard you sing that burden
    In my vernal days and bowers   10
Other praises disregarding,
    I but hearkened that of yours—

Only saying
In heart-playing,
"Blessed eyes mine eyes have been,
If the sweetest HIS have seen!"

III.

But all changes. At this vesper,
    Cold the sun shines down the door.
If you stood there, would you whisper
    "Love, I love you," as before,—   20
        Death pervading
        Now, and shading
Eyes you sang of, that yestreen,
As the sweetest ever seen?

IV.

Yes. I think, were you beside them,
    Near the bed I die upon,
Though their beauty you denied them,
    As you stood there, looking down,
        You would truly
        Call them duly,   30
For the love's sake found therein,
"Sweetest eyes were ever seen."

V.

And if *you* looked down upon them,
    And if *they* looked up to *you*,
All the light which has foregone them
    Would be gathered back anew.
        They would truly
        Be as duly
Love-transformed to beauty's sheen,
"Sweetest eyes were ever seen."   40

VI.

But, ah me: you only see me,
    In your thoughts of loving man,
Smiling soft perhaps and dreamy
    Through the wavings of my fan;
        And unweeting
        Go repeating,
In your reverie serene,
"Sweetest eyes were ever seen—"

VII.

While my spirit leans and reaches
    From my body still and pale,   50
Fain to hear what tender speech is
    In your love to help my bale.
        O my poet,
        Come and show it!
Come, of latest love, to glean
"Sweetest eyes were ever seen."

VIII.

O my poet, O my prophet,
    When you praised their sweetness so,
Did you think, in singing of it,
    That it might be near to go?   60
        Had you fancies
        From their glances,
That the grave would quickly screen
"Sweetest eyes were ever seen"?

IX.

No reply. The fountain's warble
    In the courtyard sounds alone.
As the water to the marble
    So my heart falls with a moan
        From love-sighing
        To this dying.   70
Death forerunneth Love to win
"Sweetest eyes were ever seen."

X.

Will you come? When I'm departed
    Where all sweetnesses are hid,
Where thy voice, my tender-hearted,
    Will not lift up either lid.
        Cry, O lover,
        Love is over!
Cry, beneath the cypress green,
"Sweetest eyes were ever seen!"   80

XI.

When the angelus is ringing,
　　Near the convent will you walk,
And recall the choral singing
　　Which brought angels down our talk?
　　　　Spirit-shriven
　　　　I viewed Heaven,
Till you smiled—"Is earth unclean,
Sweetest eyes were ever seen?"

XII.

When beneath the palace-lattice   90
　　You ride slow as you have done,
And you see a face there that is
　　Not the old familiar one,—
　　　　Will you oftly
　　　　Murmur softly,
"Here ye watched me morn and e'en,
Sweetest eyes were ever seen!"

XIII.

When the palace-ladies, sitting
　　Round your gittern,[62] shall have said,
"Poet, sing those verses written
　　For the lady who is dead,"   100
　　　　Will you tremble
　　　　Yet dissemble,—
Or sing hoarse, with tears between,
"Sweetest eyes were ever seen"?

XIV.

"Sweetest eyes!" how sweet in flowings
　　The repeated cadence is!
Though you sang a hundred poems,
　　Still the best one would be this.
　　　　I can hear it
　　　　'Twixt my spirit   110
And the earth-noise intervene—
"Sweetest eyes were ever seen!"

XV.

But the priest waits for the praying,
　　And the choir are on their knees,
And the soul must pass away in
　　　Strains more solemn-high than these.
　　　　Miserere
　　　　For the weary!
Oh, no longer for Catrine
"Sweetest eyes were ever seen!"   120

XVI.

Keep my riband, take and keep it,
　　(I have loosed it from my hair)
Feeling, while you overweep it,
　　　Not alone in your despair,
　　　　Since with saintly
　　　　Watch unfaintly
Out of heaven shall o'er you lean
"Sweetest eyes were ever seen."

XVII.

But—but *now*—yet unremovèd
　　Up to heaven, they glisten fast;   130
You may cast away, Belovèd,
　　　In your future all my past:
　　　　Such old phrases
　　　　May be praises
For some fairer bosom-queen—
"Sweetest eyes were ever seen!"

XVIII.

Eyes of mine, what are ye doing?
　　Faithless, faithless,—praised amiss
If a tear be of your showing,
　　　Dropt for any hope of HIS!   140
　　　　Death has boldness
　　　　Besides coldness,
If unworthy tears demean
"Sweetest eyes were ever seen."

XIX.

I will look out to his future;
    I will bless it till it shine.
Should he ever be a suitor
    Unto sweeter eyes than mine,
        Sunshine gild them,
        Angels shield them,   150
Whatsoever eyes terrene
Be the sweetest HIS have seen!

THE DEAD PAN[63]

I.

GODS of Hellas, gods of Hellas,[64]
Can ye listen in your silence?
Can your mystic voices tell us
Where ye hide? In floating islands,
With a wind that evermore
Keeps you out of sight of shore?
                    Pan, Pan is dead.

II.

In what revels are ye sunken
In old Aethiopia?
Have the Pygmies made you drunken,   10
Bathing in mandragora
Your divine pale lips that shiver
Like the lotus in the river?
                    Pan, Pan is dead.

III.

Do ye sit there still in slumber,
In gigantic Alpine rows?
The black poppies out of number
Nodding, dripping from your brows
To the red lees of your wine,
And so kept alive and fine?   20
                    Pan, Pan is dead.

IV.

Or lie crushed your stagnant corses
Where the silver spheres roll on,
Stung to life by centric forces
Thrown like rays out from the sun?—
While the smoke of your old altars
Is the shroud that round you welters?
                    Great Pan is dead.

V.

"Gods of Hellas, gods of Hellas"
Said the old Hellenic tongue,—   30
Said the hero-oaths, as well as
Poets' songs the sweetest sung:
Have ye grown deaf in a day?
Can ye speak not yea or nay,
                    Since Pan is dead?

VI.

Do ye leave your rivers flowing
All alone, O Naiades,
While your drénchèd locks dry slow in
This cold feeble sun and breeze?
Not a word the Naiads say,   40
Though the rivers run for aye;
                    For Pan is dead.

VII.

From the gloaming of the oak-wood,
O ye Dryads,[65] could ye flee?
At the rushing thunderstroke, would
No sob tremble through the tree?
Not a word the Dryads say,
Though the forests wave for aye;
                    For Pan is dead.

VIII.

Have ye left the mountain places,   50
Oreads wild, for other tryst?
Shall we see no sudden faces
Strike a glory through the mist?
Not a sound the silence thrills
Of the everlasting hills:
                    Pan, Pan is dead.

IX.

O twelve gods of Plato's vision,[66]
Crowned to starry wanderings,
With your chariots in procession
And your silver clash of wings!   60
Very pale ye seem to rise,
Ghosts of Grecian deities,
                    Now Pan is dead!

X.

Jove, that right hand is unloaded
Whence the thunder did prevail,
While in idiocy of godhead
Thou art staring the stars pale!
And thine eagle, blind and old,
Roughs his feathers in the cold.
                    Pan, Pan is dead.   70

XI.

Where, O Juno, is the glory
Of thy regal look and tread?
Will they lay, for evermore, thee
On thy dim, strait, golden bed?
Will thy queendom all lie hid
Meekly under either lid?
                    Pan, Pan is dead.

XII.

Ha, Apollo! floats his golden
Hair all mist-like where he stands,
While the Muses hang enfolding   80
Knee and foot with faint wild hands?
'Neath the clanging of thy bow,
Niobe[67] looked lost as thou!
                    Pan, Pan is dead.

XIII.

Shall the casque with its brown iron
Pallas' broad blue eyes eclipse,[68]
And no hero take inspiring
From the god-Greek of her lips?
'Neath her olive dost thou sit,
Mars the mighty, cursing it?   90
                    Pan, Pan is dead.

XIV.

Bacchus, Bacchus! on the panther
He swoons, bound with his own vines;
And his Maenads slowly saunter,[69]
Head aside, among the pines,
While they murmur dreamingly
"Evohe![70] – ah – evohe! –
                    Ah, Pan is dead!"

XV.

Neptune lies beside the trident,
Dull and senseless as a stone;   100
And old Pluto deaf and silent
Is cast out into the sun:
Ceres smileth stern thereat,[71]
"We *all* now are desolate –
                    Now Pan is dead."

XVI.

Aphrodite! dead and driven
As thy native foam thou art;
With the cestus long done heaving
On the white calm of thine heart![72]
Ai Adonis! at that shriek   110
Not a tear runs down her cheek –
                    Pan, Pan is dead.

XVII.

And the Loves, we used to know from
One another, huddled lie,
Frore[73] as taken in a snow-storm,
Close beside her tenderly;
As if each had weakly tried
Once to kiss her as he died.
                    Pan, Pan is dead.

XVIII.

What, and Hermes?[74] Time enthralleth   120
All thy cunning, Hermes, thus,
And the ivy blindly crawleth
Round thy brave caduceus?
Hast thou no new message for us,
Full of thunder and Jove-glories?
                    Nay, Pan is dead.

XIX.

Crownèd Cybele's[75] great turret
Rocks and crumbles on her head;
Roar the lions of her chariot
Toward the wilderness, unfed: 130
Scornful children are not mute,—
"Mother, mother, walk afoot,
                    Since Pan is dead!"

XX.

In the fiery-hearted centre
Of the solemn universe,
Ancient Vesta,[76]—who could enter
To consume thee with this curse?
Drop thy grey chin on thy knee,
O thou palsied Mystery!
                    For Pan is dead.   140

XXI.

Gods, we vainly do adjure you,—
Ye return nor voice nor sign!
Not a votary could secure you
Even a grave for your Divine:
Not a grave, to show thereby
Here these grey old gods do lie.
                    Pan, Pan is dead.

XXII.

Even that Greece who took your wages
Calls the obolus[77] outworn;
And the hoarse, deep-throated ages   150
Laugh your godships unto scorn:
And the poets do disclaim you,
Or grow colder if they name you—
                    And Pan is dead.

XXIII.

Gods bereavèd, gods belated,
With your purples rent asunder,
Gods discrowned and desecrated,
Disinherited of thunder!
Now, the goats may climb and crop
The soft grass on Ida's top—   160
                    Now Pan is dead.

XXIV.

Calm, of old, the bark went onward,
When a cry more loud than wind
Rose up, deepened, and swept sunward
From the pilèd Dark behind;[78]
And the sun shrank and grew pale,
Breathed against by the great wail—
              "Pan, Pan is dead."

XXV.

And the rowers from the benches
Fell, each shuddering on his face,   170
While departing Influences
Struck a cold back through the place;
And the shadow of the ship
Reeled along the passive deep—
              "Pan, Pan is dead."

XXVI.

And that dismal cry rose slowly
And sank slowly through the air,
Full of spirit's melancholy
And eternity's despair!
And they heard the words it said—   180
PAN IS DEAD—GREAT PAN IS DEAD—
              PAN, PAN IS DEAD.

XXVII.

'Twas the hour when One in Sion
Hung for love's sake on a cross;
When His brow was chill with dying
And His soul was faint with loss;
When His priestly blood dropped downward
And His kingly eyes looked throneward—
              Then, Pan was dead.

XXVIII.

By the love, He stood alone in,   190
His sole Godhead rose complete,
And the false gods fell down moaning
Each from off his golden seat;
All the false gods with a cry
Rendered up their deity—
              Pan, Pan was dead.

XXIX.

Wailing wide across the islands,
They rent, vest-like, their Divine;
And a darkness and a silence
Quenched the light of every shrine;   200
And Dodona's oak[79] swang lonely
Henceforth, to the tempest only:
                    Pan, Pan was dead.

XXX.

Pythia[80] staggered, feeling o'er her
Her lost god's forsaking look;
Straight her eyeballs filmed with horror
And her crispy fillets shook
And her lips gasped, through their foam,
For a word that did not come.
                    Pan, Pan was dead.   210

XXXI.

O ye vain false gods of Hellas,
Ye are silent evermore!
And I dash down this old chalice
Whence libations ran of yore.
See, the wine crawls in the dust
Wormlike—as your glories must,
                    Since Pan is dead.

XXXII.

Get to dust, as common mortals,
By a common doom and track!
Let no Schiller from the portals   220
Of that Hades call you back,
Or instruct us to weep all
At your antique funeral.
                    Pan, Pan is dead.

XXXIII.

By your beauty, which confesses
Some chief Beauty conquering you,—
By our grand heroic guesses
Through your falsehood at the True,—
We will weep *not!* earth shall roll
Heir to each god's aureole—   230
                    And Pan is dead.

XXXIV.

Earth outgrows the mythic fancies
Sung beside her in her youth,
And those debonair romances
Sound but dull beside the truth.
Phoebus' chariot-course is run:
Look up, poets, to the sun!
                    Pan, Pan is dead.

XXXV.

Christ hath sent us down the angels;
And the whole earth and the skies   240
Are illumed by altar-candles
Lit for blessèd mysteries;
And a priest's hand through creation
Waveth calm and consecration:
                    And Pan is dead.

XXXVI.

Truth is fair: should we forgo it?
Can we sigh right for a wrong?
God Himself is the best Poet,[81]
And the Real is His song.
Sing His truth out fair and full,   250
And secure His beautiful!
                    Let Pan be dead!

XXXVII.

Truth is large: our aspiration
Scarce embraces half we be.
Shame, to stand in His creation
And doubt truth's sufficiency! —
To think God's song unexcelling
The poor tales of our own telling —
                    When Pan is dead!

XXXVIII.

What is true and just and honest,   260
What is lovely, what is pure,
All of praise that hath admonisht,
All of virtue, — shall endure;
These are themes for poets' uses,
Stirring nobler than the Muses,
                    Ere Pan was dead.

XXXIX.

O brave poets, keep back nothing,
Nor mix falsehood with the whole!
Look up Godward; speak the truth in
Worthy song from earnest soul: 270
Hold, in high poetic duty,
Truest Truth the fairest Beauty!
                    Pan, Pan is dead.

Poems
1850[1]

THE RUNAWAY SLAVE AT PILGRIM'S POINT[2]

I.

I STAND on the mark beside the shore
    Of the first white pilgrim's bended knee,
Where exile turned to ancestor,
    And God was thanked for liberty.
I have run through the night, my skin is as dark,
I bend my knee down on this mark:
    I look on the sky and the sea.

II.

O pilgrim-souls, I speak to you!
    I see you come proud and slow
From the land of the spirits pale as dew   10
    And round me and round me ye go.
O pilgrims, I have gasped and run
All night long from the whips of one
    Who in your names works sin and woe!

III.

And thus I thought that I would come
    And kneel here where ye knelt before,
And feel your souls around me hum
    In undertone to the ocean's roar;
And lift my black face, my black hand,
Here, in your names, to curse this land   20
    Ye blessed in freedom's, evermore.

IV.

I am black, I am black,
    And yet God made me, they say:
But if He did so, smiling back
    He must have cast His work away
Under the feet of His white creatures,
With a look of scorn, that the dusky features
    Might be trodden again to clay.

V.

And yet He has made dark things
    To be glad and merry as light: 30
There's a little dark bird sits and sings,
    There's a dark stream ripples out of sight,
And the dark frogs chant in the safe morass,
And the sweetest stars are made to pass
    O'er the face of the darkest night.

VI.

But *we* who are dark, we are dark!
    Ah God, we have no stars!
About our souls in care and cark[3]
    Our blackness shuts like prison-bars:
The poor souls crouch so far behind   40
That never a comfort can they find
    By reaching through the prison-bars.

VII.

Indeed we live beneath the sky,
    That great smooth Hand of God stretched out
On all His children fatherly,
    To save them from the dread and doubt
Which would be if, from this low place,
All opened straight up to His face
    Into the grand eternity.

VIII.

And still God's sunshine and His frost,   50
    They make us hot, they make us cold,
As if we were not black and lost;
    And the beasts and birds, in wood and fold,
Do fear and take us for very men:
Could the whip-poor-will or the cat of the glen
    Look into my eyes and be bold?

IX.

I am black, I am black!
    But, once, I laughed in girlish glee,
For one of my colour stood in the track
    Where the drivers drove, and looked at me,   60
And tender and full was the look he gave—
Could a slave look *so* at another slave?—
    I look at the sky and the sea.

X.

And from that hour our spirits grew
    As free as if unsold, unbought:
Oh, strong enough, since we were two,
    To conquer the world, we thought.
The drivers drove us day by day;
We did not mind, we went one way,
    And no better a freedom sought.   70

XI.

In the sunny ground between the canes,
    He said "I love you" as he passed;
When the shingle-roof rang sharp with the rains,
    I heard how he vowed it fast:
While others shook he smiled in the hut,
As he carved me a bowl of the cocoa-nut
    Through the roar of the hurricanes.

XII.

I sang his name instead of a song,
    Over and over I sang his name,
Upward and downward I drew it along   80
    My various notes,—the same, the same!
I sang it low, that the slave-girls near
Might never guess, from aught they could hear,
    It was only a name—a name.

XIII.

I look on the sky and the sea.
    We were two to love, and two to pray:
Yes, two, O God, who cried to Thee,
    Though nothing didst Thou say!
Coldly Thou sat'st behind the sun:
And now I cry who am but one,   90
    Thou wilt not speak to-day.

XIV.

We were black, we were black,
    We had no claim to love and bliss,
What marvel if each went to wrack?
    They wrung my cold hands out of his,
They dragged him—where? I crawled to touch
His blood's mark in the dust . . . not much,
    Ye pilgrim-souls, though plain as *this*!

XV.

Wrong, followed by a deeper wrong!
    Mere grief's too good for such as I: 100
So the white men brought the shame ere long
    To strangle the sob of my agony.
They would not leave me for my dull
Wet eyes!—it was too merciful
    To let me weep pure tears and die.

XVI.

I am black, I am black!
    I wore a child upon my breast,
An amulet that hung too slack,
    And, in my unrest, could not rest:
Thus we went moaning, child and mother,   110
One to another, one to another,
    Until all ended for the best.

XVII.

For hark! I will tell you low, low,
    I am black, you see,—
And the babe who lay on my bosom so,
    Was far too white, too white for me;
As white as the ladies who scorned to pray
Beside me at church but yesterday,
    Though my tears had washed a place for my knee.

XVIII.

My own, own child! I could not bear   120
    To look in his face, it was so white;
I covered him up with a kerchief there,
    I covered his face in close and tight:
And he moaned and struggled, as well might be,
For the white child wanted his liberty—
    Ha, ha! he wanted the master-right.

XIX.

He moaned and beat with his head and feet,
    His little feet that never grew;
He struck them out, as it was meet,
    Against my heart to break it through: 130
I might have sung and made him mild,
But I dared not sing to the white-faced child
    The only song I knew.

XX.

I pulled the kerchief very close:
    He could not see the sun, I swear,
More, then, alive, than now he does
    From between the roots of the mango . . . where?
I know where. Close! A child and mother
Do wrong to look at one another
    When one is black and one is fair.   140

XXI.

Why, in that single glance I had
    Of my child's face, . . . I tell you all,
I saw a look that made me mad!
    The *master's* look, that used to fall
On my soul like his lash . . . or worse!
And so, to save it from my curse,
    I twisted it round in my shawl.

XXII.

And he moaned and trembled from foot to head,
    He shivered from head to foot;
Till after a time, he lay instead   150
    Too suddenly still and mute.
I felt, beside, a stiffening cold:
I dared to lift up just a fold,
    As in lifting a leaf of the mango-fruit.

XXIII.

But *my* fruit . . . ha, ha!—there, had been
    (I laugh to think on't at this hour!)
Your fine white angels (who have seen
    Nearest the secret of God's power)
And plucked my fruit to make them wine,
And sucked the soul of that child of mine   160
    As the humming-bird sucks the soul of the flower.

XXIV.

Ha, ha, the trick of the angels white!
    They freed the white child's spirit so.
I said not a word, but day and night
    I carried the body to and fro,
And it lay on my heart like a stone, as chill.
—The sun may shine out as much as he will:
    I am cold, though it happened a month ago.

XXV.

From the white man's house, and the black man's hut,
    I carried the little body on;   170
The forest's arms did round us shut,
    And silence through the trees did run:
They asked no question as I went,
They stood too high for astonishment,
    They could see God sit on His throne.

XXVI.

My little body, kerchiefed fast,
    I bore it on through the forest, on;
And when I felt it was tired at last,
    I scooped a hole beneath the moon:
Through the forest-tops the angels far,   180
With a white sharp finger from every star,
    Did point and mock at what was done.

XXVII.

Yet when it was all done aright,—
    Earth, 'twixt me and my baby, strewed,—
All, changed to black earth,—nothing white,—
    A dark child in the dark!—ensued
Some comfort, and my heart grew young;
I sate down smiling there and sung
    The song I learnt in my maidenhood.

XXVIII.

And thus we two were reconciled,   190
    The white child and black mother, thus;
For as I sang it soft and wild,
    The same song, more melodious,
Rose from the grave whereon I sate:
It was the dead child singing that,
    To join the souls of both of us.

XXIX.

I look on the sea and the sky.
    Where the pilgrims' ships first anchored lay
The free sun rideth gloriously,
    But the pilgrim-ghosts have slid away   200
Through the earliest streaks of the morn:
My face is black, but it glares with a scorn
    Which they dare not meet by day.

XXX.

Ha!—in their stead, their hunter sons!
    Ha, ha! they are on me—they hunt in a ring!
Keep off! I brave you all at once,
    I throw off your eyes like snakes that sting!
You have killed the black eagle at nest, I think:
Did you ever stand still in your triumph, and shrink
    From the stroke of her wounded wing?   210

XXXI.

(Man, drop that stone you dared to lift!—)
    I wish you who stand there five abreast,
Each, for his own wife's joy and gift,
    A little corpse as safely at rest
As mine in the mangoes! Yes, but *she*
May keep live babies on her knee,
    And sing the song she likes the best.

XXXII.

I am not mad: I am black.
    I see you staring in my face—
I know you staring, shrinking back,   220
    Ye are born of the Washington-race,
And this land is the free America,
And this mark on my wrist—(I prove what I say)
    Ropes tied me up here to the flogging-place.

XXXIII.

You think I shrieked then? Not a sound!
    I hung, as a gourd hangs in the sun;
I only cursed them all around
    As softly as I might have done
My very own child: from these sands
Up to the mountains, lift your hands,   230
    O slaves, and end what I begun!

XXXIV.

Whips, curses; these must answer those!
    For in this UNION you have set
Two kinds of men in adverse rows,
    Each loathing each; and all forget
The seven wounds[4] in Christ's body fair,
While HE sees gaping everywhere
    Our countless wounds that pay no debt.

XXXV.

Our wounds are different. Your white men
    Are, after all, not gods indeed,   240
Nor able to make Christs again
    Do good with bleeding. *We* who bleed
(Stand off!) we help not in our loss!
We are too heavy for our cross,
    And fall and crush you and your seed.

XXXVI.

I fall, I swoon! I look at the sky.
    The clouds are breaking on my brain;
I am floated along, as if I should die
    Of liberty's exquisite pain.
In the name of the white child waiting for me   250
In the death-dark where we may kiss and agree,
White men, I leave you all curse-free
    In my broken heart's disdain!

FINITE AND INFINITE

The wind sounds only in opposing straits,
The sea, beside the shore; man's spirit rends
Its quiet only up against the ends
Of wants and oppositions, loves and hates,
Where, worked and worn by passionate debates,
And losing by the loss it apprehends,
The flesh rocks round and every breath it sends
Is ravelled to a sigh. All tortured states
Suppose a straitened place. Jehovah Lord,
Make room for rest, around me! out of sight   10
Now float me of the vexing land abhorred,
Till in deep calms of space my soul may right
Her nature, shoot large sail on lengthening cord,
And rush exultant on the Infinite.

MOUNTAINEER AND POET[5]

The simple goatherd between Alp and sky,
Seeing his shadow, in that awful tryst,
Dilated to a giant's on the mist,
Esteems not his own stature larger by
The apparent image, but more patiently
Strikes his staff down beneath his clenching fist,
While the snow-mountains lift their amethyst
And sapphire crowns of splendour, far and nigh,
Into the air around him. Learn from hence
Meek morals, all ye poets that pursue   10
Your way still onward up to eminence!
Ye are not great because creation drew
Large revelations round your earliest sense,
Nor bright because God's glory shines for you.

THE POET

The poet hath the child's sight in his breast
And sees all *new*. What oftenest he has viewed
He views with the first glory.[6] Fair and good
Pall never on him, at the fairest, best,
But stand before him holy and undressed
In week-day false conventions, such as would
Drag other men down from the altitude
Of primal types, too early dispossessed.
Why, God would tire of all His heavens, as soon
As thou, O godlike, childlike poet, didst   10
Of daily and nightly sights of sun and moon!
And therefore hath He set thee in the midst
Where men may hear thy wonder's ceaseless tune
And praise His world for ever, as thou bidst.

HIRAM POWERS' "GREEK SLAVE"[7]

They say Ideal beauty cannot enter
The house of anguish. On the threshold stands
An alien Image with enshackled hands,
Called the Greek Slave! as if the artist meant her
(That passionless perfection which he lent her,
Shadowed not darkened where the sill expands)
To so confront man's crimes in different lands
With man's ideal sense. Pierce to the centre,
Art's fiery finger, and break up ere long
The serfdom of this world. Appeal, fair stone,   10
From God's pure heights of beauty against man's wrong!
Catch up in thy divine face, not alone
East griefs but west, and strike and shame the strong,
By thunders of white silence, overthrown.

A REED[8]

I.

I am no trumpet, but a reed;
No flattering breath shall from me lead
    A silver sound, a hollow sound:
I will not ring, for priest or king,
One blast that in re-echoing
    Would leave a bondsman faster bound.

II.

I am no trumpet, but a reed,—
A broken reed,[9] the wind indeed
    Left flat upon a dismal shore;
Yet if a little maid or child
Should sigh within it, earnest-mild
    This reed will answer evermore.

III.

I am no trumpet, but a reed;
Go, tell the fishers, as they spread
    Their nets along the river's edge,
I will not tear their nets at all,
Nor pierce their hands, if they should fall:
    Then let them leave me in the sedge.

10

A WOMAN'S SHORTCOMINGS

I.

She has laughed as softly as if she sighed,
    She has counted six, and over,
Of a purse well filled and a heart well tried—
    Oh, each a worthy lover!
They "give her time;" for her soul must slip
    Where the world has set the grooving;
She will lie to none with her fair red lip:
    But love seeks truer loving.

II.

She trembles her fan in a sweetness dumb,
　　As her thoughts were beyond recalling,   10
With a glance for *one*, and a glance for *some*,
　　From her eyelids rising and falling;
Speaks common words with a blushful air,
　　Hears bold words, unreproving;
But her silence says—what she never will swear—
　　And love seeks better loving.

III.

Go, lady, lean to the night-guitar
　　And drop a smile to the bringer;
Then smile as sweetly, when he is far,
　　At the voice of an in-door singer.   20
Bask tenderly beneath tender eyes;
　　Glance lightly, on their removing;
And join new vows to old perjuries—
　　But dare not call it loving.

IV.

Unless you can think, when the song is done,
　　No other is soft in the rhythm;
Unless you can feel, when left by One,
　　That all men else go with him;
Unless you can know, when unpraised by his breath,
　　That your beauty itself wants proving;   30
Unless you can swear "For life, for death!"—
　　Oh, fear to call it loving!

V.

Unless you can muse in a crowd all day
　　On the absent face that fixed you;
Unless you can love, as the angels may,
　　With the breadth of heaven betwixt you;
Unless you can dream that his faith is fast,
　　Through behoving[10] and unbehoving;
Unless you can *die* when the dream is past—
　　Oh, never call it loving!   40

A MAN'S REQUIREMENTS

I.

Love me, Sweet, with all thou art,
    Feeling, thinking, seeing;
Love me in the lightest part,
    Love me in full being.

II.

Love me with thine open youth
    In its frank surrender;
With the vowing of thy mouth
    With its silence tender.

III.

Love me with thine azure eyes,
    Made for earnest granting;   10
Taking colour from the skies,
    Can Heaven's truth be wanting?

IV.

Love me with their lids, that fall
    Snow-like at first meeting;
Love me with thine heart, that all
    Neighbours then see beating.

V.

Love me with thine hand stretched out
    Freely—open-minded:
Love me with thy loitering foot,—
    Hearing one behind it.   20

VI.

Love me with thy voice, that turns
    Sudden faint above me;
Love me with thy blush that burns
    When I murmur *Love me!*

VII.

Love me with thy thinking soul,
    Break it to love-sighing;
Love me with thy thoughts that roll
    On through living—dying.

VIII.

Love me in thy gorgeous airs,
    When the world has crowned thee;   30
Love me, kneeling at thy prayers,
    With the angels round thee.

IX.

Love me pure, as musers do,
    Up the woodlands shady:
Love me gaily, fast and true,
    As a winsome lady.

X.

Through all hopes that keep us brave,
    Farther off or nigher,
Love me for the house and grave,
    And for something higher.   40

XI.

Thus, if thou wilt prove me, Dear,
    Woman's love no fable,
I will love *thee*—half a year—
    As a man is able.

INSUFFICIENCY[11]

I.

There is no one beside thee and no one above thee,
    Thou standest alone as the nightingale sings!
    And my words that would praise thee are impotent things,
For none can express thee though all should approve thee.
    I love thee so, Dear, that I only can love thee.

II.

Say, what can I do for thee? weary thee, grieve thee?
    Lean on thy shoulder, new burdens to add?
    Weep my tears over thee, making thee sad?
Oh, hold me not—love me not! let me retrieve thee.
    I love thee so, Dear, that I only can leave thee.   10

SONNETS FROM THE PORTUGUESE[12]

I.

I thought once how Theocritus[13] had sung
Of the sweet years, the dear and wished-for years,
Who each one in a gracious hand appears
To bear a gift for mortals, old or young:
And, as I mused it in his antique tongue,
I saw, in gradual vision through my tears,
The sweet, sad years, the melancholy years,
Those of my own life, who by turns had flung
A shadow across me. Straightway I was 'ware,
So weeping, how a mystic Shape did move   10
Behind me, and drew me backward by the hair;[14]
And a voice said in mastery, while I strove,—
"Guess now who holds thee?"—"Death," I said.
                But, there,
The silver answer rang,—"Not Death, but Love."

II.

But only three in all God's universe
Have heard this word thou hast said,—Himself, beside
Thee speaking, and me listening! and replied
One of us . . . *that* was God, . . . and laid the curse
So darkly on my eyelids, as to amerce[15]
My sight from seeing thee,—that if I had died,
The deathweights,[16] placed there, would have signified
Less absolute exclusion. "Nay" is worse
From God than from all others, O my friend!
Men could not part us with their worldly jars,   10
Nor the seas change us, nor the tempests bend;
Our hands would touch for all the mountain bars:
And, heaven being rolled between us at the end,
We should but vow the faster for the stars.

III.

Unlike are we, unlike, O princely Heart!
Unlike our uses and our destinies.
Our ministering two angels look surprise
On one another, as they strike athwart
Their wings in passing. Thou, bethink thee, art
A quest for queens to social pageantries,
With gages[17] from a hundred brighter eyes

Than tears even can make mine, to play thy part
Of chief musician. What hast *thou* to do
With looking from the lattice-lights at me,   10
A poor, tired, wandering singer, singing through
The dark, and leaning up a cypress tree?
The chrism is on thine head,—on mine, the dew,—
And Death must dig the level where these agree.

IV.

Thou hast thy calling to some palace-floor,
Most gracious singer of high poems! where
The dancers will break footing, from the care
Of watching up thy pregnant lips for more.
And dost thou lift this house's latch too poor
For hand of thine? and canst thou think and bear
To let thy music drop here unaware
In folds of golden fulness at my door?
Look up and see the casement broken in,
The bats and owlets builders in the roof!   10
My cricket chirps against thy mandolin.
Hush, call no echo up in further proof
Of desolation! there's a voice within
That weeps . . . as thou must sing . . . alone, aloof.

V.

I lift my heavy heart up solemnly,
As once Electra her sepulchral urn,[18]
And, looking in thine eyes, I overturn
The ashes at thy feet. Behold and see
What a great heap of grief lay hid in me,
And how the red wild sparkles dimly burn
Through the ashen greyness. If thy foot in scorn
Could tread them out to darkness utterly,
It might be well perhaps. But if instead
Thou wait beside me for the wind to blow   10
The grey dust up, . . . those laurels on thine head,
O my Belovèd, will not shield thee so,
That none of all the fires shall scorch and shred
The hair beneath. Stand farther off then! go.

VI.

Go from me. Yet I feel that I shall stand
Henceforward in thy shadow. Nevermore
Alone upon the threshold of my door
Of individual life, I shall command
The uses of my soul, nor lift my hand
Serenely in the sunshine as before,
Without the sense of that which I forbore —
Thy touch upon the palm. The widest land
Doom takes to part us, leave thy heart in mine
With pulses that beat double. What I do   10
And what I dream include thee, as the wine
Must taste of its own grapes. And when I sue
God for myself, He hears that name of thine,
And sees within my eyes the tears of two.

VII.

The face of all the world is changed, I think,
Since first I heard the footsteps of thy soul
Move still, oh, still, beside me, as they stole
Betwixt me and the dreadful outer brink
Of obvious death, where I, who thought to sink,
Was caught up into love, and taught the whole
Of life in a new rhythm. The cup of dole
God gave for baptism, I am fain to drink,
And praise its sweetness, Sweet, with thee anear.
The names of country, heaven, are changed away   10
For where thou art or shalt be, there or here;
And this . . . this lute and song . . . loved yesterday,
(The singing angels know) are only dear
Because thy name moves right in what they say.

VIII.

What can I give thee back, O liberal
And princely giver, who hast brought the gold
And purple of thine heart, unstained, untold,
And laid them on the outside of the wall
For such as I to take or leave withal,
In unexpected largesse? am I cold,
Ungrateful, that for these most manifold
High gifts, I render nothing back at all?
Not so; not cold, — but very poor instead.
Ask God who knows. For frequent tears have run   10

The colours from my life, and left so dead
And pale a stuff, it were not fitly done
To give the same as pillow to thy head.
Go farther! let it serve to trample on.

IX.

Can it be right to give what I can give?
To let thee sit beneath the fall of tears
As salt as mine, and hear the sighing years
Re-sighing on my lips renunciative
Through those infrequent smiles which fail to live
For all thy adjurations? O my fears,
That this can scarce be right! We are not peers,
So to be lovers; and I own, and grieve,
That givers of such gifts as mine are, must
Be counted with the ungenerous. Out, alas!   10
I will not soil thy purple with my dust,
Nor breathe my poison on thy Venice-glass,[19]
Nor give thee any love—which were unjust.
Beloved, I only love thee! let it pass.

X.

Yet, love, mere love, is beautiful indeed
And worthy of acceptation. Fire is bright,
Let temple burn, or flax; an equal light
Leaps in the flame from cedar-plank or weed:
And love is fire. And when I say at need
I love thee . . . mark! . . . I love thee—in thy sight
I stand transfigured, glorified aright,
With conscience of the new rays that proceed
Out of my face toward thine. There's nothing low
In love, when love the lowest: meanest creatures   10
Who love God, God accepts while loving so.
And what I *feel*, across the inferior features
Of what I *am*, doth flash itself, and show
How that great work of Love enhances Nature's.

XIII.

And wilt thou have me fashion into speech
The love I bear thee, finding words enough,
And hold the torch out, while the winds are rough,
Between our faces, to cast light on each?—
I drop it at thy feet. I cannot teach

My hand to hold my spirit so far off
From myself—me—that I should bring thee proof
In words, of love hid in me out of reach.
Nay, let the silence of my womanhood
Commend my woman-love to thy belief,—   10
Seeing that I stand unwon, however wooed,
And rend the garment of my life,[20] in brief,
By a most dauntless, voiceless fortitude,
Lest one touch of this heart convey its grief.

XIV.

If thou must love me, let it be for nought
Except for love's sake only. Do not say
"I love her for her smile—her look—her way
Of speaking gently,—for a trick of thought
That falls in well with mine, and certes brought
A sense of pleasant ease on such a day"—
For these things in themselves, Belovèd, may
Be changed, or change for thee,—and love, so wrought,
May be unwrought so. Neither love me for
Thine own dear pity's wiping my cheeks dry,—   10
A creature might forget to weep, who bore
Thy comfort long, and lose thy love thereby!
But love me for love's sake, that evermore
Thou mayst love on, through love's eternity.

XV.

Accuse me not, beseech thee, that I wear
Too calm and sad a face in front of thine;
For we two look two ways, and cannot shine
With the same sunlight on our brow and hair.
On me thou lookest with no doubting care,
As on a bee shut in a crystalline;
Since sorrow hath shut me safe in love's divine,
And to spread wing and fly in the outer air
Were most impossible failure, if I strove
To fail so. But I look on thee—on thee—   10
Beholding, besides love, the end of love,
Hearing oblivion beyond memory;
As one who sits and gazes from above,
Over the rivers to the bitter sea.

XVI.

And yet, because thou overcomest so,
Because thou art more noble and like a king,
Thou canst prevail against my fears and fling
Thy purple round me, till my heart shall grow
Too close against thine heart henceforth to know
How it shook when alone. Why, conquering
May prove as lordly and complete a thing
In lifting upward, as in crushing low!
And as a vanquished soldier yields his sword
To one who lifts him from the bloody earth,   10
Even so, Belovèd, I at last record,
Here ends my strife. If *thou* invite me forth,
I rise above abasement at the word.
Make thy love larger to enlarge my worth.

XVII.

My poet, thou canst touch on all the notes
God set between His After and Before,
And strike up and strike off the general roar
Of the rushing worlds a melody that floats
In a serene air purely. Antidotes
Of medicated music, answering for
Mankind's forlornest uses, thou canst pour
From thence into their ears. God's will devotes
Thine to such ends, and mine to wait on thine.
How, Dearest, wilt thou have me for most use?   10
A hope, to sing by gladly? or a fine
Sad memory, with thy songs to interfuse?
A shade, in which to sing—of palm or pine?
A grave, on which to rest from singing? Choose.

XVIII.

I never gave a lock of hair away
To a man, Dearest, except this to thee,
Which now upon my fingers thoughtfully,
I ring out to the full brown length and say
"Take it." My day of youth went yesterday;
My hair no longer bounds to my foot's glee,
Nor plant I it from rose or myrtle-tree,
As girls do, any more: it only may
Now shade on two pale cheeks the mark of tears,
Taught drooping from the head that hangs aside   10

Through sorrow's trick. I thought the funeral-shears
Would take this first, but Love is justified,—
Take it thou,—finding pure, from all those years,
The kiss my mother left here when she died.

XIX.

The soul's Rialto hath its merchandise;
I barter curl for curl upon that mart,
And from my poet's forehead to my heart
Receive this lock which outweighs argosies,—
As purply black, as erst to Pindar's eyes
The dim purpureal tresses gloomed athwart
The nine white Muse-brows. For this counterpart, . . .
The bay-crown's shade, Beloved, I surmise,
Still lingers on thy curl, it is so black!
Thus, with a fillet of smooth-kissing breath,   10
I tie the shadows safe from gliding back,
And lay the gift where nothing hindereth;
Here on my heart, as on thy brow, to lack
No natural heat till mine grows cold in death.

XX.

Beloved, my Belovèd, when I think
That thou wast in the world a year ago,
What time I sat alone here in the snow
And saw no footprint, heard the silence sink
No moment at thy voice, but, link by link,
Went counting all my chains as if that so
They never could fall off at any blow
Struck by thy possible hand,—why, thus I drink
Of life's great cup of wonder! Wonderful,
Never to feel thee thrill the day or night   10
With personal act or speech,—nor ever cull
Some prescience of thee with the blossoms white
Thou sawest growing! Atheists are as dull,
Who cannot guess God's presence out of sight.

XXI.

Say over again, and yet once over again,
That thou dost love me. Though the word repeated
Should seem "a cuckoo-song," as thou dost treat it,
Remember, never to the hill or plain,
Valley and wood, without her cuckoo-strain

Comes the fresh Spring in all her green completed.
Belovèd, I, amid the darkness greeted
By a doubtful spirit-voice, in that doubt's pain
Cry, "Speak once more—thou lovest!" Who can fear
Too many stars, though each in heaven shall roll,   10
Too many flowers, though each shall crown the year?
Say thou dost love me, love me, love me—toll
The silver iterance!—only minding, Dear,
To love me also in silence with thy soul.

XXII.

When our two souls stand up erect and strong,
Face to face, silent, drawing nigh and nigher,
Until the lengthening wings break into fire
At either curvèd point,[21]—what bitter wrong
Can the earth do to us, that we should not long
Be here contented? Think. In mounting higher,
The angels would press on us and aspire
To drop some golden orb of perfect song
Into our deep, dear silence. Let us stay
Rather on earth, Belovèd,—where the unfit   10
Contrarious moods of men recoil away
And isolate pure spirits, and permit
A place to stand and love in for a day,
With darkness and the death-hour rounding it.

XXIII.

Is it indeed so? If I lay here dead,
Wouldst thou miss any life in losing mine?
And would the sun for thee more coldly shine
Because of grave-damps falling round my head?
I marvelled, my Belovèd, when I read
Thy thought so in the letter. I am thine—
But . . . *so* much to thee? Can I pour thy wine
While my hands tremble? Then my soul, instead
Of dreams of death, resumes life's lower range.
Then, love me, Love! look on me—breathe on me!   10
As brighter ladies do not count it strange,
For love, to give up acres and degree,
I yield the grave for thy sake, and exchange
My near sweet view of Heaven, for earth with thee!

XXV.

A heavy heart, Belovèd, have I borne
From year to year until I saw thy face,
And sorrow after sorrow took the place
Of all those natural joys as lightly worn
As the stringed pearls, each lifted in its turn
By a beating heart at dance-time. Hopes apace
Were changed to long despairs, till God's own grace
Could scarcely lift above the world forlorn
My heavy heart. Then *thou* didst bid me bring
And let it drop adown thy calmly great   10
Deep being! Fast it sinketh, as a thing
Which its own nature doth precipitate,
While thine doth close above it, mediating
Betwixt the stars and the unaccomplished fate.

XXVI.

I lived with visions for my company
Instead of men and women, years ago,
And found them gentle mates, nor thought to know
A sweeter music than they played to me.
But soon their trailing purple was not free
Of this world's dust, their lutes did silent grow,
And I myself grew faint and blind below
Their vanishing eyes. Then THOU didst come—to be,
Belovèd, what they seemed. Their shining fronts,
Their songs, their splendours (better, yet the same,   10
As river-water hallowed into fonts),
Met in thee, and from out thee overcame
My soul with satisfaction of all wants:
Because God's gifts put man's best dreams to shame.

XXVIII.

My letters! all dead paper, mute and white![22]
And yet they seem alive and quivering
Against my tremulous hands which loose the string
And let them drop down on my knee to-night.
This said,—he wished to have me in his sight
Once, as a friend: this fixed a day in spring
To come and touch my hand[23] . . . a simple thing,
Yet I wept for it!—this, . . . the paper's light . . .
Said, *Dear, I love thee*; and I sank and quailed
As if God's future thundered on my past.   10

This said, *I am thine*—and so its ink has paled
With lying at my heart that beat too fast.
And this . . . O Love, thy words have ill availed
If, what this said, I dared repeat at last!

XXXII.

The first time that the sun rose on thine oath
To love me, I looked forward to the moon
To slacken all those bonds which seemed too soon
And quickly tied to make a lasting troth.
Quick-loving hearts, I thought, may quickly loathe;
And, looking on myself, I seemed not one
For such man's love!—more like an out-of-tune
Worn viol, a good singer would be wroth
To spoil his song with, and which, snatched in haste,
Is laid down at the first ill-sounding note.   10
I did not wrong myself so, but I placed
A wrong on *thee*. For perfect strains may float
'Neath master-hands, from instruments defaced,—
And great souls, at one stroke may do and doat.[24]

XXXV.

If I leave all for thee, wilt thou exchange
And be all to me? Shall I never miss
Home-talk and blessing and the common kiss
That comes to each in turn, nor count it strange,
When I look up, to drop on a new range
Of walls and floors, another home than this?[25]
Nay, wilt thou fill that place by me which is
Filled by dead eyes[26] too tender to know change?
That's hardest. If to conquer love, has tried,
To conquer grief, tries more, as all things prove;   10
For grief indeed is love and grief beside.
Alas, I have grieved so I am hard to love.
Yet love me—wilt thou? Open thine heart wide,
And fold within the wet wings of thy dove.

XXXVII.

Pardon, oh, pardon, that my soul should make,
Of all that strong divineness which I know
For thine and thee, an image only so
Formed of the sand, and fit to shift and break.
It is that distant years which did not take

Thy sovranty, recoiling with a blow,
Have forced my swimming brain to undergo
Their doubt and dread, and blindly to forsake
Thy purity of likeness and distort
Thy worthiest love to a worthless counterfeit: 10
As if a shipwrecked Pagan, safe in port,
His guardian sea-god to commemorate,
Should set a sculptured porpoise, gills a-snort
And vibrant tail, within the temple-gate.

XXXVIII.

First time he kissed me, he but only kissed
The fingers of this hand wherewith I write;
And ever since, it grew more clean and white,
Slow to world-greetings, quick with its "Oh, list,"
When the angels speak. A ring of amethyst
I could not wear here, plainer to my sight,
Than that first kiss. The second passed in height
The first, and sought the forehead, and half missed,
Half falling on the hair. O beyond meed!²⁷
That was the chrism of love, which love's own crown,   10
With sanctifying sweetness, did precede.
The third upon my lips was folded down
In perfect, purple state; since when, indeed,
I have been proud and said, "My love, my own."

XXXIX.

Because thou hast the power and own'st the grace
To look through and behind this mask of me
(Against which years have beat thus blanchingly
With their rains), and behold my soul's true face,
The dim and weary witness of life's race,—
Because thou hast the faith and love to see,
Through that same soul's distracting lethargy,
The patient angel waiting for a place
In the new Heavens,—because nor sin nor woe,
Nor God's infliction, nor death's neighbourhood,   10
Nor all which others viewing, turn to go,
Nor all which makes me tired of all, self-viewed,—
Nothing repels thee, . . . Dearest, teach me so
To pour out gratitude, as thou dost, good!

XLI.

I thank all who have loved me in their hearts,
With thanks and love from mine. Deep thanks to all
Who paused a little near the prison-wall ·
To hear my music in its louder parts
Ere they went onward, each one to the mart's
Or temple's occupation, beyond call.
But thou, who, in my voice's sink and fall
When the sob took it, thy divinest Art's
Own instrument didst drop down at thy foot
To hearken what I said between my tears, . . .   10
Instruct me how to thank thee! Oh, to shoot
My soul's full meaning into future years,
That *they* should lend it utterance, and salute
Love that endures, from Life that disappears!

XLII.

"My future will not copy fair my past"—[28]
I wrote that once; and thinking at my side
My ministering life-angel justified
The word by his appealing look upcast
To the white throne of God, I turned at last,
And there, instead, saw thee, not unallied
To angels in thy soul! Then I, long tried
By natural ills, received the comfort fast,
While budding, at thy sight, my pilgrim's staff
Gave out green leaves with morning dews impearled.   10
I seek no copy now of life's first half:
Leave here the pages with long musing curled,
And write me new my future's epigraph,
New angel mine, unhoped for in the world!

XLIII.

How do I love thee? Let me count the ways.
I love thee to the depth and breadth and height
My soul can reach, when feeling out of sight
For the ends of Being and ideal Grace.
I love thee to the level of everyday's
Most quiet need, by sun and candle-light.
I love thee freely, as men strive for Right;
I love thee purely, as they turn from Praise.
I love thee with the passion put to use
In my old griefs, and with my childhood's faith.   10

I love thee with a love I seemed to lose
With my lost saints,[29] — I love thee with the breath,
Smiles, tears, of all my life! — and, if God choose,
I shall but love thee better after death.

XLIV.

Belovèd, thou hast brought me many flowers
Plucked in the garden, all the summer through
And winter, and it seemed as if they grew
In this close room, nor missed the sun and showers.
So, in the like name of that love of ours,
Take back these thoughts which here unfolded too,
And which on warm and cold days I withdrew
From my heart's ground. Indeed, those beds and bowers
Be overgrown with bitter weeds and rue,
And wait thy weeding; yet here's eglantine,   10
Here's ivy! — take them, as I used to do
Thy flowers, and keep them where they shall not pine.
Instruct thine eyes to keep their colours true,
And tell thy soul their roots are left in mine.

Casa Guidi Windows[1]
1851

Part I.

I heard last night a little child go singing
   'Neath Casa Guidi windows, by the church,
O bella libertà, O bella![2]—stringing
   The same words still on notes he went in search
So high for, you concluded the upspringing
   Of such a nimble bird to sky from perch
Must leave the whole bush in a tremble green,
   And that the heart of Italy must beat,
While such a voice had leave to rise serene
   'Twixt church and palace of a Florence street: 10
A little child, too, who not long had been
   By mother's finger steadied on his feet,
And still O bella libertà he sang.

Then I thought, musing, of the innumerous
   Sweet songs which still for Italy outrang
From older singers' lips who sang not thus
   Exultingly and purely, yet, with pang
Fast sheathed in music, touched the heart of us
   So finely that the pity scarcely pained.
I thought how Filicaja[3] led on others,   20
   Bewailers for their Italy enchained,
And how they called her childless among mothers,
   Widow of empires, ay, and scarce refrained
Cursing her beauty to her face, as brothers
   Might a shamed sister's,—"Had she been less fair
She were less wretched;"—how, evoking so
   From congregated wrong and heaped despair
Of men and women writhing under blow,
   Harrowed and hideous in a filthy lair,
Some personating Image wherein woe   30

Was wrapt in beauty from offending much,
They called it Cybele, or Niobe,[4]
　　Or laid it corpse-like on a bier for such,
Where all the world might drop for Italy
　　Those cadenced tears which burn not where they touch,—
"Juliet of nations,[5] canst thou die as we?
　　And was the violet crown that crowned thy head
So over-large, though new buds made it rough,
　　It slipped down and across thine eyelids dead,
O sweet, fair Juliet?" Of such songs enough,　　　　40
　　Too many of such complaints! behold, instead,
Void at Verona, Juliet's marble trough:
　　As void as that is, are all images
Men set between themselves and actual wrong,
　　To catch the weight of pity, meet the stress
Of conscience,—since 'tis easier to gaze long
　　On mournful masks and sad effigies
Than on real, live, weak creatures crushed by strong.

For me who stand in Italy to-day
Where worthier poets stood and sang before,　　　　50
　　I kiss their footsteps yet their words gainsay.
I can but muse in hope upon this shore
　　Of golden Arno[6] as it shoots away
Through Florence' heart beneath her bridges four:
　　Bent bridges, seeming to strain off like bows,
And tremble while the arrowy undertide
　　Shoots on and cleaves the marble as it goes,
And strikes up palace-walls on either side,
　　And froths the cornice out in glittering rows,
With doors and windows quaintly multiplied,　　　　60
　　And terrace-sweeps, and gazers upon all,
By whom if flower or kerchief were thrown out
　　From any lattice there, the same would fall
Into the river underneath, no doubt,
　　It runs so close and fast 'twixt wall and wall.
How beautiful! the mountains from without
　　In silence listen for the word said next.
What word will men say,—here where Giotto planted
　　His campanile[7] like an unperplexed
Fine question Heavenward, touching the things granted　　70
　　A noble people who, being greatly vexed
In act, in inspiration keep undaunted?

What word will God say? Michel's Night and Day
And Dawn and Twilight[8] wait in marble scorn
    Like dogs upon a dunghill, couched on clay
From whence the Medicean stamp's outworn,
    The final putting off of all such sway
By all such hands, and freeing of the unborn
    In Florence and the great world outside Florence.
Three hundred years his patient statues wait   80
    In that small chapel of the dim Saint Lawrence:
Day's eyes are breaking bold and passionate
    Over his shoulder, and will flash abhorrence
On darkness and with level looks meet fate,
    When once loose from that marble film of theirs;
The Night has wild dreams in her sleep, the Dawn
    Is haggard as the sleepless, Twilight wears
A sort of horror; as the veil withdrawn
    'Twixt the artist's soul and works had left them heirs
Of speechless thoughts which would not quail nor fawn,   90
    Of anger and contempts, of hope and love:
For not without a meaning did he place
    The princely Urbino on the seat above
With everlasting shadow on his face,
    While the slow dawns and twilights disapprove
The ashes of his long-extinguished race
    Which never more shall clog the feet of men.
I do believe, divinest Angelo,
    That winter-hour in Via Larga, when
They bade thee build a statue up in snow[9]   100
    And straight that marvel of thine art again
Dissolved beneath the sun's Italian glow,
    Thine eyes, dilated with the plastic passion,
Thawing too in drops of wounded manhood, since,
    To mock alike thine art and indignation,
Laughed at the palace-window the new prince,—
    ("Aha! this genius needs for exaltation,
When all's said and howe'er the proud may wince,
    A little marble from our princely mines!")
I do believe that hour thou laughedst too   110
    For the whole sad world and for thy Florentines,
After those few tears, which were only few!
    That as, beneath the sun, the grand white lines
Of thy snow-statue trembled and withdrew,—
    The head, erect as Jove's, being palsied first,

The eyelids flattened, the full brow turned blank,
    The right-hand, raised but now as if it cursed,
Dropt, a mere snowball, (till the people sank
    Their voices, though a louder laughter burst
From the royal window)—thou couldst proudly thank   120
    God and the prince for promise and presage,
And laugh the laugh back, I think verily,
    Thine eyes being purged by tears of righteous rage
To read a wrong into a prophecy,
    And measure a true great man's heritage
Against a mere great-duke's posterity.
    I think thy soul said then, "I do not need
A princedom and its quarries, after all;
    For if I write, paint, carve a word, indeed,
On book or board or dust, on floor or wall,   130
    The same is kept of God who taketh heed
That not a letter of the meaning fall
    Or ere it touch and teach His world's deep heart,
Outlasting, therefore, all your lordships, sir!
    So keep your stone, beseech you, for your part,
To cover up your grave-place and refer
    The proper titles; *I* live by my art.
The thought I threw into this snow shall stir
    This gazing people when their gaze is done;
And the tradition of your act and mine,   140
    When all the snow is melted in the sun,
Shall gather up, for unborn men, a sign
    Of what is the true princedom,—ay, and none
Shall laugh that day, except the drunk with wine."

    Amen, great Angelo! the day's at hand.
If many laugh not on it, shall we weep?
    Much more we must not, let us understand.
Through rhymers sonneteering in their sleep,
    And archaists mumbling dry bones up the land,
And sketchers lauding ruined towns a-heap,—   150
    Through all that drowsy hum of voices smooth,
The hopeful bird mounts carolling from brake,
    The hopeful child, with leaps to catch his growth,
Sings open-eyed for liberty's sweet sake:
    And I, a singer also from my youth,
Prefer to sing with these who are awake,
    With birds, with babes, with men who will not fear

The baptism of the holy morning dew,
        (And many of such wakers now are here,
Complete in their anointed manhood, who   160
        Will greatly dare and greatlier persevere,)
Than join those old thin voices with my new,
        And sigh for Italy with some safe sigh
Cooped up in music 'twixt an oh and ah,—
        Nay, hand in hand with that young child, will I
Go singing rather, *"Bella libertà,"*
        Than, with those poets, croon the dead or cry
"Se tu men bella fossi, Italia!"
        "Less wretched if less fair." Perhaps a truth
Is so far plain in this, that Italy,   170
        Long trammelled with the purple of her youth
Against her age's ripe activity,
        Sits still upon her tombs, without death's ruth
But also without life's brave energy.
        "Now tell us what is Italy?" men ask:
And others answer, "Virgil, Cicero,
        Catullus, Caesar." What beside? to task
The memory closer—"Why, Boccaccio,
        Dante, Petrarca,"—and if still the flask
Appears to yield its wine by drops too slow,—   180
        "Angelo, Raffael, Pergolese,"—all
Whose strong hearts beat through stone, or charged again
        The paints with fire of souls electrical,
Or broke up heaven for music. What more then?
        Why, then, no more. The chaplet's last beads fall
In naming the last saintship within ken,
        And, after that, none prayeth in the land.
Alas, this Italy has too long swept
        Heroic ashes up for hour-glass sand;
Of her own past, impassioned nympholept![10]   190
        Consenting to be nailed here by the hand
To the very bay-tree under which she stept
        A queen of old, and plucked a leafy branch;
And, licensing the world too long indeed
        To use her broad phylacteries[11] to staunch
And stop her bloody lips, she takes no heed
        How one clear word would draw an avalanche
Of living sons around her, to succeed
        The vanished generations. Can she count
These oil-eaters with large live mobile mouths   200

Agape for macaroni, in the amount
Of consecrated heroes of her south's
    Bright rosary? The pitcher at the fount,
The gift of gods, being broken, she much loathes
    To let the ground-leaves of the place confer
A natural bowl. So henceforth she would seem
    No nation, but the poet's pensioner,
With alms from every land of song and dream,
    While aye her pipers sadly pipe of her
Until their proper breaths, in that extreme   210
    Of sighing, split the reed on which they played:
Of which, no more. But never say "no more"
    To Italy's life! Her memories undismayed
Still argue "evermore;" her graves implore
    Her future to be strong and not afraid;
Her very statues send their looks before.
    We do not serve the dead—the past is past.
God lives, and lifts His glorious mornings up
    Before the eyes of men awake at last,
Who put away the meats they used to sup,   220
    And down upon the dust of earth outcast
The dregs remaining of the ancient cup,
    Then turn to wakeful prayer and worthy act.
The Dead, upon their awful 'vantage ground,
    The sun not in their faces, shall abstract
No more our strength; we will not be discrowned
    As guardians of their crowns, nor deign transact
A barter of the present, for a sound
    Of good so counted in the foregone days.
O Dead, ye shall no longer cling to us   230
    With rigid hands of desiccating praise,
And drag us backward by the garment thus,
    To stand and laud you in long-drawn virelays![12]
We will not henceforth be oblivious
    Of our own lives, because ye lived before,
Nor of our acts, because ye acted well.
    We thank you that ye first unlatched the door,
But will not make it inaccessible
    By thankings on the threshold any more.
We hurry onward to extinguish hell   240
    With our fresh souls, our younger hope, and God's
Maturity of purpose. Soon shall we
    Die also! and, that then our periods

Of life may round themselves to memory
    As smoothly as on our graves the burial-sods,
We now must look to it to excel as ye,
    And bear our age as far, unlimited
By the last mind-mark; so, to be invoked
    By future generations, as their Dead.
'Tis true that when the dust of death has choked   250
    A great man's voice, the common words he said
Turn oracles, the common thoughts he yoked
    Like horses, draw like griffins: this is true
And acceptable. I, too, should desire,
    When men make record, with the flowers they strew,
"Savonarola's[13] soul went out in fire
    Upon our Grand-duke's piazza, and burned through
A moment first, or ere he did expire,
    The veil betwixt the right and wrong, and showed
How near God sat and judged the judges there,—"   260
    Upon the self-same pavement overstrewed
To cast my violets with as reverent care,
    And proved that all the winters which have snowed
Cannot snow out the scent from stones and air,
    Of a sincere man's virtues. This was he,
Savonarola, who, while Peter sank
    With his whole boat-load, called courageously
"Wake Christ, wake Christ!"—who, having tried the tank
    Of old church-waters used for baptistry
Ere Luther came to spill them, swore they stank;   270
    Who also by a princely deathbed cried,
"Loose Florence, or God will not loose thy soul!"
    Then fell back the Magnificent and died
Beneath the star-look shooting from the cowl,
    Which turned to wormwood-bitterness the wide
Deep sea of his ambitions. It were foul
    To grudge Savonarola and the rest
Their violets: rather pay them quick and fresh!
    The emphasis of death makes manifest
The eloquence of action in our flesh;   280
    And men who, living, were but dimly guessed,
When once free from their life's entangled mesh,
    Show their full length in graves, or oft indeed
Exaggerate their stature, in the flat,
    To noble admirations which exceed
Most nobly, yet will calculate in that

But accurately. We, who are the seed
Of buried creatures, if we turned and spat
    Upon our antecedents, we were vile.
Bring violets rather. If these had not walked   290
    Their furlong, could we hope to walk our mile?
Therefore bring violets. Yet if we self-baulked
    Stand still, a-strewing violets all the while,
These moved in vain, of whom we have vainly talked.
    So rise up henceforth with a cheerful smile,
And having strewn the violets, reap the corn,
    And having reaped and garnered, bring the plough
And draw new furrows 'neath the healthy morn,
    And plant the great Hereafter in this Now.

Of old 'twas so. How step by step was worn,   300
    As each man gained on each securely!—how
Each by his own strength sought his own Ideal,—
    The ultimate Perfection leaning bright
From out the sun and stars to bless the leal[14]
    And earnest search of all for Fair and Right
Through doubtful forms by earth accounted real!
    Because old Jubal[15] blew into delight
The souls of men with clear-piped melodies,
    If youthful Asaph[16] were content at most
To draw from Jubal's grave, with listening eyes,   310
    Traditionary music's floating ghost
Into the grass-grown silence, were it wise?
    And was't not wiser, Jubal's breath being lost,
That Miriam[17] clashed her cymbals to surprise
    The sun between her white arms flung apart,
With new glad golden sounds? that David's strings
    O'erflowed his hand with music from his heart?
So harmony grows full from many springs,
    And happy accident turns holy art.

*   *   *   *   *[18]

I would but turn these lachrymals to use,
    And pour fresh oil in from the olive-grove,
To furnish them as new lamps. Shall I say
    What made my heart beat with exulting love
A few weeks back?—

                    The day was such a day
        As Florence owes the sun. The sky above,
Its weight upon the mountains seemed to lay,
        And palpitate in glory, like a dove
Who has flown too fast, full-hearted—take away   450
        The image! for the heart of man beat higher
That day in Florence, flooding all her streets
        And piazzas with a tumult and desire.
The people, with accumulated heats
        And faces turned one way, as if one fire
Both drew and flushed them, left their ancient beats
        And went up toward the palace-Pitti wall
To thank their Grand-duke who, not quite of course,
        Had graciously permitted, at their call,
The citizens to use their civic force   460
        To guard their civic homes. So, one and all,
The Tuscan cities streamed up to the source
        Of this new good at Florence, taking it
As good so far, presageful of more good,—
        The first torch of Italian freedom, lit
To toss in the next tiger's face who should
        Approach too near them in a greedy fit,—
The first pulse of an even flow of blood
        To prove the level of Italian veins
Towards rights perceived and granted. How we gazed   470
        From Casa Guidi windows while, in trains
Of orderly procession—banners raised,
        And intermittent bursts of martial strains
Which died upon the shout, as if amazed
        By gladness beyond music—they passed on!

                *   *   *   *   *[19]

The people who are simple, blind and rough,
        Know their own angels, after looking round.   600
Whom chose they then? where met they?
                                On the stone
Called Dante's,[20]—a plain flat stone scarce discerned
From others in the pavement,—whereupon
        He used to bring his quiet chair out, turned
To Brunelleschi's church,[21] and pour alone
        The lava of his spirit when it burned:

It is not cold to-day. O passionate
   Poor Dante who, a banished Florentine,
Didst sit austere at banquets of the great
   And muse upon this far-off stone of thine   610
And think how oft some passer used to wait
   A moment, in the golden day's decline,
With "Good night, dearest Dante!"–well, good night!
   I muse now, Dante, and think verily,
Though chapelled in the byeway out of sight,
   Ravenna's bones would thrill with ecstasy,
Couldst know thy favourite stone's elected right
   As tryst-place for thy Tuscans to foresee
Their earliest chartas from. Good night, good morn,
   Henceforward, Dante: now my soul is sure   620
That thine is better comforted of scorn,
   And looks down earthward in completer cure
Than when, in Santa Croce church forlorn
   Of any corpse, the architect and hewer
Did pile the empty marbles as thy tomb.
   For now thou art no longer exiled, now
Best honoured: we salute thee who art come
   Back to the old stone[22] with a softer brow
Than Giotto drew upon the wall, for some
   Good lovers of our age to track and plough   630
Their way to, through time's ordures stratified,
   And startle broad awake into the dull
Bargello chamber: now thou'rt milder-eyed,–
   Now Beatrix may leap up glad to cull
Thy first smile, even in heaven and at her side,
   Like that which, nine years old, looked beautiful
At May-game. What do I say? I only meant
   That tender Dante loved his Florence well,
While Florence, now, to love him is content;
   And, mark ye, that the piercingest sweet smell   640
Of love's dear incense by the living sent
   To find the dead, is not accessible
To lazy livers–no narcotic,–not
   Swung in a censer to a sleepy tune,–
But trod out in the morning air by hot
   Quick spirits who tread firm to ends foreshown,
And use the name of greatness unforgot,
   To meditate what greatness may be done.

For Dante sits in heaven and ye stand here,
    And more remains for doing, all must feel   650
Than trysting on his stone from year to year
    To shift processions, civic toe to heel,
The town's thanks to the Pitti. Are ye freer
    For what was felt that day? a chariot-wheel
May spin fast, yet the chariot never roll.
    But if that day suggested something good,
And bettered, with one purpose, soul by soul,—
    Better means freer. A land's brotherhood
Is most puissant: men, upon the whole,
    Are what they can be,—nations, what they would.   660

Will, therefore, to be strong, thou Italy!
    Will to be noble! Austrian Metternich[23]
Can fix no yoke unless the neck agree;
    And thine is like the lion's when the thick
Dews shudder from it, and no man would be
    The stroker of his mane, much less would prick
His nostril with a reed. When nations roar
    Like lions, who shall tame them and defraud
Of the due pasture by the river-shore?
    Roar, therefore! shake your dewlaps dry abroad: 670
The amphitheatre with open door
    Leads back upon the benches who applaud
The last spear-thruster.

                    Yet the Heavens forbid
    That we should call on passion to confront
The brutal with the brutal and, amid
    This ripening world, suggest a lion-hunt
And lion's-vengeance for the wrongs men did
    And do now, though the spears are getting blunt.
We only call, because the sight and proof
    Of lion-strength hurts nothing; and to show   680
A lion-heart, and measure paw with hoof,
    Helps something, even, and will instruct a foe
As well as the onslaught, how to stand aloof:
    Or else the world gets past the mere brute blow
Or given or taken. Children use the fist
    Until they are of age to use the brain;
And so we needed Caesars to assist
    Man's justice, and Napoleons to explain

God's counsel, when a point was nearly missed,
    Until our generations should attain   690
Christ's stature nearer. Not that we, alas,
    Attain already; but a single inch
Will raise to look down on the swordsman's pass,
    As knightly Roland on the coward's flinch:
And, after chloroform and ether-gas,
    We find out slowly what the bee and finch
Have ready found, through Nature's lamp in each,
    How to our races we may justify
Our individual claims and, as we reach
    Our own grapes, bend the top vines to supply   700
The children's uses,—how to fill a breach
    With olive-branches,—how to quench a lie
With truth, and smite a foe upon the cheek
    With Christ's most conquering kiss. Why, these
        are things
Worth a great nation's finding, to prove weak
    The "glorious arms" of military kings.
And so with wide embrace, my England, seek
    To stifle the bad heat and flickerings
Of this world's false and nearly expended fire!
    Draw palpitating arrows to the wood,   710
And twang abroad thy high hopes and thy higher
    Resolves, from that most virtuous altitude!
Till nations shall unconsciously aspire
    By looking up to thee, and learn that good
And glory are not different. Announce law
    By freedom; exalt chivalry by peace;
Instruct how clear calm eyes can overawe,
    And how pure hands, stretched simply to release
A bond-slave, will not need a sword to draw
    To be held dreadful. O my England, crease   720
Thy purple with no alien agonies,
    No struggles toward encroachment, no vile war!
Disband thy captains, change thy victories,
    Be henceforth prosperous as the angels are,
Helping, not humbling.

                        Drums and battle-cries
Go out in music of the morning-star—
And soon we shall have thinkers in the place
    Of fighters, each found able as a man

To strike electric influence through a race,
    Unstayed by city-wall and barbican.   730
The poet shall look grander in the face
    Than even of old (when he of Greece began
To sing "that Achillean wrath which slew
    So many heroes")—seeing he shall treat
The deeds of souls heroic toward the true,
    The oracles of life, previsions sweet
And awful like divine swans gliding through
    White arms of Ledas,[24] which will leave the heat
Of their escaping godship to endue
    The human medium with a heavenly flush.   740

Meanwhile, in this same Italy we want
    Not popular passion, to arise and crush,
But popular conscience, which may covenant
    For what it knows. Concede without a blush,
To grant the "civic guard" is not to grant
    The civic spirit, living and awake:
Those lappets on your shoulders, citizens,
    Your eyes strain after sideways till they ache
(While still, in admirations and amens,
    The crowd comes up on festa-days to take   750
The great sight in)—are not intelligence,
    Nor courage even—alas, if not the sign
Of something very noble, they are nought;
    For every day ye dress your sallow kine
With fringes down their cheeks, though unbesought
    They loll their heavy heads and drag the wine
And bear the wooden yoke as they were taught
    The first day. What ye want is light—indeed
Not sunlight—(ye may well look up surprised
    To those unfathomable heavens that feed   760
Your purple hills)—but God's like organised
    In some high soul, crowned capable to lead
The conscious people, conscious and advised,—
    For if we lift a people like mere clay,
It falls the same. We want thee, O unfound
    And sovran teacher! if thy beard be grey
Or black, we bid thee rise up from the ground
    And speak the word God giveth thee to say,
Inspiring into all this people round,
    Instead of passion, thought, which pioneers   770

All generous passion, purifies from sin,
  And strikes the hour for. Rise up, teacher! here's
A crowd to make a nation!—best begin
  By making each a man, till all be peers
Of earth's true patriots and pure martyrs in
  Knowing and daring. Best unbar the doors
Which Peter's heirs keep locked so overclose
  They only let the mice across the floors,
While every churchman dangles, as he goes,
  The great key at his girdle, and abhors   780
In Christ's name, meekly. Open wide the house,
  Concede the entrance with Christ's liberal mind,
And set the tables with His wine and bread.
  What! "commune in both kinds?" In every kind—
Wine, wafer, love, hope, truth, unlimited,
  Nothing kept back. For when a man is blind
To starlight, will he see the rose is red?
  A bondsman shivering at a Jesuit's foot—
"Vae! mea culpa!"[25]—is not like to stand
  A freedman at a despot's and dispute   790
His titles by the balance in his hand,
  Weighing them "suo jure." Tend the root
If careful of the branches, and expand
  The inner souls of men before you strive
For civic heroes.

                                    But the teacher, where?
  From all these crowded faces, all alive,
Eyes, of their own lids flashing themselves bare,
  And brows that with a mobile life contrive
A deeper shadow,—may we in no wise dare
  To put a finger out and touch a man,   800
And cry "this is the leader"? What, all these!
  Broad heads, black eyes,—yet not a soul that ran
From God down with a message? All, to please
  The donna waving measures with her fan,
And not the judgment-angel on his knees
  (The trumpet just an inch off from his lips),
Who when he breathes next, will put out the sun?

Yet mankind's self were foundered in eclipse,
  If lacking doers, with great works to be done;
And lo, the startled earth already dips   810

Back into light; a better day's begun;
    And soon this leader, teacher, will stand plain,
And build the golden pipes and synthesize
    This people-organ for a holy strain.
We hold this hope, and still in all these eyes
    Go sounding for the deep look which shall drain
Suffused thought into channelled enterprise.
    Where is the teacher? What now may he do,
Who shall do greatly? Doth he gird his waist
    With a monk's rope, like Luther? or pursue   820
The goat, like Tell? or dry his nets in haste,
    Like Masaniello[26] when the sky was blue?
Keep house, like other peasants, with inlaced
    Bare brawny arms about a favourite child,
And meditative looks beyond the door
    (But not to mark the kidling's teeth have filed
The green shoots of his vine which last year bore
    Full twenty bunches), or, on triple-piled
Throne-velvets sit at ease to bless the poor,
    Like other pontiffs, in the Poorest's name?   830
The old tiara keeps itself aslope
    Upon his steady brows which, all the same,
Bend mildly to permit the people's hope?

    Whatever hand shall grasp this oriflamme,
Whatever man (last peasant or first pope
    Seeking to free his country) shall appear,
Teach, lead, strike fire into the masses, fill
    These empty bladders with fine air, insphere
These wills into a unity of will,
    And make of Italy a nation—dear   840
And blessed be that man! the Heavens shall kill
    No leaf the earth lets grow for him, and Death
Shall cast him back upon the lap of Life
    To live more surely, in a clarion-breath
Of hero-music. Brutus with the knife,
    Rienzi[27] with the fasces, throb beneath
Rome's stones,—and more who threw away joy's fife
    Like Pallas, that the beauty of their souls
Might ever shine untroubled and entire:
    But if it can be true that he who rolls   850
The Church's thunders will reserve her fire
    For only light,—from eucharistic bowls

Will pour new life for nations that expire,
And rend the scarlet of his papal vest
To gird the weak loins of his countrymen,—
I hold that he surpasses all the rest
Of Romans, heroes, patriots; and that when
He sat down on the throne, he dispossessed
The first graves of some glory. See again,
This country-saving is a glorious thing: 860
And if a common man achieved it? well.
Say, a rich man did? excellent. A king?
That grows sublime. A priest? improbable.
A pope? Ah, there we stop, and cannot bring
Our faith up to the leap, with history's bell
So heavy round the neck of it—albeit
We fain would grant the possibility
For *thy* sake, Pio Nono![28]

                                        Stretch thy feet
In that case—I will kiss them reverently
As any pilgrim to the papal seat: 870
And, such proved possible, thy throne to me
Shall seem as holy a place as Pellico's[29]
Venetian dungeon, or as Spielberg's grate
At which the Lombard woman hung the rose
Of her sweet soul by its own dewy weight,
To feel the dungeon round her sunshine close,
And pining so, died early, yet too late
For what she suffered. Yea, I will not choose
Betwixt thy throne, Pope Pius, and the spot
Marked red for ever, spite of rains and dews,   880
Where Two fell riddled by the Austrian's shot,
The brothers Bandiera,[30] who accuse,
With one same mother-voice and face (that what
They speak may be invincible) the sins
Of earth's tormentors before God the just,
Until the unconscious thunderbolt begins
To loosen in His grasp.
                                        And yet we must
Beware, and mark the natural kiths and kins
Of circumstance and office, and distrust
The rich man reasoning in a poor man's hut,   890
The poet who neglects pure truth to prove
Statistic fact, the child who leaves a rut

For a smoother road, the priest who vows his glove
    Exhales no grace, the prince who walks afoot,
The woman who has sworn she will not love,
    And this Ninth Pius in Seventh Gregory's chair,
With Andrea Doria's forehead!

                            Count what goes
    To making up a pope, before he wear
That triple crown. We pass the world-wide throes
    Which went to make the popedom,—the despair   900
Of free men, good men, wise men; the dread shows
    Of women's faces, by the faggot's flash
Tossed out, to the minutest stir and throb
    O' the white lips, the least tremble of a lash,
To glut the red stare of a licensed mob;
    The short mad cries down oubliettes,[31] and plash
So horribly far off; priests, trained to rob,
    And kings that, like encouraged nightmares, sat
On nations' hearts most heavily distressed
    With monstrous sights and apophthegms of fate—   910
We pass these things,—because "the times" are prest
    With necessary charges of the weight
Of all this sin, and "Calvin, for the rest,
    Made bold to burn Servetus.[32] Ah, men err!"—
And so do *churches!* which is all we mean
    To bring to proof in any register
Of theological fat kine and lean:
    So drive them back into the pens! refer
Old sins (with pourpoint, "quotha" and "I ween")
    Entirely to the old times, the old times;   920
Nor ever ask why this preponderant
    Infallible pure Church could set her chimes
Most loudly then, just then,—most jubilant,
    Precisely then, when mankind stood in crimes
Full heart-deep, and Heaven's judgments were not scant.
    Inquire still less, what signifies a church
Of perfect inspiration and pure laws
    Who burns the first man with a brimestone-torch,
And grinds the second, bone by bone, because
    The times, forsooth, are used to rack and scorch!   930
What *is* a holy Church unless she awes
    The times down from their sins? Did Christ select
Such amiable times to come and teach

Love to, and mercy? The whole world were wrecked
If every mere great man, who lives to reach
 A little leaf of popular respect,
Attained not simply by some special breach
 In the age's customs, by some precedence
In thought and act, which, having proved him higher
 Than those he lived with, proved his competence 940
In helping them to wonder and aspire.

My words are guiltless of the bigot's sense;
My soul has fire to mingle with the fire
 Of all these souls, within or out of doors
Of Rome's church or another. I believe
 In one Priest, and one temple with its floors
Of shining jasper gloom'd at morn and eve
 By countless knees of earnest auditors,
And crystal walls too lucid to perceive,
 That none may take the measure of the place 950
And say "So far the porphyry, then, the flint—
 To this mark mercy goes, and there ends grace,"
Though still the permeable crystals hint
 At some white starry distance, bathed in space.
I feel how nature's ice-crusts keep the dint
 Of undersprings of silent Deity.
I hold the articulated gospels which
 Show Christ among us crucified on tree.
I love all who love truth, if poor or rich
 In what they have won of truth possessively. 960
No altars and no hands defiled with pitch
 Shall scare me off, but I will pray and eat
With all these—taking leave to choose my ewers—
 And say at last "Your visible churches cheat
Their inward types; and, if a church assures
 Of standing without failure and defeat,
The same both fails and lies."

        To leave which lures
 Of wider subject through past years,—behold,
We come back from the popedom to the pope,
 To ponder what he *must* be, ere we are bold 970
For what he *may* be, with our heavy hope
 To trust upon his soul. So, fold by fold,
Explore this mummy in the priestly cope,

Transmitted through the darks of time, to catch
The man within the wrappage, and discern
     How he, an honest man, upon the watch
Full fifty years for what a man may learn,
     Contrived to get just there; with what a snatch
Of old world oboli[33] he had to earn
     The passage through; with what a drowsy sop,   980
To drench the busy barkings of his brain;
     What ghosts of pale tradition, wreathed with hope
'Gainst wakeful thought, he had to entertain
     For heavenly visions; and consent to stop
The clock at noon, and let the hour remain
     (Without vain windings-up) inviolate
Against all chimings from the belfry. Lo,
     From every given pope you must abate,
Albeit you love him, some things—good, you know—
     Which every given heretic you hate,   990
Assumes for his, as being plainly so.
     A pope must hold by popes a little,—yes,
By councils, from the Nicaea up to Trent,[34]—
     By hierocratic empire, more or less
Irresponsible to men,—he must resent
     Each man's particular conscience, and repress
Inquiry, meditation, argument,
     As tyrants faction. Also, he must not
Love truth too dangerously, but prefer
     "The interests of the Church" (because a blot   1000
Is better than a rent, in miniver)—
     Submit to see the people swallow hot
Husk-porridge, which his chartered churchmen stir
     Quoting the only true God's epigraph,
"Feed my lambs, Peter!"—must consent to sit
     Attesting with his pastoral ring and staff
To such a picture of our Lady, hit
     Off well by artist-angels (though not half
As fair as Giotto would have painted it)—
     To such a vial, where a dead man's blood   1010
Runs yearly warm beneath a churchman's finger,—
     To such a holy house of stone and wood,
Whereof a cloud of angels was the bringer
     From Bethlehem to Loreto. Were it good
For any pope on earth to be a flinger
     Of stones against these high-niched counterfeits?

Apostates only are iconoclasts.
    He dares not say, while this false thing abets
That true thing, "This is false." He keeps his fasts
    And prayers, as prayer and fast were silver frets   1020
To change a note upon a string that lasts,
    And make a lie a virtue. Now, if he
Did more than this, higher hoped, and braver dared,
    I think he were a pope in jeopardy,
Or no pope rather, for his truth had barred
    The vaulting of his life,—and certainly,
If he do only this, mankind's regard
    Moves on from him at once, to seek some new
Teacher and leader. He is good and great
    According to the deeds a pope can do;   1030
Most liberal, save those bonds; affectionate,
    As princes may be, and, as priests are, true;
But only the Ninth Pius after eight,
    When all's praised most. At best and hopefullest,
He's pope—we want a man! his heart beats warm,
    But, like the prince enchanted to the waist,
He sits in stone and hardens by a charm
    Into the marble of his throne high-placed.
Mild benediction waves his saintly arm—
    So, good! but what we want's a perfect man,   1040
Complete and all alive: half travertine
    Half suits our need, and ill subserves our plan.
Feet, knees, nerves, sinews, energies divine
    Were never yet too much for men who ran
In such hard ways as must be this of thine,
    Deliverer whom we seek, whoe'er thou art,
Pope, prince, or peasant! If, indeed, the first,
    The noblest, therefore! since the heroic heart
Within thee must be great enough to burst
    Those trammels buckling to the baser part   1050
Thy saintly peers in Rome, who crossed and cursed
    With the same finger.

                            Come, appear, be found,
If pope or peasant, come! we hear the cock,
    The courtier of the mountains when first crowned
With golden dawn; and orient glories flock
    To meet the sun upon the highest ground.
Take voice and work! we wait to hear thee knock

At some one of our Florentine nine gates,
On each of which was imaged a sublime
    Face of a Tuscan genius, which, for hate's   1060
And love's sake, both, our Florence in her prime
    Turned boldly on all comers to her states,
As heroes turned their shields in antique time
    Emblazoned with honourable acts. And though
The gates are blank now of such images,
    And Petrarch looks no more from Nicolo
Toward dear Arezzo, 'twixt the acacia-trees,
    Nor Dante, from gate Gallo — still we know,
Despite the razing of the blazonries,
    Remains the consecration of the shield: 1070
The dead heroic faces will start out
    On all these gates, if foes should take the field,
And blend sublimely, at the earliest shout,
    With living heroes who will scorn to yield
A hair's-breadth even, when, gazing round about,
    They find in what a glorious company
They fight the foes of Florence. Who will grudge
    His one poor life, when that great man we see
Has given five hundred years, the world being judge,
    To help the glory of his Italy?   1080
Who, born the fair side of the Alps, will budge,
    When Dante stays, when Ariosto stays,
When Petrarch stays for ever? Ye bring swords,
    My Tuscans? Ay, if wanted in this haze,
Bring swords: but first bring souls! — bring thoughts
        and words,
    Unrusted by a tear of yesterday's,
Yet awful by its wrong, — and cut these cords,
    And mow this green lush falseness to the roots,
And shut the mouth of hell below the swathe!
    And, if ye can bring songs too, let the lute's   1090
Recoverable music softly bathe
    Some poet's hand, that, through all bursts and bruits
Of popular passion, all unripe and rathe
    Convictions of the popular intellect,
Ye may not lack a finger up the air,
    Annunciative, reproving, pure, erect,
To show which way your first Ideal bare
    The whiteness of its wings when (sorely pecked

By falcons on your wrists) it unaware
    Arose up overhead and out of sight.   1100

Meanwhile, let all the far ends of the world
    Breathe back the deep breath of their old delight,
To swell the Italian banner just unfurled.
    Help, lands of Europe! for, if Austria fight,
The drums will bar your slumber. Had ye curled
    The laurel for your thousand artists' brows,
If these Italian hands had planted none?
    Can any sit down idle in the house
Nor hear appeals from Buonarroti's stone
    And Raffael's canvas,[35] rousing and to rouse?   1110
Where's Poussin's master?[36] Gallic Avignon
    Bred Laura, and Vaucluse's fount has stirred
The heart of France too strongly, as it lets
    Its little stream out (like a wizard's bird
Which bounds upon its emerald wing and wets
    The rocks on each side), that she should not gird
Her loins with Charlemagne's sword when foes beset
    The country of her Petrarch. Spain may well
Be minded how from Italy she caught,
    To mingle with her tinkling Moorish bell,   1120
A fuller cadence and a subtler thought.
    And even the New World, the receptacle
Of freemen, may send glad men, as it ought,
    To greet Vespucci Amerigo's door.
While England claims, by trump of poetry,
    Verona, Venice, the Ravenna-shore,
And dearer holds John Milton's Fiesole
    Than Langland's Malvern with the stars in flower.

And Vallombrosa,[37] we two went to see
    Last June, beloved companion,—where sublime   1130
The mountains live in holy families,
    And the slow pine woods ever climb and climb
Half up their breasts, just stagger as they seize
    Some grey crag, drop back with it many a time,
And straggle blindly down the precipice.
    The Vallombrosan brooks were strewn as thick
That June-day, knee-deep with dead beechen leaves,
    As Milton saw them ere his heart grew sick

And his eyes blind. I think the monks and beeves
    Are all the same too: scarce have they changed
        the wick   1140
On good Saint Gualbert's[38] altar which receives
    The convent's pilgrims; and the pool in front
(Wherein the hill-stream trout are cast, to wait
    The beatific vision and the grunt
Used at refectory) keeps its weedy state,
    To baffle saintly abbots who would count
The fish across their breviary nor 'bate
    The measure of their steps. O waterfalls
And forests! sound and silence! mountains bare
    That leap up peak by peak and catch the palls   1150
Of purple and silver mist to rend and share
    With one another, at electric calls
Of life in the sunbeams,—till we cannot dare
    Fix your shapes, count your number! we must think
Your beauty and your glory helped to fill
    The cup of Milton's soul so to the brink,
He never more was thirsty when God's will
    Had shattered to his sense the last chain-link
By which he had drawn from Nature's visible
    The fresh well-water. Satisfied by this,   1160
He sang of Adam's paradise and smiled,
    Remembering Vallombrosa. Therefore is
The place divine to English man and child,
    And pilgrims leave their souls here in a kiss.

For Italy's the whole earth's treasury, piled
    With reveries of gentle ladies, flung
Aside, like ravelled silk, from life's worn stuff;
    With coins of scholars' fancy, which, being rung
On work-day counter, still sound silver-proof;
    In short, with all the dreams of dreamers young,   1170
Before their heads have time for slipping off
    Hope's pillow to the ground. How oft, indeed,
We've sent our souls out from the rigid north,
    On bare white feet which would not print nor bleed,
To climb the Alpine passes and look forth,
    Where booming low the Lombard rivers lead
To gardens, vineyards, all a dream is worth,—
    Sights, thou and I, Love, have seen afterward
From Tuscan Bellosguardo, wide awake,

When, standing on the actual blessed sward   1180
Where Galileo stood at nights to take
    The vision of the stars, we have found it hard,
Gazing upon the earth and heaven, to make
    A choice of beauty.
                                    Therefore let us all
Refreshed in England or in other land,
    By visions, with their fountain-rise and fall,
Of this earth's darling,—we, who understand
    A little how the Tuscan musical
Vowels do round themselves as if they planned
    Eternities of separate sweetness,—we,   1190
Who loved Sorrento vines in picture-book,
    Or ere in wine-cup we pledged faith or glee,—
Who loved Rome's wolf with demi-gods at suck,
    Or ere we loved truth's own divinity,—
Who loved, in brief, the classic hill and brook,
    And Ovid's dreaming tales and Petrarch's song,
Or ere we loved Love's self even,—let us give
    The blessing of our souls (and wish them strong
To bear it to the height where prayers arrive,
    When faithful spirits pray against a wrong,)   1200
To this great cause of southern men who strive
    In God's name for man's rights, and shall not fail.

Behold, they shall not fail. The shouts ascend
    Above the shrieks, in Naples, and prevail.
Rows of shot corpses, waiting for the end
    Of burial, seem to smile up straight and pale
Into the azure air and apprehend
    That final gun-flash from Palermo's coast
Which lightens their apocalypse of death.
    So let them die! The world shows nothing lost;   1210
Therefore, not blood. Above or underneath,
    What matter, brothers, if ye keep your post
On duty's side? As sword returns to sheath,
    So dust to grave, but souls find place in Heaven.
Heroic daring is the true success,
    The eucharistic bread requires no leaven;
And though your ends were hopeless, we should bless
    Your cause as holy. Strive—and, having striven,
Take, for God's recompense, that righteousness!

Aurora Leigh
1857

Upon the completion of *Aurora Leigh* in 1856, EBB dedicated the poem to her cousin and benefactor, John Kenyon, stating that it contained her "highest convictions upon Life and Art." The central conflict between Aurora and her cousin, Romney Leigh, is the conflict of whether to dedicate one's life to artistic endeavor or to improvement of the impoverished masses. The inferior position of women proves to be closely allied with this conflict. Related questions of prostitution, social disease, and illegitimacy are also raised, principally through the subplot involving the character Marian Erle. Through her portrayal of Romney Leigh as sympathetic but possessing limited vision, of the aristocratic Lady Waldemar as cold and vulgar, and of Lord Howe's vacillating personality, EBB presents various attitudes of the aristocracy toward these problems. The voice is that of the narrator-poet, Aurora Leigh.

[PRÉCIS]

In Books I–IV, the speaker, reflecting on her past, describes the first twenty-seven years of her life. In Book I, included here in full, Aurora, born in Italy of an English aristocratic father and a Florentine mother, relates how she was orphaned at age thirteen and subsequently placed under the care of her paternal aunt in Shropshire where she developed her early interest in nature and in reading poetry. In Books II–IV, she carries on her story from the age of twenty when her cousin Romney Leigh proposes to her, but in a way which indicates his interest is mainly in having her as a help-mate to his cause of alleviating the condition of victims of the social-economic system. Actually, however, there is an undercurrent of romantic attraction between them, but each is bent on following a separate course—Aurora her art, and Romney his philanthropy. After the death of her aunt, Aurora, with some inherited money, moves to London where, after seven years, she manages to achieve a certain fame in critical and creative writing. In Book III, Lady Waldemar informs Aurora that Romney Leigh is about to marry Marian Erle, a girl of the lowest class, and asks Aurora to try to break off this unsuitable match, an action clearly motivated by Lady Waldemar's desire to marry Romney herself. Aurora interviews Marian, but does nothing to prevent the marriage, being persuaded of Marian's integrity and Romney's sincerity. Neither Marian nor Romney seems to consider love a requirement for marriage. A lavish public wedding is set up as a statement against class distinctions, but Marian fails to appear, her decision explained by a letter stating that incompatibility makes the marriage impossible. The debate between Aurora and Romney on art versus philanthropy continues with some increasing appreciation of each other's position, but with both still going separate ways.

In Book V Aurora articulates her "convictions of Life and Art" as she evolves a rationale to go to Italy. By her musings on the role of the woman artist in which she affirms "Art for Art, / And good for God Himself, the essential Good!," she selects the epic as the proper medium "to represent the age" in its timelessness. At the same time, it is clear that she has not resolved woman's dilemma of hungering for love as well as for God's truth. In a retrospective passage on an evening party at Lord Howe's, Aurora portrays the coldness and hypocrisy of compromising artistocrats, overhears gossip (incorrect) of the upcoming marriage of Lady Waldemar and Romney, refuses a proposal from a wealthy landlord, and, in a dialogue with herself on the nature of sexual love, rationalizes her jealousy of Lady Waldemar, and then writes a congratulatory note to her. The result of her ruminations is a decision to sell her father's books to provide a means of escape to Italy.

Books VI–IX connect the Marian Erle plot to the main conflict, with the scene changed to Paris and Florence. Meditating on life and art as she strolls through the crowded streets of Paris, Aurora begins to sympathize with Romney's view and sees the need of the poet and philanthropist standing side by side. Suddenly she recognizes Marian Erle, who is holding a baby. She befriends her and learns that Lady Waldemar had cunningly plotted Marian's emigration from England to Australia with the help of her former maid. This woman took Marian to a house of ill-fame in Paris where she was drugged and raped. After wandering in the countryside, she was eventually hired by a seamstress. Marian's experience changes Aurora's opinion of Romney and she writes to Lord Howe, informing him of Marian's story and requesting that he tell it to Romney. If Romney has already married Lady Waldemar, however, then she requests he mention only that Marian has been found. Aurora also writes to Lady Waldemar, telling her she knows the sordid story and will divulge it if Lady Waldemar does not play fairly with Romney.

Aurora decides to take Marian and her baby to Florence, where they live in some degree of tranquillity. Eventually, Aurora receives a letter from Vincent Carrington, an artist and a mutual friend of hers and

Romney's, who informs her of his own marriage and the success of her latest book. His remarks lead Aurora to believe Lady Waldemar and Romney are, indeed, married. The news causes her to ruminate further on the need of the union of the natural and the spiritual, the ideal and the real, and hence, the need of a balance between her own and Romney's views of life: "Earth's crammed with heaven, / And every common bush afire with God." By degrees, she is becoming more and more aware of her love for him.

The denouement is prolonged, commencing with Romney's sudden appearance, during which he tells Aurora of his admiration for her new book, whereupon they virtually arrive at philosophic agreement. He also tells her of the failure of his social experiment—how the inhabitants of his phalanstery had no idea of order and how the neighbors and members of the church burned his Hall. Not only did he lose his buildings, but he was blinded during the fire, a fact which Aurora learns only later in their reunion. Romney has not married Lady Waldemar and has come with the idea of dutifully fulfilling his original plans to marry Marian Erle. In the final book, after reading an explanatory letter from Lady Waldemar, Aurora assents to the marriage of Marian and Romney. Marian, however, refuses Romney's offer. Aurora and Romney, realizing their love, decide to marry and thus unite the spiritual and the natural.

DEDICATION TO JOHN KENYON, ESQ.

The words "cousin" and "friend" are constantly recurring in this poem, the last pages of which have been finished under the hospitality of your roof, my own dearest cousin and friend; —cousin and friend, in a sense of less equality and greater disinterestedness than "Romney's".

Ending, therefore, and preparing once more to quit England, I venture to leave in your hands this book, the most mature of my works, and the one into which my highest convictions upon Life and Art have entered; that as, through my various efforts in Literature and steps in life, you have believed in me, borne with me, and been generous to me, far beyond the common uses of mere relationship or sympathy of mind, so you may kindly accept, in sight of the public, this poor sign of esteem, gratitude, and affection from—Your unforgetting

E. B. B.

39 Devonshire Place
October 17, 1856

AURORA LEIGH

First Book

Of writing many books there is no end;[1]
And I who have written much in prose and verse
For others' uses, will write now for mine, —
Will write my story for my better self,
As when you paint your portrait for a friend,
Who keeps it in a drawer and looks at it
Long after he has ceased to love you, just
To hold together what he was and is.
I, writing thus, am still what men call young;
I have not so far left the coasts of life   10
To travel inward, that I cannot hear
That murmur of the outer Infinite
Which unweaned babies smile at in their sleep
When wondered at for smiling; not so far,
But still I catch my mother at her post
Beside the nursery door, with finger up,
"Hush, hush — here's too much noise!" while her
     sweet eyes
Leap forward, taking part against her word
In the child's riot. Still I sit and feel
My father's slow hand, when she had left us both,   20
Stroke out my childish curls across his knee,
And hear Assunta's daily jest (she knew
He liked it better than a better jest)
Inquire how many golden scudi went
To make such ringlets. O my father's hand,
Stroke heavily, heavily the poor hair down,
Draw, press the child's head closer to thy knee!
I'm still too young, too young, to sit alone.
I write. My mother was a Florentine,
Whose rare blue eyes were shut from seeing me   30
When scarcely I was four years old, my life
A poor spark snatched up from a failing lamp
Which went out therefore. She was weak and frail;
She could not bear the joy of giving life,
The mother's rapture slew her. If her kiss
Had left a longer weight upon my lips
It might have steadied the uneasy breath,
And reconciled and fraternised my soul

With the new order. As it was, indeed,
I felt a mother-want about the world,   40
And still went seeking, like a bleating lamb
Left out at night in shutting up the fold,—
As restless as a nest-deserted bird
Grown chill through something being away, though what
It knows not. I, Aurora Leigh, was born
To make my father sadder, and myself
Not overjoyous, truly. Women know
The way to rear up children (to be just),
They know a simple, merry, tender knack
Of tying sashes, fitting baby-shoes,   50
And stringing pretty words that make no sense,
And kissing full sense into empty words,
Which things are corals to cut life upon,
Although such trifles: children learn by such,
Love's holy earnest in a pretty play
And get not over-early solemnised,
But seeing, as in a rose-bush, Love's Divine
Which burns and hurts not,—not a single bloom,—
Become aware and unafraid of Love.
Such good do mothers. Fathers love as well   60
—Mine did, I know,—but still with heavier brains,
And wills more consciously responsible,
And not as wisely, since less foolishly;
So mothers have God's license to be missed.

My father was an austere Englishman,
Who, after a dry lifetime spent at home
In college-learning, law, and parish talk,
Was flooded with a passion unaware,
His whole provisioned and complacent past
Drowned out from him that moment. As he stood   70
In Florence, where he had come to spend a month
And note the secret of Da Vinci's drains,
He musing somewhat absently perhaps
Some English question . . . whether men should pay
The unpopular but necessary tax
With left or right hand—in the alien sun
In that great square of the Santissima
There drifted past him (scarcely marked enough
To move his comfortable island scorn)
A train of priestly banners, cross and psalm,   80

The white-veiled rose-crowned maidens holding up
Tall tapers, weighty for such wrists, aslant
To the blue luminous tremor of the air,
And letting drop the white wax as they went
To eat the bishop's wafer at the church;
From which long trail of chanting priests and girls,
A face flashed like a cymbal on his face
And shook with silent clangour brain and heart,
Transfiguring him to music. Thus, even thus,
He too received his sacramental gift   90
With eucharistic meanings; for he loved.

And thus beloved, she died. I've heard it said
That but to see him in the first surprise
Of widower and father, nursing me,
Unmothered little child of four years old,
His large man's hands afraid to touch my curls,
As if the gold would tarnish,—his grave lips
Contriving such a miserable smile
As if he knew needs must, or I should die,
And yet 'twas hard,—would almost make the stones   100
Cry out for pity. There's a verse he set
In Santa Croce[2] to her memory,—
"Weep for an infant too young to weep much
When death removed this mother"—stops the mirth
To-day on women's faces when they walk
With rosy children hanging on their gowns,
Under the cloister to escape the sun
That scorches in the piazza. After which
He left our Florence and made haste to hide
Himself, his prattling child, and silent grief,   110
Among the mountains above Pelago;[3]
Because unmothered babes, he thought, had need
Of mother nature more than others use,
And Pan's white goats, with udders warm and full
Of mystic contemplations, come to feed
Poor milkless lips of orphans like his own—
Such scholar-scraps he talked, I've heard from friends,
For even prosaic men who wear grief long
Will get to wear it as a hat aside
With a flower stuck in't. Father, then, and child,   120
We lived among the mountains many years,
God's silence on the outside of the house,

And we who did not speak too loud within,
And old Assunta to make up the fire,
Crossing herself whene'er a sudden flame
Which lightened from the firewood, made alive
That picture of my mother on the wall.
The painter drew it after she was dead,
And when the face was finished, throat and hands,
Her cameriera[4] carried him, in hate   130
Of the English-fashioned shroud, the last brocade
She dressed in at the Pitti; "he should paint
No sadder thing than that," she swore, "to wrong
Her poor signora." Therefore very strange
The effect was. I, a little child, would crouch
For hours upon the floor with knees drawn up,
And gaze across them, half in terror, half
In adoration, at the picture there,—
That swan-like supernatural white life
Just sailing upward from the red stiff silk   140
Which seemed to have no part in it nor power
To keep it from quite breaking out of bounds.
For hours I sat and stared. Assunta's awe
And my poor father's melancholy eyes
Still pointed that way. That way went my thoughts
When wandering beyond sight. And as I grew
In years, I mixed, confused, unconsciously,
Whatever I last read or heard or dreamed,
Abhorrent, admirable, beautiful,
Pathetical, or ghastly, or grotesque,   150
With still that face . . . which did not
          therefore change,
But kept the mystic level of all forms,
Hates, fears, and admirations, was by turns
Ghost, fiend, and angel, fairy, witch, and sprite,
A dauntless Muse who eyes a dreadful Fate,
A loving Psyche who loses sight of Love,
A still Medusa with mild milky brows
All curdled and all clothed upon with snakes
Whose slime falls fast as sweat will; or anon
Our Lady of the Passion, stabbed with swords   160
Where the Babe sucked; or Lamia in her first
Moonlighted pallor, ere she shrunk and blinked
And shuddering wriggled down to the unclean;
Or my own mother, leaving her last smile

In her last kiss upon the baby-mouth
My father pushed down on the bed for that,—
Or my dead mother, without smile or kiss,
Buried at Florence. All which images,
Concentred on the picture, glassed themselves
Before my meditative childhood, as   170
The incoherencies of change and death
Are represented fully, mixed and merged,
In the smooth fair mystery of perpetual Life.
And while I stared away my childish wits
Upon my mother's picture (ah, poor child!),
My father, who through love had suddenly
Thrown off the old conventions, broken loose
From chin-bands of the soul, like Lazarus,
Yet had no time to learn to talk and walk
Or grow anew familiar with the sun,—   180
Who had reached to freedom, not to action, lived,
But lived as one entranced, with thoughts, not aims,—
Whom love had unmade from a common man
But not completed to an uncommon man,—
My father taught me what he had learnt the best
Before he died and left me,—grief and love.
And, seeing we had books among the hills,
Strong words of counselling souls confederate
With vocal pines and waters,—out of books
He taught me all the ignorance of men,   190
And how God laughs in heaven when any man
Says "Here I'm learned; this, I understand;
In that, I am never caught at fault or doubt."
He sent the schools to school, demonstrating
A fool will pass for such through one mistake,
While a philosopher will pass for such,
Through said mistakes being ventured in the gross
And heaped up to a system.

                          I am like,
They tell me, my dear father. Broader brows
Howbeit, upon a slenderer undergrowth   200
Of delicate features,—paler, near as grave;
But then my mother's smile breaks up the whole,
And makes it better sometimes than itself.
So, nine full years, our days were hid with God
Among his mountains: I was just thirteen,
Still growing like the plants from unseen roots

In tongue-tied Springs,—and suddenly awoke
To full life and life's needs and agonies
With an intense, strong, struggling heart beside
A stone-dead father. Life, struck sharp on death,   210
Makes awful lightning. His last word was "Love—"
"Love, my child, love, love!"—(then he had
    done with grief)
"Love, my child." Ere I answered he was gone,
And none was left to love in all the world.

There, ended childhood. What succeeded next
I recollect as, after fevers, men
Thread back the passage of delirium,
Missing the turn still, baffled by the door;
Smooth endless days, notched here and there with
    knives,
A weary, wormy darkness, spurred i' the flank   220
With flame, that it should eat and end itself
Like some tormented scorpion. Then at last
I do remember clearly how there came
A stranger with authority, not right
(I thought not), who commanded, caught me up
From old Assunta's neck; how, with a shriek,
She let me go,—while I, with ears too full
Of my father's silence to shriek back a word,
In all a child's astonishment at grief
Stared at the wharf-edge where she stood and moaned,   230
My poor Assunta, where she stood and moaned!
The white walls, the blue hills, my Italy,
Drawn backward from the shuddering steamer-deck,
Like one in anger drawing back her skirts
Which suppliants catch at. Then the bitter sea
Inexorably pushed between us both
And, sweeping up the ship with my despair,
Threw us out as a pasture to the stars.

Ten nights and days we voyaged on the deep;
Ten nights and days without the common face   240
Of any day or night; the moon and sun
Cut off from the green reconciling earth,
To starve into a blind ferocity
And glare unnatural; the very sky
(Dropping its bell-net down upon the sea,

As if no human heart should 'scape alive)
Bedraggled with the desolating salt,
Until it seemed no more that holy heaven
To which my father went. All new and stange;
The universe turned stranger, for a child. 250

Then, land!—then, England! oh, the frosty cliffs
Looked cold upon me. Could I find a home
Among those mean red houses through the fog?
And when I heard my father's language first
From alien lips which had no kiss for mine
I wept aloud, then laughed, then wept, then wept,
And some one near me said the child was mad
Through much sea-sickness. The train swept us on:
Was this my father's England? the great isle?
The ground seemed cut up from the fellowship 260
Of verdure, field from field, as man from man;
The skies themselves looked low and positive,
As almost you could touch them with a hand,
And dared to do it they were so far off
From God's celestial crystals; all things blurred
And dull and vague. Did Shakespeare and his mates
Absorb the light here?—not a hill or stone
With heart to strike a radiant colour up
Or active outline on the indifferent air.

I think I see my father's sister stand 270
Upon the hall-step of her country-house
To give me welcome. She stood straight and calm,
Her somewhat narrow forehead braided tight
As if for taming accidental thoughts
From possible pulses; brown hair pricked with gray
By frigid use of life (she was not old,
Although my father's elder by a year),
A nose drawn sharply, yet in delicate lines;
A close mild mouth, a little soured about
The ends, through speaking unrequited loves 280
Or peradventure niggardly half-truths;
Eyes of no colour,—once they might have smiled,
But never, never have forgot themselves
In smiling; cheeks, in which was yet a rose
Of perished summers, like a rose in a book,

Kept more for ruth than pleasure,—if past bloom,
Past fading also.
                              She had lived, we'll say,
A harmless life, she called a virtuous life,
A quiet life, which was not life at all
(But that, she had not lived enough to know),   290
Between the vicar and the county squires,
The lord-lieutenant looking down sometimes
From the empyrean to assure their souls
Against chance vulgarisms, and, in the abyss,
The apothecary, looked on once a year
To prove their soundness of humility.
The poor-club exercised her Christian gifts
Of knitting stockings, stitching petticoats,
Because we are of one flesh, after all,
And need one flannel (with a proper sense   300
Of difference in the quality)—and still
The book-club, guarded from your modern trick
Of shaking dangerous questions from the crease,
Preserved her intellectual. She had lived
A sort of cage-bird life, born in a cage,
Accounting that to leap from perch to perch
Was act and joy enough for any bird.
Dear heaven, how silly are the things that live
In thickets, and eat berries!
                                      I, alas,
A wild bird scarcely fledged, was brought to her cage,   310
And she was there to meet me. Very kind.
Bring the clean water, give out the fresh seed.

She stood upon the steps to welcome me,
Calm, in black garb. I clung about her neck,—
Young babes, who catch at every shred of wool
To draw the new light closer, catch and cling
Less blindly. In my ears my father's word
Hummed ignorantly, as the sea in shells,
"Love, love, my child." She, black there with my grief,
Might feel my love—she was his sister once—   320
I clung to her. A moment she seemed moved,
Kissed me with cold lips, suffered me to cling,
And drew me feebly through the hall into
The room she sat in.
                            There, with some strange spasm

Of pain and passion, she wrung loose my hands
Imperiously, and held me at arm's length,
And with two grey-steel naked-bladed eyes
Searched through my face,—ay, stabbed in through
    and through,
Through brows and cheeks and chin, as if to find
A wicked murderer in my innocent face, 330
If not here, there perhaps. Then, drawing breath,
She struggled for her ordinary calm—
And missed it rather,—told me not to shrink,
As if she had told me not to lie or swear,—
"She loved my father and would love me too
As long as I deserved it." Very kind.

I understood her meaning afterward;
She thought to find my mother in my face,
And questioned it for that. For she, my aunt,
Had loved my father truly, as she could, 340
And hated, with the gall of gentle souls,
My Tuscan mother who had fooled away
A wise man from wise courses, a good man
From obvious duties, and, depriving her,
His sister, of the household precedence,
Had wronged his tenants, robbed his native land,
And made him mad, alike by life and death,
In love and sorrow. She had pored for years
What sort of woman could be suitable
To her sort of hate, to entertain it with, 350
And so, her very curiosity
Became hate too, and all the idealism
She ever used in life was used for hate,
Till hate, so nourished, did exceed at last
The love from which it grew, in strength and heat,
And wrinkled her smooth conscience with a sense
Of disputable virtue (say not, sin)
When Christian doctrine was enforced at church.

And thus my father's sister was to me
My mother's hater. From that day she did 360
Her duty to me (I appreciate it
In her own word as spoken to herself),
Her duty, in large measure, well pressed out
But measured always. She was generous, bland,

More courteous than was tender, gave me still
The first place,—as if fearful that God's saints
Would look down suddenly and say "Herein
You missed a point, I think, through lack of love."
Alas, a mother never is afraid
Of speaking angerly to any child,   370
Since love, she knows, is justified of love.

And I, I was a good child on the whole,
A meek and manageable child. Why not?
I did not live, to have the faults of life:
There seemed more true life in my father's grave
Than in all England. Since *that* threw me off
Who fain would cleave (his latest will, they say,
Consigned me to his land), I only thought
Of lying quiet there where I was thrown
Like sea-weed on the rocks, and suffering her   380
To prick me to a pattern with her pin,
Fibre from fibre, delicate leaf from leaf,
And dry out from my drowned anatomy
The last sea-salt left in me.
                                             So it was.
I broke the copious curls upon my head
In braids, because she liked smooth-ordered hair.
I left off saying my sweet Tuscan words
Which still at any stirring of the heart
Came up to float across the English phrase
As lilies (*Bene* or *Che che*), because   390
She liked my father's child to speak his tongue.
I learnt the collects and the catechism,
The creeds, from Athanasius back to Nice,[5]
The Articles, the Tracts *against* the times[6]
(By no means Buonaventure's "Prick of Love"),
And various popular synopses of
Inhuman doctrines never taught by John,
Because she liked instructed piety.
I learnt my complement of classic French
(Kept pure of Balzac and neologism)   400
And German also, since she liked a range
Of liberal education,—tongues, not books.
I learnt a little algebra, a little
Of the mathematics,—brushed with extreme flounce
The circle of the sciences, because

She misliked women who are frivolous.
I learnt the royal genealogies
Of Oviedo,[7] the internal laws
Of the Burmese empire,—by how many feet
Mount Chimborazo outsoars Teneriffe.[8]   410
What navigable river joins itself
To Lara, and what census of the year five
Was taken at Klagenfurt,—because she liked
A general insight into useful facts.
I learnt much music,—such as would have been
As quite impossible in Johnson's day
As still it might be wished—fine sleights of hand
And unimagined fingering, shuffling off
The hearer's soul through hurricanes of notes
To a noisy Tophet; and I drew . . . costumes   420
From French engravings, nereids neatly draped
(With smirks of simmering godship): I washed in
Landscapes from nature (rather say, washed out).
I danced the polka and Cellarius,
Spun glass, stuffed birds, and modelled flowers in wax,
Because she liked accomplishments in girls.
I read a score of books on womanhood
To prove, if women do not think at all,
They may teach thinking (to a maiden aunt
Or else the author),—books that boldly assert   430
Their right of comprehending husband's talk
When not too deep, and even of answering
With pretty "may it please you," or "so it is,"—
Their rapid insight and fine aptitude,
Particular worth and general missionariness,
As long as they keep quiet by the fire
And never say "no" when the world says "ay,"
For that is fatal,—their angelic reach
Of virtue, chiefly used to sit and darn,
And fatten household sinners,—their, in brief,   440
Potential faculty in everything
Of abdicating power in it: she owned
She liked a woman to be womanly,
And English women, she thanked God and sighed
(Some people always sigh in thanking God)
Were models to the universe. And last
I learnt cross-stitch, because she did not like
To see me wear the night with empty hands

A-doing nothing. So, my shepherdess
Was something after all (the pastoral saints   450
Be praised for't), leaning lovelorn with pink eyes
To match her shoes, when I mistook the silks;
Her head uncrushed by that round weight of hat
So strangely similar to the tortoise-shell
Which slew the tragic poet.[9]
                                              By the way,
The works of women are symbolical.
We sew, sew, prick our fingers, dull our sight,
Producing what? A pair of slippers, sir,
To put on when you're weary—or a stool
To stumble over and vex you . . . "curse that stool!"   460
Or else at best, a cushion, where you lean
And sleep, and dream of something we are not
But would be for your sake. Alas, alas!
This hurts most, this—that, after all, we are paid
The worth of our work, perhaps.
                                         In looking down
Those years of education (to return)
I wonder if Brinvilliers[10] suffered more
In the water-torture . . . flood succeeding flood
To drench the incapable throat and split the veins . . .
Than I did. Certain of your feebler souls   470
Go out in such a process; many pine
To a sick, inodorous light; my own endured:
I had relations in the Unseen, and drew
The elemental nutriment and heat
From nature, as earth feels the sun at nights,
Or as a babe sucks surely in the dark.
I kept the life thrust on me, on the outside
Of the inner life with all its ample room
For heart and lungs, for will and intellect,
Inviolable by conventions. God,   480
I thank thee for that grace of thine!
                                              At first
I felt no life which was not patience,—did
The thing she bade me, without heed to a thing
Beyond it, sat in just the chair she placed,
With back against the window, to exclude
The sight of the great lime-tree on the lawn,
Which seemed to have come on purpose from the woods
To bring the house a message,—ay, and walked

Demurely in her carpeted low rooms,
As if I should not, hearkening my own steps,   490
Misdoubt I was alive. I read her books,
Was civil to her cousin, Romney Leigh,
Gave ear to her vicar, tea to her visitors,
And heard them whisper, when I changed a cup
(I blushed for joy at that),—"The Italian child,
For all her blue eyes and her quiet ways,
Thrives ill in England: she is paler yet
Than when we came the last time; she will die."

"Will die." My cousin, Romney Leigh, blushed too,
With sudden anger, and approaching me   500
Said low between his teeth, "You're wicked now?
You wish to die and leave the world a-dusk
For others, with your naughty light blown out?"
I looked into his face defyingly;
He might have known that, being what I was,
'Twas natural to like to get away
As far as dead folk can: and then indeed
Some people make no trouble when they die.
He turned and went abruptly, slammed the door,
And shut his dog out.
                              Romney, Romney Leigh. 510
I have not named my cousin hitherto,
And yet I used him as a sort of friend;
My elder by few years, but cold and shy
And absent . . . tender, when he thought of it,
Which scarcely was imperative, grave betimes,
As well as early master of Leigh Hall,
Whereof the nightmare sat upon his youth,
Repressing all its seasonable delights,
And agonising with a ghastly sense
Of universal hideous want and wrong   520
To incriminate possession. When he came
From college to the country, very oft
He crossed the hill on visits to my aunt,
With gifts of blue grapes from the hothouses,
A book in one hand,—mere statistics (if
I chanced to lift the cover), count of all
The goats whose beards grow sprouting down toward hell
Against God's separative judgment-hour.
And she, she almost loved him,—even allowed

That sometimes he should seem to sigh my way;   530
It made him easier to be pitiful,
And sighing was his gift. So, undisturbed,
At whiles she let him shut my music up
And push my needles down, and lead me out
To see in that south angle of the house
The figs grow black as if by a Tuscan rock,
On some light pretext. She would turn her head
At other moments, go to fetch a thing,
And leave me breath enough to speak with him,
For his sake; it was simple.
                                     Sometimes too   540
He would have saved me utterly, it seemed,
He stood and looked so.
                             Once, he stood so near,
He dropped a sudden hand upon my head
Bent down on woman's work, as soft as rain—
But then I rose and shook it off as fire,
The stranger's touch that took my father's place
Yet dared seem soft.
                             I used him for a friend
Before I ever knew him for a friend.
'Twas better, 'twas worse also, afterward:
We came so close, we saw our differences   550
Too intimately. Always Romney Leigh
Was looking for the worms, I for the gods.
A godlike nature his; the gods look down,
Incurious of themselves; and certainly
'Tis well I should remember, how, those days,
I was a worm too, and he looked on me.

A little by his act perhaps, yet more
By something in me, surely not my will,
I did not die. But slowly, as one in swoon,
To whom life creeps back in the form of death,   560
With a sense of separation, a blind pain
Of blank obstruction, and a roar i' the ears
Of visionary chariots which retreat
As earth grows clearer . . . slowly, by degrees;
I woke, rose up . . . where was I? in the world;
For uses therefore I must count worth while.

I had a little chamber in the house,
As green as any privet-hedge a bird
Might choose to build in, though the nest itself
Could show but dead-brown sticks and straws; the walls 570
Were green, the carpet was pure green, the straight
Small bed was curtained greenly, and the folds
Hung green about the window which let in
The out-door world with all its greenery.
You could not push your head out and escape
A dash of dawn-dew from the honeysuckle,
But so you were baptized into the grace
And privilege of seeing. . . .
                                                    First, the lime
(I had enough there, of the lime, be sure,—
My morning-dream was often hummed away   580
By the bees in it); past the lime, the lawn,
Which, after sweeping broadly round the house,
Went trickling through the shrubberies in a stream
Of tender turf, and wore and lost itself
Among the acacias, over which you saw
The irregular line of elms by the deep lane
Which stopped the grounds and dammed the overflow
Of arbutus and laurel. Out of sight
The lane was; sunk so deep, no foreign tramp
Nor drover of wild ponies out of Wales   590
Could guess if lady's hall or tenant's lodge
Dispensed such odours,—though his stick well-crooked
Might reach the lowest trail of blossoming briar
Which dipped upon the wall. Behind the elms,
And through their tops, you saw the folded hills
Striped up and down with hedges (burly oaks
Projecting from the line to show themselves),
Through which my cousin Romney's chimneys smoked
As still as when a silent mouth in frost
Breathes, showing where the woodlands hid Leigh Hall; 600
While, far above, a jut of table-land,
A promontory without water, stretched,—
You could not catch it if the days were thick,
Or took it for a cloud; but, otherwise,
The vigorous sun would catch it up at eve
And use it for an anvil till he had filled
The shelves of heaven with burning thunder-bolts,
Protesting against night and darkness:—then,

When all his setting trouble was resolved
To a trance of passive glory, you might see   610
In apparition on the golden sky
(Alas, my Giotto's[11] background!) the sheep run
Along the fine clear outline, small as mice
That run along a witch's scarlet thread.

Not a grand nature. Not my chestnut-woods
Of Vallombrosa, cleaving by the spurs
To the precipices. Not my headlong leaps
Of waters, that cry out for joy or fear
In leaping through the palpitating pines,
Like a white soul tossed out to eternity   620
With thrills of time upon it. Not indeed
My multitudinous mountains, sitting in
The magic circle, with the mutual touch
Electric, panting from their full deep hearts
Beneath the influent heavens, and waiting for
Communion and commission. Italy
Is one thing, England one.
                                    On English ground
You understand the letter,—ere the fall
How Adam lived in a garden. All the fields
Are tied up fast with hedges, nosegay-like;   630
The hills are crumpled plains, the plains parterres,
The trees, round, woolly, ready to be clipped,
And if you seek for any wilderness
You find, at best, a park. A nature tamed
And grown domestic like a barn-door fowl,
Which does not awe you with its claws and beak,
Nor tempt you to an eyrie too high up,
But which, in cackling, sets you thinking of
Your eggs to-morrow at breakfast, in the pause
Of finer meditation.
                                    Rather say,   640
A sweet familar nature, stealing in
As a dog might, or child, to touch your hand
Or pluck your gown, and humbly mind you so
Of presence and affection, excellent
For inner uses, from the things without.

I could not be unthankful, I who was
Entreated thus and holpen. In the room
I speak of, ere the house was well awake,

And also after it was well asleep,
I sat alone, and drew the blessing in   650
Of all that nature. With a gradual step,
A stir among the leaves, a breath, a ray,
It came in softly, while the angels made
A place for it beside me. The moon came,
And swept my chamber clean of foolish thoughts.
The sun came, saying, "Shall I lift this light
Against the lime-tree, and you will not look?
I make the birds sing—listen! but, for you,
God never hears your voice, excepting when
You lie upon the bed at nights and weep."   660

Then, something moved me. Then, I wakened up
More slowly than I verily write now,
But wholly, at last, I wakened, opened wide
The window and my soul, and let the airs
And out-door sights sweep gradual gospels in,
Regenerating what I was. O, Life,
How oft we throw it off and think,—"Enough,
Enough of life in so much!—here's a cause
For rupture;—herein we must break with Life,
Or be ourselves unworthy; here we are wronged,   670
Maimed, spoiled for aspiration: farewell, Life!"
And so, as froward babes, we hide our eyes
And think all ended.—Then, Life calls to us
In some transformed, apocalyptic voice,
Above us, or below us, or around:
Perhaps we name it Nature's voice, or Love's,
Tricking ourselves, because we are more ashamed
To own our compensations than our griefs:
Still, Life's voice!—still, we make our peace with Life.

And I, so young then, was not sullen. Soon   680
I used to get up early, just to sit
And watch the morning quicken in the gray,
And hear the silence open like a flower
Leaf after leaf,—and stroke with listless hand
The woodbine through the window, till at last
I came to do it with a sort of love,
At foolish unaware: whereat I smiled,—

A melancholy smile, to catch myself
Smiling for joy.
                                        Capacity for joy
Admits temptation. It seemed, next, worth while   690
To dodge the sharp sword set against my life;
To slip down stairs through all the sleepy house,
As mute as any dream there, and escape
As a soul from the body, out of doors,
Glide through the shrubberies, drop into the lane,
And wander on the hills an hour or two,
Then back again before the house should stir.
Or else I sat on in my chamber green,
And lived my life, and thought my thoughts, and prayed
My prayers without the vicar; read my books   700
Without considering whether they were fit
To do me good. Mark, there. We get no good
By being ungenerous, even to a book,
And calculating profits,—so much help
By so much reading. It is rather when
We gloriously forget ourselves and plunge
Soul-forward, headlong, into a book's profound,
Impassioned for its beauty and salt of truth—
'Tis then we get the right good from a book.

I read much. What my father taught before   710
From many a volume, Love re-emphasised
Upon the self-same pages: Theophrast[12]
Grew tender with the memory of his eyes,
And Aelian[13] made mine wet. The trick of Greek
And Latin he had taught me, as he would
Have taught me wrestling or the game of fives
If such he had known,—most like a shipwrecked man
Who heaps his single platter with goats' cheese
And scarlet berries; or like any man
Who loves but one, and so gives all at once,   720
Because he has it, rather than because
He counts it worthy. Thus, my father gave;
And thus, as did the women formerly
By young Achilles, when they pinned a veil
Across the boy's audacious front, and swept
With tuneful laughs the silver-fretted rocks,
He wrapt his little daughter in his large
Man's doublet, careless did it fit or no.

But, after I had read for memory,
I read for hope. The path my father's foot   730
Had trod me out (which suddenly broke off
What time he dropped the wallet of the flesh
And passed), alone I carried on, and set
My child-heart 'gainst the thorny underwood,
To reach the grassy shelter of the trees.
Ah babe i' the wood, without a brother-babe!
My own self-pity, like the red-breast bird,
Flies back to cover all that past with leaves.

Sublimest danger, over which none weeps,
When any young wayfaring soul goes forth   740
Alone, unconscious of the perilous road,
The day-sun dazzling in his limpid eyes,
To thrust his own way, he an alien, through
The world of books! Ah, you!—you think it fine,
You clap hands—"A fair day!"—you cheer him on,
As if the worst, could happen, were to rest
Too long beside a fountain. Yet, behold,
Behold!—the world of books is still the world,
And worldings in it are less merciful
And more puissant. For the wicked there   750
Are winged like angels; every knife that strikes
Is edged from elemental fire to assail
A spiritual life; the beautiful seems right
By force of beauty, and the feeble wrong
Because of weakness; power is justified
Though armed against Saint Michael; many a crown
Covers bald foreheads. In the book-world, true,
There's no lack, neither, of God's saints and kings,
That shake the ashes of the grave aside
From their calm locks and undiscomfited   760
Look steadfast truths against Time's changing mask.
True, many a prophet teaches in the roads;
True, many a seer pulls down the flaming heavens
Upon his own head in strong martyrdom
In order to light men a moment's space.
But stay!—who judges?—who distinguishes
'Twixt Saul and Nahash justly, at first sight,
And leaves king Saul precisely at the sin,
To serve king David?[14] who discerns at once
The sound of the trumpets, when the trumpets blow   770

For Alaric as well as Charlemagne?
Who judges wizards, and can tell true seers
From conjurers? the child, there? Would you leave
That child to wander in a battle-field
And push his innocent smile against the guns;
Or even in a catacomb,—his torch
Grown ragged in the fluttering air, and all
The dark a-mutter round him? not a child.

I read books bad and good—some bad and good
At once (good aims not always make good books: 780
Well-tempered spades turn up ill-smelling soils
In digging vineyards even); books that prove
God's being so definitely, that man's doubt
Grows self-defined the other side the line,
Made atheist by suggestion; moral books,
Exasperating to license; genial books,
Discounting from the human dignity;
And merry books, which set you weeping when
The sun shines,—ay, and melancholy books,
Which make you laugh that any one should weep   790
In this disjointed life for one wrong more.

The world of books is still the world, I write,
And both worlds have God's providence, thank God,
To keep and hearten: with some struggle, indeed,
Among the breakers, some hard swimming through
The deeps—I lost breath in my soul sometimes
And cried "God save me if there's any God,"
But, even so, God saved me; and, being dashed
From error on to error, every turn
Still brought me nearer to the central truth.   800

I thought so. All this anguish in the thick
Of men's opinions . . . press and counter-press,
Now up, now down, now underfoot, and now
Emergent . . . all the best of it, perhaps,
But throws you back upon a noble trust
And use of your own instinct,—merely proves
Pure reason stronger than bare inference
At strongest. Try it,—fix against heaven's wall
The scaling-ladders of school logic—mount
Step by step!—sight goes faster; that still ray   810

Which strikes out from you, how, you cannot tell,
And why, you know not (did you eliminate,
That such as you indeed should analyse?)
Goes straight and fast as light, and high as God.

The cygnet finds the water, but the man
Is born in ignorance of his element
And feels out blind at first, disorganised
By sin i' the blood,—his spirit-insight dulled
And crossed by his sensations. Presently
He feels it quicken in the dark sometimes,   820
When, mark, be reverent, be obedient,
For such dumb motions of imperfect life
Are oracles of vital Deity
Attesting the Hereafter. Let who says
"The soul's a clean white paper," rather say,
A palimpsest, a prophet's holograph
Defiled, erased and covered by a monk's,—
The apocalypse, by a Longus! poring on
Which obscene text, we may discern perhaps
Some fair, fine trace of what was written once,   830
Some upstroke of an alpha and omega
Expressing the old scripture.
                                        Books, books, books!
I had found the secret of a garret-room
Piled high with cases in my father's name,
Piled high, packed large,—where, creeping in and out
Among the giant fossils of my past,
Like some small nimble mouse between the ribs
Of a mastodon, I nibbled here and there
At this or that box, pulling through the gap,
In heats of terror, haste, victorious joy,   840
The first book first. And how I felt it beat
Under my pillow, in the morning's dark,
An hour before the sun would let me read!
My books! At last because the time was ripe,
I chanced upon the poets.
                                        As the earth
Plunges in fury, when the internal fires
Have reached and pricked her heart, and, throwing flat
The marts and temples, the triumphal gates
And towers of observation, clears herself
To elemental freedom—thus, my soul,   850

At poetry's divine first finger-touch,
Let go conventions and sprang up surprised,
Convicted of the great eternities
Before two worlds.

                What's this, Aurora Leigh,
You write so of the poets, and not laugh?
Those virtuous liars, dreamers after dark,
Exaggerators of the sun and moon,
And soothsayers in a tea-cup?

                              I write so
Of the only truth-tellers now left to God,
The only speakers of essential truth,   860
Opposed to relative, comparative,
And temporal truths; the only holders by
His sun-skirts, through conventional gray glooms;
The only teachers who instruct mankind
From just a shadow on a charnel-wall
To find man's veritable stature out
Erect, sublime,—the measure of a man,
And that's the measure of an angel, says
The apostle. Ay, and while your common men
Lay telegraphs, gauge railroads, reign, reap, dine,   870
And dust the flaunty carpets of the world
For kings to walk on, or our president,
The poet suddenly will catch them up
With his voice like a thunder,—"This is soul,
This is life, this word is being said in heaven,
Here's God down on us! what are you about?"
How all those workers start amid their work,
Look round, look up, and feel, a moment's space,
That carpet-dusting, though a pretty trade,
Is not the imperative labour after all.   880

My own best poets, am I one with you,
That thus I love you,—or but one through love?
Does all this smell of thyme about my feet
Conclude my visit to your holy hill
In personal presence, or but testify
The rustling of your vesture through my dreams
With influent odours? When my joy and pain,
My thought and aspiration like the stops
Of pipe or flute, are absolutely dumb
Unless melodious, do you play on me   890

My pipers,—and if, sooth, you did not blow,
Would no sound come? or is the music mine,
As a man's voice or breath is called his own,
Inbreathed by the Life-breather? There's a doubt
For cloudy seasons!
                              But the sun was high
When first I felt my pulses set themselves
For concord; when the rhythmic turbulence
Of blood and brain swept outward upon words,
As wind upon the alders, blanching them
By turning up their under-natures till   900
They trembled in dilation. O delight
And triumph of the poet, who would say
A man's mere "yes," a woman's common "no,"
A little human hope of that or this,
And says the word so that it burns you through
With a special revelation, shakes the heart
Of all the men and women in the world,
As if one came back from the dead and spoke,
With eyes too happy, a familiar thing
Become divine i' the utterance! while for him   910
The poet, speaker, he expands with joy;
The palpitating angel in his flesh
Thrills inly with consenting fellowship
To those innumerous spirits who sun themselves
Outside of time.
                              O life, O poetry,
—Which means life in life! cognisant of life
Beyond this blood-beat, passionate for truth
Beyond these senses!—poetry, my life,
My eagle, with both grappling feet still hot
From Zeus's thunder, who hast ravished me   920
Away from all the shepherds, sheep, and dogs,
And set me in the Olympian roar and round
Of luminous faces for a cup-bearer,
To keep the mouths of all the godheads moist
For everlasting laughters,—I myself
Half drunk across the beaker with their eyes!
How those gods look!
                              Enough so, Ganymede,[15]
We shall not bear above a round or two.
We drop the golden cup at Heré's foot[16]
And swoon back to the earth,—and find ourselves   930

Face-down among the pine-cones, cold with dew,
While the dogs bark, and many a shepherd scoffs,
"What's come now to the youth?" Such ups and downs
Have poets.
      Am I such indeed? The name
Is royal, and to sign it like a queen
Is what I dare not,—though some royal blood
Would seem to tingle in me now and then,
With sense of power and ache,—with imposthumes
And manias usual to the race. Howbeit
I dare not: 'tis too easy to go mad   940
And ape a Bourbon[17] in a crown of straws;
The thing's too common.
       Many fervent souls
Strike rhyme on rhyme, who would strike steel on steel
If steel had offered, in a restless heat
Of doing something. Many tender souls
Have strung their losses on a rhyming thread,
As children cowslips:—the more pains they take,
The work more withers. Young men, ay, and maids,
Too often sow their wild oats in tame verse,
Before they sit down under their own vine   950
And live for use. Alas, near all the birds
Will sing at dawn,—and yet we do not take
The chaffering swallow for the holy lark.
In those days, though, I never analysed,
Not even myself. Analysis comes late.
You catch a sight of Nature, earliest,
In full front sun-face, and your eyelids wink
And drop before the wonder of't; you miss
The form, through seeing the light. I lived, those days,
And wrote because I lived—unlicensed else;   960
My heart beat in my brain. Life's violent flood
Abolished bounds,—and, which my neighbour's field,
Which mine, what mattered? it is thus in youth!
We play at leap-frog over the god Term;
The love within us and the love without
Are mixed, confounded; if we are loved or love,
We scarce distinguish: thus, with other power;
Being acted on and acting seem the same:
In that first onrush of life's chariot-wheels,
We know not if the forests move or we.   970

And so, like most young poets, in a flush
Of individual life I poured myself
Along the veins of others, and achieved
Mere lifeless imitations of live verse,
And made the living answer for the dead,
Profaning nature. "Touch not, do not taste,
Nor handle,"—we're too legal, who write young:
We beat the phorminx[18] till we hurt our thumbs,
As if still ignorant of counterpoint;
We call the Muse,—"O Muse, benignant Muse,"—   980
As if we had seen her purple-braided head,
With the eyes in it, start between the boughs
As often as a stag's. What make-believe,
With so much earnest! what effete results
From virile efforts! what cold wire-drawn odes
From such white heats!—bucolics, where the cows
Would scare the writer if they splashed the mud
In lashing off the flies,—didactics, driven
Against the heels of what the master said;
And counterfeiting epics, shrill with trumps   990
A babe might blow between two straining cheeks
Of bubbled rose, to make his mother laugh;
And elegiac griefs, and songs of love,
Like cast-off nosegays picked up on the road,
The worse for being warm: all these things, writ
On happy mornings, with a morning heart,
That leaps for love, is active for resolve,
Weak for art only. Oft, the ancient forms
Will thrill, indeed, in carrying the young blood.
The wine-skins, now and then, a little warped,   1000
Will crack even, as the new wine gurgles in.
Spare the old bottles!—spill not the new wine.

By Keats's soul, the man who never stepped
In gradual progress like another man,
But, turning grandly on his central self,
Ensphered himself in twenty perfect years
And died, not young (the life of a long life
Distilled to a mere drop, falling like a tear
Upon the world's cold cheek to make it burn
For ever); by that strong excepted soul,   1010
I count it strange and hard to understand
That nearly all young poets should write old,

That Pope was sexagenary at sixteen,
And beardless Byron academical,
And so with others. It may be perhaps
Such have not settled long and deep enough
In trance, to attain to clairvoyance,—and still
The memory mixes with the vision, spoils,
And works it turbid.
                    Or perhaps, again,
In order to discover the Muse-Sphinx,   1020
The melancholy desert must sweep round,
Behind you as before.—
                        For me, I wrote
False poems, like the rest, and thought them true
Because myself was true in writing them.
I peradventure have writ true ones since
With less complacence.
                    But I could not hide
My quickening inner life from those at watch.
They saw a light at a window, now and then,
They had not set there: who had set it there?
My father's sister started when she caught   1030
My soul agaze in my eyes. She could not say
I had no business with a sort of soul,
But plainly she objected,—and demurred
That souls were dangerous things to carry straight
Through all the spilt saltpetre of the world.
She said sometimes "Aurora, have you done
Your task this morning? have you read that book?
And are you ready for the crochet here?"—
As if she said "I know there's something wrong;
I know I have not ground you down enough   1040
To flatten and bake you to a wholesome crust
For household uses and proprieties,
Before the rain has got into my barn
And set the grains a-sprouting. What, you're green
With out-door impudence? you almost grow?"
To which I answered, "Would she hear my task,
And verify my abstract of the book?
Or should I sit down to the crochet work?
Was such her pleasure?" Then I sat and teased
The patient needle till it split the thread,   1050
Which oozed off from it in meandering lace
From hour to hour. I was not, therefore, sad;

My soul was singing at a work apart
Behind the wall of sense, as safe from harm
As sings the lark when sucked up out of sight
In vortices of glory and blue air.

And so, through forced work and spontaneous work,
The inner life informed the outer life,
Reduced the irregular blood to a settled rhythm,
Made cool the forehead with fresh-sprinkling dreams,   1060
And, rounding to the spheric soul the thin,
Pined body, struck a colour up the cheeks
Though somewhat faint. I clenched my brows across
My blue eyes greatening in the looking-glass,
And said "We'll live, Aurora! we'll be strong.
The dogs are on us—but we will not die."

Whoever lives true life will love true love.
I learnt to love that England. Very oft,
Before the day was born, or otherwise
Through secret windings of the afternoons,   1070
I threw my hunters off and plunged myself
Among the deep hills, as a hunted stag
Will take the waters, shivering with the fear
And passion of the course. And when at last
Escaped, so many a green slope built on slope
Betwixt me and the enemy's house behind,
I dared to rest, or wander, in a rest
Made sweeter for the step upon the grass,
And view the ground's most gentle dimplement
(As if God's finger touched but did not press   1080
In making England), such an up and down
Of verdure,—nothing too much up or down,
A ripple of land; such little hills, the sky
Can stoop to tenderly and the wheatfields climb;
Such nooks of valleys lined with orchises,
Fed full of noises by invisible streams;
And open pastures where you scarcely tell
White daisies from white dew,—at intervals
The mythic oaks and elm-trees standing out
Self-poised upon their prodigy of shade,—   1090
I thought my father's land was worthy too
Of being my Shakespeare's.
                                        Very oft alone,

Unlicensed; not unfrequently with leave
To walk the third with Romney and his friend
The rising painter, Vincent Carrington,
Whom men judge hardly as bee-bonneted,
Because he holds that, paint a body well,
You paint a soul by implication, like
The grand first Master. Pleasant walks! for if
He said "When I was last in Italy,"   1100
It sounded as an instrument that's played
Too far off for the tune—and yet it's fine
To listen.
                    Often we walked only two
If cousin Romney pleased to walk with me.
We read, or talked, or quarrelled, as it chanced.
We were not lovers, nor even friends well-matched:
Say rather, scholars upon different tracks,
And thinkers disagreed: he, overfull
Of what is, and I, haply, overbold
For what might be.
                    But then the thrushes sang,   1110
And shook my pulses and the elms' new leaves:
At which I turned, and held my finger up,
And bade him mark that, howsoe'er the world
Went ill, as he related, certainly
The thrushes still sang in it. At the word
His brow would soften,—and he bore with me
In melancholy patience, not unkind,
While breaking into voluble ecstasy
I flattered all the beauteous country round,
As poets use, the skies, the clouds, the fields,   1120
The happy violets hiding from the roads
The primroses run down to, carrying gold;
The tangled hedgerows, where the cows push out
Impatient horns and tolerant churning mouths
'Twixt dripping ash-boughs,—hedgerows all alive
With birds and gnats and large white butterflies
Which look as if the May-flower had caught life
And palpitated forth upon the wind;
Hills, vales, woods, netted in a silver mist,
Farms, granges, doubled up among the hills;   1130
And cattle grazing in the watered vales,
And cottage-chimneys smoking from the woods,
And cottage-gardens smelling everywhere,

Confused with smell of orchards. "See," I said,
"And see! is God not with us on the earth?
And shall we put Him down by aught we do?
Who says there's nothing for the poor and vile
Save poverty and wickedness? behold!"
And ankle-deep in English grass I leaped
And clapped my hands, and called all very fair.   1140
In the beginning when God called all good,
Even then was evil near us, it is writ;
But we indeed who call things good and fair,
The evil is upon us while we speak;
Deliver us from evil, let us pray.

Poems Before Congress[1]
1860

PREFACE

These poems were written under the pressure of the events they indicate, after a residence in Italy of so many years that the present triumph of great principles is heightened to the writer's feelings by the disastrous issue of the last movement, witnessed from "Casa Guidi Windows" in 1849. Yet, if the verses should appear to English readers too pungently rendered to admit of a patriotic respect to the English sense of things, I will not excuse myself on such grounds, nor on the grounds of my attachment to the Italian people and my admiration of their heroic constancy and union. What I have written has simply been written because I love truth and justice *quand même*,[2]—"more than Plato" and Plato's country, more than Dante and Dante's country, more even than Shakespeare and Shakespeare's country.

And if patriotism means the flattery of one's nation in every case, then the patriot, take it as you please, is merely the courtier, which I am not, though I have written "Napoleon III. in Italy."[3] It is time to limit the significance of certain terms, or to enlarge the significance of certain things. Nationality is excellent in its place; and the instinct of self-love is the root of a man, which will develop into sacrificial virtues. But all the virtues are means and uses; and, if we hinder their tendency to growth and expansion, we both destroy them as virtues, and degrade them to that rankest species of corruption reserved for the most noble organisms. For instance,—non-intervention in the affairs of neighbouring states is a high political virtue; but non-intervention does not mean, passing by on the other side when your neighbour falls among thieves,[4]—or Phariseeism would recover it from Christianity. Freedom itself is virtue, as well as privilege; but freedom of the seas does not mean piracy, nor freedom of the land, brigandage; nor freedom of the senate, freedom to cudgel a dissident member; nor freedom of the press, freedom to calumniate and lie. So, if patriotism be a virtue indeed, it cannot mean an exclusive devotion to our country's interests,— for that is only another form of devotion to personal interests, family interests, or provincial interests, all of which, if not driven past themselves, are vulgar and immoral objects. Let us put away the Little

Peddlingtonism[5] unworthy of a great nation, and too prevalent among us. If the man who does not look beyond this natural life is of a somewhat narrow order, what must be the man who does not look beyond his own frontier or his own sea?

I confess that I dream of the day when an English statesman shall arise with a heart too large for England; having courage in the face of his countrymen to assert of some suggested policy,—"This is good for your trade; this is necessary for your domination: but it will vex a people hard by; it will hurt a people farther off; it will profit nothing to the general humanity: therefore, away with it!—it is not for you or for me." When a British minister dares speak so, and when a British public applauds him speaking, then shall the nation be glorious, and her praise, instead of exploding from within, from loud civic mouths, come to her from without, as all worthy praise must, from the alliances she has fostered and the population she has saved.

And poets who write of the events of that time shall not need to justify themselves in prefaces for ever so little jarring of the national sentiment imputable to their rhymes.

Rome: February 1860

A TALE OF VILLAFRANCA.
TOLD IN TUSCANY[6]

I.

My little son, my Florentine,[7]
    Sit down beside my knee,
And I will tell you why the sign
    Of joy which flushed our Italy
Has faded since but yesternight;
And why your Florence of delight
    Is mourning as you see.

II.

A great man (who was crowned one day)
    Imagined a great Deed:[8]
He shaped it out of cloud and clay,   10
    He touched it finely till the seed
Possessed the flower: from heart and brain
He fed it with large thoughts humane,
    To help a people's need.

III.

He brought it out into the sun—
    They blessed it to his face:
"O great pure Deed, that hast undone
    So many bad and base!
O generous Deed, heroic Deed,
Come forth, be perfected, succeed,   20
    Deliver by God's grace."

IV.

Then sovereigns, statesmen, north and south,
    Rose up in wrath and fear,
And cried, protesting by one mouth,
    "What monster have we here?
A great Deed at this hour of day?
A great just Deed—and not for pay?
    Absurd,—or insincere."

V.

"And if sincere, the heavier blow
    In that case we shall bear,   30
For where's our blessed 'status quo,'
    Our holy treaties, where,—
Our rights to sell a race, or buy,
Protect and pillage, occupy,
    And civilise despair?"

VI.

Some muttered that the great Deed meant
    A great pretext to sin;
And others, the pretext, so lent,
    Was heinous (to begin).
Volcanic terms of "great" and "just"?   40
Admit such tongues of flame, the crust
    Of time and law falls in.

VII.

A great Deed in this world of ours?
    Unheard of the pretence is:
It threatens plainly the great Powers;
    Is fatal in all senses.
A just Deed in the world?—call out
The rifles! be not slack about
    The national defences.

VIII.

And many murmured, "From this source   50
    What red blood must be poured!"
And some rejoined, "'Tis even worse;
    What red tape is ignored!"
All cursed the Doer for an evil
Called here, enlarging on the Devil,—
    There, monkeying the Lord!

IX.

Some said it could not be explained,
    Some, could not be excused;
And others, "Leave it unrestrained,
    Gehenna's[9] self is loosed."   60
And all cried "Crush it, maim it, gag it!
Set dog-toothed lies to tear it ragged,
    Truncated and traduced!"

X.

But HE stood sad before the sun
    (The peoples felt their fate).
"The world is many,—I am one;
    My great Deed was too great.
God's fruit of justice ripens slow:
Men's souls are narrow; let them grow.
    My brothers, we must wait."   70

XI.

The tale is ended, child of mine,
    Turned graver at my knee.
They say your eyes, my Florentine,
    Are English: it may be.
And yet I've marked as blue a pair
Following the doves across the square
    At Venice by the sea.

XII.

Ah child! ah child! I cannot say
    A word more. You conceive
The reason now, why just to-day   80
    We see our Florence grieve.
Ah child, look up into the sky!
In this low world, where great Deeds die,
    What matter if we live?

A CURSE FOR A NATION[10]

Prologue

I heard an angel speak last night,
    And he said "Write!
Write a Nation's curse for me,
And send it over the Western Sea."

I faltered, taking up the word:
    "Not so, my lord!
If curses must be, choose another
To send thy curse against my brother.

"For I am bound by gratitude,
    By love and blood,   10
To brothers of mine across the sea,
Who stretch out kindly hands to me."

"Therefore," the voice said, "shalt thou write
    My curse to-night.
From the summits of love a curse is driven,
As lightning is from the tops of heaven."

"Not so," I answered. "Evermore
    My heart is sore
For my own land's sins: for little feet
Of children bleeding along the street: 20

"For parked-up honours that gainsay
    The right of way:
For almsgiving through a door that is
Not open enough for two friends to kiss:

"For love of freedom which abates
    Beyond the Straits:
For patriot virtue starved to vice on
Self-praise, self-interest, and suspicion:

"For an oligarchic parliament,
    And bribes well-meant.   30
What curse to another land assign,
When heavy-souled for the sins of mine?"

"Therefore," the voice said, "shalt thou write
     My curse to-night.
Because thou hast strength to see and hate
A foul thing done *within* thy gate."

"Not so," I answered once again.
     "To curse, choose men.
For I, a woman, have only known
How the heart melts and the tears run down."   40

"Therefore," the voice said, "shalt thou write
     My curse to-night.
Some women weep and curse, I say
(And no one marvels), night and day.

"And thou shalt take their part to-night,
     Weep and write.
A curse from the depths of womanhood
Is very salt, and bitter, and good."

So thus I wrote, and mourned indeed,
     What all may read.   50
And thus, as was enjoined on me,
I send it over the Western Sea.

Last Poems[1]
1862

LORD WALTER'S WIFE[2]

I.

"But why do you go?" said the lady, while both
    sat under the yew,
And her eyes were alive in their depth, as the kraken[3]
    beneath the sea-blue.

II.

"Because I fear you," he answered; —"because
    you are far too fair,
And able to strangle my soul in a mesh of your gold-
    coloured hair."

III.

"Oh, that," she said, "is no reason! Such knots
    are quickly undone,
And too much beauty, I reckon, is nothing but too
    much sun."

IV.

"Yet farewell so," he answered; —"the sunstroke's
    fatal at times.
I value your husband, Lord Walter, whose gallop rings
    still from the limes."

V.

"Oh, that," she said, "is no reason. You smell a
    rose through a fence:
If two should smell it, what matter? who grumbles,
    and where's the pretence?"

10

VI.

"But I," he replied, "have promised another, when
    love was free,
To love her alone, alone, who alone and afar loves
    me."

VII.

"Why, that," she said, "is no reason. Love's
    always free, I am told.
Will you vow to be safe from the headache on Tues-
    day, and think it will hold?"

VIII.

"But you," he replied, "have a daughter, a young
    little child, who was laid
In your lap to be pure; so I leave you: the angels
    would make me afraid."

IX.

"Oh, that," she said, "is no reason. The angels
    keep out of the way;
And Dora, the child, observes nothing, although you
    should please me and stay."

X.

At which he rose up in his anger—"Why, now,
    you no longer are fair!
Why, now, you no longer are fatal, but ugly and
    hateful, I swear."   20

XI.

At which she laughed out in her scorn: "These men!
    Oh, these men overnice,
Who are shocked if a colour not virtuous is frankly put
    on by a vice."

XII.

Her eyes blazed upon him—"And *you*! You bring
    us your vices so near
That we smell them! You think in our presence a
    thought 'twould defame us to hear!

XIII.

"What reason had you, and what right,—I appeal
        to your soul from my life,—
To find me too fair as a woman? Why, sir, I am
        pure, and a wife.

XIV.

"Is the day-star too fair up above you? It burns you
        not. Dare you imply
I brushed you more close than the star does, when
        Walter had set me as high?

XV.

"If a man finds a woman too fair, he means simply
        adapted too much
To use unlawful and fatal. The praise!—shall I
        thank you for such?   30

XVI.

"Too fair?—not unless you misuse us! and surely
        if, once in a while,
You attain to it, straightway you call us no longer too
        fair, but too vile.

XVII.

"A moment,—I pray your attention!—I have a
        poor word in my head
I must utter, though womanly custom would set it
        down better unsaid.

XVIII.

"You grew, sir, pale to impertinence, once when I
        showed you a ring.
You kissed my fan when I dropped it. No matter!
        —I've broken the thing.

XIX.

"You did me the honour, perhaps, to be moved at
        my side now and then
In the senses—a vice, I have heard, which is common
        to beasts and some men.

XX.

"Love's a virtue for heroes!—as white as the snow
       on high hills,
And immortal as every great soul is that struggles,
       endures, and fulfils.   40

XXI.

"I love my Walter profoundly,—you, Maude, though
       you faltered a week,
For the sake of . . . what was it—an eyebrow?
       or, less still, a mole on a cheek?

XXII.

"And since, when all's said, you're too noble to
       stoop to the frivolous cant
About crimes irresistible, virtues that swindle, betray
       and supplant,

XXIII.

"I determined to prove to yourself that, whate'er you
       might dream or avow
By illusion, you wanted precisely no more of me than
       you have now.

XXIV.

"There! Look me full in the face!—in the face.
       Understand, if you can,
That the eyes of such women as I am are clean as the
       palm of a man.

XXV.

"Drop his hand, you insult him. Avoid us for fear
       we should cost you a scar—
You take us for harlots, I tell you, and not for the
       women we are.   50

XXVI.

"You wronged me: but then I considered . . .
       there's Walter! And so at the end
I vowed that he should not be mulcted, by me, in the
       hand of a friend.

XXVII.

"Have I hurt you indeed? We are quits then. Nay,
     friend of my Walter, be mine!
Come, Dora, my darling, my angel, and help me to
     ask him to dine."

BIANCA AMONG THE NIGHTINGALES

I.

The cypress stood up like a church
     That night we felt our love would hold,
And saintly moonlight seemed to search
     And wash the whole world clean as gold;
The olives crystallised the vales'
     Broad slopes until the hills grew strong:
The fire-flies and the nightingales
     Throbbed each to either, flame and song.
The nightingales, the nightingales!

II.

Upon the angle of its shade   10
     The cypress stood, self-balanced high;
Half up, half down, as double-made,
     Along the ground, against the sky;
And *we*, too! from such soul-height went
     Such leaps of blood, so blindly driven,
We scarce knew if our nature meant
     Most passionate earth or intense heaven,
The nightingales, the nightingales!

III.

We paled with love, we shook with love,
     We kissed so close we could not vow;   20
Till Giulio whispered "Sweet, above
     God's Ever guaranties this Now."
And through his words the nightingales
     Drove straight and full their long clear call,
Like arrows through heroic mails,[4]
     And love was awful in it all.
The nightingales, the nightingales!

IV.

O cold white moonlight of the north,
  Refresh these pulses, quench this hell!
O coverture of death drawn forth   30
  Across this garden-chamber . . . well!
But what have nightingales to do
  In gloomy England, called the free . . .
(Yes, free to die in! . . .) when we two
  Are sundered, singing still to me?
And still they sing, the nightingales!

V.

I think I hear him, how he cried
  "My own soul's life!" between their notes.
Each man has but one soul supplied,
  And that's immortal. Though his throat's   40
On fire with passion now, to *her*
  He can't say what to me he said!
And yet he moves her, they aver.
  The nightingales sing through my head,—
The nightingales, the nightingales!

VI.

He says to her what moves her most.
  He would not name his soul within
Her hearing,—rather pays her cost
  With praises to her lips and chin.
Man has but one soul, 'tis ordained,   50
  And each soul but one love, I add;
Yet souls are damned and love's profaned;
  These nightingales will sing me mad!
The nightingales, the nightingales!

VII.

I marvel how the birds can sing.
  There's little difference, in their view,
Betwixt our Tuscan trees that spring
  As vital flames into the blue,
And dull round blots of foliage meant,
  Like saturated sponges here   60
To suck the fogs up. As content
  Is he too in this land, 'tis clear.
And still they sing, the nightingales.

VIII.

My native Florence! dear, forgone!
    I see across the Alpine ridge
How the last feast-day of Saint John
    Shot rockets from Carraia bridge.
The luminous city, tall with fire,
    Trod deep down in that river of ours,
While many a boat with lamp and choir   70
    Skimmed birdlike over glittering towers.
I will not hear these nightingales.

IX.

I seem to float, *we* seem to float
    Down Arno's stream in festive guise;
A boat strikes flame into our boat,
    And up that lady seems to rise
As then she rose. The shock had flashed
    A vision on us! What a head,
What leaping eyeballs!—beauty dashed
    To splendour by a sudden dread.   80
And still they sing, the nightingales.

X.

Too bold to sin, too weak to die;
    Such women are so. As for me,
I would we had drowned there, he and I,
    That moment, loving perfectly.
He had not caught her with her loosed
    Gold ringlets . . . rarer in the south . . .
Nor heard the "Grazie tanto"[5] bruised
    To sweetness by her English mouth.
And still they sing, the nightingales.   90

XI.

She had not reached him at my heart
    With her fine tongue, as snakes indeed
Kill flies; nor had I, for my part,
    Yearned after, in my desperate need,
And followed him as he did her
    To coasts left bitter by the tide,
Whose very nightingales, elsewhere
    Delighting, torture and deride!
For still they sing, the nightingales.

XII.

A worthless woman; mere cold clay 100
    As all false things are: but so fair,
She takes the breath of men away
    Who gaze upon her unaware.
I would not play her larcenous tricks
    To have her looks! She lied and stole,
And spat into my love's pure pyx[6]
    The rank saliva of her soul.
And still they sing, the nightingales.

XIII.

I would not for her white and pink,
    Though such he likes—her grace of limb, 110
Though such he has praised—nor yet, I think,
    For life itself, though spent with him,
Commit such sacrilege, affront
    God's nature which is love, intrude
'Twixt two affianced souls, and hunt
    Like spiders, in the altar's wood.
I cannot bear these nightingales.

XIV.

If she chose sin, some gentler guise
    She might have sinned in, so it seems:
She might have pricked out both my eyes, 120
    And I still seen him in my dreams!
—Or drugged me in my soup or wine,
    Nor left me angry afterward:
To die here with his hand in mine,
    His breath upon me, were not hard.
(Our Lady hush these nightingales!)

XV.

But set a springe for *him*, "mio ben,"[7]
    My only good, my first last love!—
Though Christ knows well what sin is, when
    He sees some things done they must move 130
Himself to wonder. Let her pass.
    I think of her by night and day.
Must *I* too join her . . . out, alas! . . .
    With Giulio, in each word I say?
And evermore the nightingales!

XVI.

Giulio, my Giulio!—sing they so,
     And you be silent? Do I speak,
And you not hear? An arm you throw
     Round some one, and I feel so weak?
—Oh, owl-like birds! They sing for spite,   140
     They sing for hate, they sing for doom,
They'll sing through death who sing through night,
     They'll sing and stun me in the tomb—
The nightingales, the nightingales!

MOTHER AND POET

(Turin, After News From Gaeta,[8] 1861)

I.

Dead! One of them shot by the sea in the east,
     And one of them shot in the west by the sea.
Dead! both my boys! When you sit at the feast
     And are wanting a great song for Italy free,
          Let none look at *me*!

II.

Yet I was a poetess only last year,
     And good at my art, for a woman, men said;
But *this* woman, *this*, who is agonised here,
     —The east sea and west sea rhyme on in her head
          For ever instead.   10

III.

What art can a woman be good at? Oh, vain!
     What art *is* she good at, but hurting her breast
With the milk-teeth of babes, and a smile at the pain?
     Ah boys, how you hurt! you were strong as you pressed,
          And I proud, by that test.

IV.

What art's for a woman? To hold on her knees
     Both darlings! to feel all their arms round her throat,
Cling, strangle a little! to sew by degrees
     And 'broider the long-clothes and neat little coat;
          To dream and to doat.   20

V.

To teach them . . . It stings there! *I* made them indeed
   Speak plain the word *country*. *I* taught them, no doubt,
That a country's a thing men should die for at need.
    I prated of liberty, rights, and about
      The tyrant cast out.

VI.

And when their eyes flashed . . . O my beautiful eyes! . . .
   I exulted; nay, let them go forth at the wheels
Of the guns, and denied not. But then the surprise
    When one sits quite alone! Then one weeps, then one kneels!
      God, how the house feels!   30

VII.

At first, happy news came, in gay letters moiled
   With my kisses,—of camp-life and glory, and how
They both loved me; and, soon coming home to be spoiled
    In return would fan off every fly from my brow
      With their green laurel-bough.

VIII.

Then was triumph at Turin: "Ancona was free!"
   And some one came out of the cheers in the street,
With a face pale as stone, to say something to me.
    My Guido was dead! I fell down at his feet,
      While they cheered in the street.   40

IX.

I bore it; friends soothed me; my grief looked sublime
   As the ransom of Italy. One boy remained
To be leant on and walked with, recalling the time
    When the first grew immortal, while both of us strained
      To the height he had gained.

X.

And letters still came, shorter, sadder, more strong,
   Writ now but in one hand, "I was not to faint,—
One loved me for two—would be with me ere long:
    And *Viva l'Italia!—he* died for, our saint,
      Who forbids our complaint."   50

XI.

My Nanni would add, "he was safe, and aware
    Of a presence that turned off the balls,—was imprest
It was Guido himself, who knew what I could bear,
    And how 'twas impossible, quite dispossessed
        To live on for the rest."

XII.

On which, without pause, up the telegraph line
    Swept smoothly the next news from Gaeta:—*Shot.*
Tell his mother. Ah, ah, "his," "their" mother,—
        not "mine,"
    No voice says "*My* mother" again to me. What!
        You think Guido forgot?   60

XIII.

Are souls straight so happy that, dizzy with Heaven,
    They drop earth's affections, conceive not of woe?
I think not. Themselves were too lately forgiven
    Through THAT Love and Sorrow which reconciled so
        The Above and Below.

XIV.

O Christ of the five wounds, who look'dst through the dark
    To the face of Thy mother! consider, I pray
How we common mothers stand desolate, mark,
    Whose sons, not being Christs, die with eyes turned away,
        And no last word to say!   70

XV.

Both boys dead? but that's out of nature. We all
    Have been patriots, yet each house must always keep one.
'Twere imbecile, hewing out roads to a wall;
    And, when Italy's made, for what end is it done
        If we have not a son?

XVI.

Ah, ah, ah! when Gaeta's taken, what then?
    When the fair wicked queen sits no more at her sport
Of the fire-balls of death crashing souls out of men?
    When the guns of Cavalli with final retort
        Have cut the game short?   80

XVII.

When Venice and Rome keep their new jubilee,
     When your flag takes all heaven for its white,
          green, and red,
When *you* have your country from mountain to sea,
     When King Victor has Italy's crown on his head,
          (And *I* have my Dead)—

XVIII.

What then? Do not mock me. Ah, ring your bells low,
     And burn your lights faintly! *My* country is *there*,
Above the star pricked by the last peak of snow:
     My Italy's THERE, with my brave civic Pair,
          To disfranchise despair!   90

XIX.

Forgive me. Some women bear children in strength,
     And bite back the cry of their pain in self-scorn;
But the birth-pangs of nations will wring us at length
     Into wail such as this—and we sit on forlorn
          When the man-child is born.

XX.

Dead! One of them shot by the sea in the east,
     And one of them shot in the west by the sea.
Both! both my boys! If in keeping the feast
     You want a great song for your Italy free,
          Let none look at *me*!   100

AMY'S CRUELTY

I.

     Fair Amy of the terraced house,
          Assist me to discover
     Why you who would not hurt a mouse
          Can torture so your lover.

II.

     You give your coffee to the cat,
          You stroke the dog for coming,
     And all your face grows kinder at
          The little brown bee's humming.

III.

But when *he* haunts your door . . . the town
    Marks coming and marks going . . .   10
You seem to have stitched your eyelids down
    To that long piece of sewing!

IV.

You never give a look, not you,
    Nor drop him a "Good morning,"
To keep his long day warm and blue,
    So fretted by your scorning.

V.

She shook her head—"The mouse and bee
    For crumb or flower will linger:
The dog is happy at my knee,
    The cat purrs at my finger.   20

VI.

"But *he* . . . to *him*, the least thing given
    Means great things at a distance;
He wants my world, my sun, my heaven,
    Soul, body, whole existence.

VII.

"They say love gives as well as takes;
    But I'm a simple maiden,—
My mother's first smile when she wakes
    I still have smiled and prayed in.

VIII.

"I only know my mother's love
    Which gives all and asks nothing;   30
And this new loving sets the groove
    Too much the way of loathing.

IX.

"Unless he gives me all in change,
    I forfeit all things by him:
The risk is terrible and strange—
    I tremble, doubt, . . . deny him.

X.

"He's sweetest friend or hardest foe,
　　Best angel or worst devil;
I either hate or . . . love him so,
　　I can't be merely civil!　　　　　　　　　　40

XI.

"You trust a woman who puts forth
　　Her blossoms thick as summer's?
You think she dreams what love is worth,
　　Who casts it to new-comers?

XII.

"Such love's a cowslip-ball to fling,
　　A moment's pretty pastime;
I give . . . all me, if anything,
　　The first time and the last time.

XIII.

"Dear neighbour of the trellised house,
　　A man should murmur never,　　　　　　　50
Though treated worse than dog and mouse,
　　Till doated on for ever!"

A MUSICAL INSTRUMENT[9]

I.

What was he doing, the great god Pan,
　　Down in the reeds by the river?
Spreading ruin and scattering ban,
Splashing and paddling with hoofs of a goat,
And breaking the golden lilies afloat
　　With the dragon-fly on the river.

II.

He tore out a reed, the great god Pan,
　　From the deep cool bed of the river:
The limpid water turbidly ran,
And the broken lilies a-dying lay,　　　　　　　10
And the dragon-fly had fled away,
　　Ere he brought it out of the river.

III.

High on the shore sat the great god Pan
    While turbidly flowed the river;
And hacked and hewed as a great god can,
With his hard bleak steel at the patient reed,
Till there was not a sign of the leaf indeed
    To prove it fresh from the river.

IV.

He cut it short, did the great god Pan,
    (How tall it stood in the river!)   20
Then drew the pith, like the heart of a man,
Steadily from the outside ring,
And notched the poor dry empty thing
    In holes, as he sat by the river.

V.

"This is the way," laughed the great god Pan
    (Laughed while he sat by the river),
"The only way, since gods began
To make sweet music, they could succeed."
Then, dropping his mouth to a hole in the reed,
    He blew in power by the river.   30

VI.

Sweet, sweet, sweet, O Pan!
    Piercing sweet by the river!
Blinding sweet, O great god Pan!
The sun on the hill forgot to die,
And the lilies revived, and the dragon-fly
    Came back to dream on the river.

VII.

Yet half a beast is the great god Pan,
    To laugh as he sits by the river,
Making a poet out of a man:
The true gods sigh for the cost and pain,—   40
For the reed which grows nevermore again
    As a reed with the reeds in the river.

Letters[1]

TO MARY RUSSELL MITFORD
17 July 1841
[1 Beacon Terrace, Torquay]

*   *   *   *   *

Thank you, thank you for Browning's poem.[2] My thought of it crossed your question about my thought, M^r. Kenyon having kindly sent me *his* copy ten days since. But I must tell you besides that I read it three times—in correspondence with M^r. Chorley's[3] four—& in testimony both to the genius & the obscurity. Nobody sh^d. complain of being forced to read it three or four or ten times. Only they w^d. do it more gratefully if they were not forced. I who am used to mysteries, caught the light at my second reading—but the full glory, not until the third. The conception of the whole is fine, very fine—& there are noble, beautiful things everywhere to be broken up & looked at. That great tragic scene, which you call "exquisite"—& which pants again with its own power! Did it strike you that there was an occasional *manner*, in the portions most strictly dramatic, like Landor's,[4] in Landor's dramas, when Landor writes best. Now read—

–"How these tall
Naked geraniums straggle! Push the lattice—
Behind that frame.—Nay, do I bid you?—Sebald,
It shakes the dust down on me! Why of course
The slide-bolt catches—Well—are you content
Or must I find you something else to spoil?
Kiss & be friends, my Sebald!"

Is'nt that Landor? Is'nt it his very trick of phrase? Yet M^r. Browning is no imitator. He asserts *himself* in his writings, with a strong & deep in-dividuality: and if he does it in Chaldee, why he makes it worth our while to get out our dictionaries! Oh most excellent critic 'in the glass house[']!—

After all, what I miss most in M^r. Browning, is *music*. There is a want of harmony, particularly when he is lyrical—& *that* struck me with a hard hand, while I was in my admiration over his Paracelsus.

This is for *you*—I *do not know him*.

(LMRM)

*   *   *   *   *

TO MARY RUSSELL MITFORD
14 January 1843
[50 Wimpole Street, London]

*   *   *   *   *

"So she sets up to be original−does she?−this modest EBB"!−

Ah, be merciful! She w^d. not "set up"−she admits your right to set her down, if she did. And yet she acknowledges freely that any single poem of hers which was to her conviction, *not* original−that is, which did not express a direct impression from nature to the mind of the writer unintermediately received & which did not convey to the reader's mind a fresh breath or new aspect of Nature,−intermediately received,−such a poem I w^d. destroy willingly, gladly, righteously, & never look back upon its ashes. Perhaps this proves a want of modesty in me: for certainly it proves my convictions of what Poetry ought to be to assume the name, & of what poets ought to be to assume the name. And now, dont let us talk any more about *me*−I only *aspire*.

But Tennyson . . . not original!−Ah my beloved friend!−what is genius−but the power of expressing a new individuality? W^d. all the finishing in the world move the soul into another attitude, as certain of those poems[5] do? Surely, surely not! No more originality now? Have we seen to the bottom of that infinite of Nature, which reflects God's! Surely, surely not! If I thought so; I w^d. throw away all these poems, & "walk softly all day long"[6] as in a universe worn out & annulled. Art & literature sh^d. be names of memories to me, for evermore−mocking an impossible substance−

But my hope & belief are, that to be "original" is as possible & not harder now, than in the first days of the creation−& that every writer who is at once true enough & strong enough to express his own individuality, is original as Shakespeare was. I hold Tennyson to be, strictly speaking, original−& Browning!−& Milnes,[7] in a less degree. Passing to prose, your own Village & Belford Regis are original−& if others write in your manner, they *Mitfordize*. Grant to me, my dearest friend, that originality has not perished from the world−

(*LMRM*)

*   *   *   *   *

TO HUGH STUART BOYD

22 September 1844
[50 Wimpole Street, London]

*   *   *   *   *

And oh, such a letter as I have had from Harriet Martineau! She had bound herself by a promise to tell me the full truth about the books,—let it be pleasant or unpleasant truth—and because her letter was long in coming, I began to fear that it would be unpleasant. But there never was a more delightful generous letter, or one fuller of fervent sympathy. She tells me that every day she has had the volumes open before her, and that their power over her is of the deepest. What particularly pleases me, is, that her predominant impression, she says, is of their entire *"originality"*. Also she observes upon what she calls the "immense advance" on the former work—being of opinion, nevertheless, that "a few of the pieces" of that former work, might be considered "worthy of a place in this." I was very much delighted by this letter from such a person, who unites to high logic, a deep sensibility to poetry—certainly the most manlike woman (in the best sense of man) in the three Kingdoms.

I should tell you however that she complains of a general impression of monotony, after reading the "Drama of Exile,"—and that she prefers upon the whole, the smaller poems. "Lady Geraldine's Courtship" she singles out for praise, and says of it that she felt herself *"swept through it."* Now it is curious, that people in general are pleased with "Lady Geraldine"—and it is true that I always hear of their being pleased with it, with a feeling like a *sense of escape,*—seeing that some peculiar circumstances attended its composition. Do not tell anybody—people might and would immediately call me a careless, hasty writer,—but the last *thirteen* of those printed pages were written,—composed and written—in one day. It was dangerous and might have been fatal speed. When people praise the poem, I always think, "What stuff it *might* have been!"—and *that* is very natural.

(*EB to HSB*)

*   *   *   *   *

TO ROBERT BROWNING

15 January 1845
50 Wimpole Street [London]

*   *   *   *   *

In art, however, I understand that it does not do to be headlong, but patient & laborious—& there is a love strong enough, even in me, to overcome nature. I apprehend what you mean in the criticism you just intimate, & shall turn it over & over in my mind until I get practical good from it. What no mere critic sees, but what you, an artist, know, is the difference between the thing desired & the thing attained, between the idea in the writer's mind & the $\epsilon\iota\delta\omega\lambda o\nu$[8] cast off in his work. All the effort—the quickening of the breath & beating of the heart in pursuit, which is ruffling & injurious to the general effect of a composition; all which you call 'insistency,' & which many w^d call superfluity, and which *is* superfluous in a sense . . *you* can pardon, because you understand. The great chasm between the thing I say, & the thing I would say, w^d. be quite dispiriting to me, in spite even of such kindnesses as yours, if the desire did not master the despondency. "Oh for a horse with wings!"[9] It is wrong of me to write so of myself—only you put your finger on the root of a fault, which has, to my fancy, been a little misapprehended. I do not *say everything I think* (as has been said of me by master-critics) but I *take every means to say what I think*, which is different!—or I fancy so!

In one thing, however, you are wrong. Why sh^d. you deny the full measure of my delight & benefit from your writings? I could tell you why you should not. You have in your vision two worlds—or to use the language of the schools of the day, you are both subjective & objective in the habits of your mind. You can deal both with abstract thought & with human passion in the most passionate sense. Thus, you have an immense grasp in Art; and no one at all accustomed to consider the usual forms of it, could help regarding with reverence & gladness the gradual expansion of your powers. Then you are 'masculine' to the height—and I, as a woman, have studied some of your gestures of language & intonation wistfully, as a thing beyond me far! & the more admirable for being beyond.

(*LRB and EBB*)

*   *   *   *   *

TO ROBERT BROWNING

[16–17 July 1845]
[50 Wimpole Street, London]

*   *   *   *   *

Probably or certainly rather, I have one advantage over you . . one, of which women are not fond of boasting—that of *being older by years*—for the Essay on Mind, which was the first poem published by me,—(and rather more printed than published after all) the work of my earliest youth, half childhood half womanhood, was published in 1826 I see—and if I told Mr. Kenyon not to let you see that book, it was not for the date, but because Coleridge's daughter was right in calling it a mere "girl's exercise," because it is just *that* and no more, . . no expression whatever of my nature as it ever was,. . . pedantic, & in some things, pert, . . & such as altogether, & to do myself justice (which I w^d. fain do of course) I was not in my whole life. Bad books are never like their writers, you know—& those under-age books are generally bad. Also I have found it hard work to *get into expression*, though I began rhyming from my very infancy, much as you did (& this, with no sympathy near to me—I have had to do without sympathy in the full sense—) & even in my 'Seraphim' days, my tongue clove to the roof of my mouth . . from leading so conventual recluse a life, perhaps—& all my better/bitterness[?] poems were written last year, the very best being to come . . . if there sh^d be any life or courage to come—

(LRB and EBB)

*   *   *   *   *

TO MARY RUSSELL MITFORD

November [1850]
[Casa Guidi, Florence]

*   *   *   *   *

I long to see your papers & dare say they are charming. At the same time just because they are sure to be charming (and notwithstanding their kindness to me . . notwithstanding that I live in a glass house myself, warmed by such rare stoves!) I am a little in fear that your generosity & excess of kindliness may run the risk of lowering the ideal of poetry in England by lifting above the mark the names of some poetasters.[10] Do you know, you take up your heart sometimes by mistake to admire with, when you ought to use it only to love with? & this is apt to be dangerous, with your reputation & authority in matters of literature. See how impertinent I am! But we should all take care to teach the world that poetry is a divine thing, . . should we not, . . that it is not mere verse-making, though the verses be pretty in their way.

Rather perish every verse *I* ever wrote, for one, than help to drag down an inch that standard of poetry which for the sake of humanity as well as literature, should be kept high. As for simplicity & clearness, did I ever deny that they were excellent qualities? Never, surely. Only, they will not *make* poetry; & absolutely vain they are, & indeed all other qualities, without the essential thing, the genius, the inspiration, the insight, . . let us call it what we please—without which, the most accomplished verse-writers had far better write prose, . . for their own sakes as for the world's—dont you think so? Which I say, because I sighed aloud over many names in your list, & now have taken pertly to write out the sigh at length.

(LMRM)

*   *   *   *   *

TO MRS. JAMES MARTIN

February [1857]
[Casa Guidi, Florence]

My dearest Mrs. Martin,—I needn't say how much, how very much, pleasure your letter gave me. That the poem[11] should really have touched you, reached you, with whatever drawbacks, is a joy. And then that Mr. Martin should have read it with any sort of interest! It was more than I counted on, as you know. Thank you, dearest Mrs. Martin—thank both of you for so much sympathy.

In respect to certain objections, I am quite sure you do me the justice to believe that I do not willingly give cause for offence. Without going as far as Robert, who holds that I "couldn't be coarse if I tried," (only that!) you will grant that I don't habitually dabble in the dirt; it's not the way of my mind or life. If, therefore, I move certain subjects in this work, it is because my conscience was first moved in me not to ignore them. What has given most offence in the book, more than the story of Marian—far more!—has been the reference to the condition of women in our cities, which a woman oughtn't to refer to, by any manner of means, says the conventional tradition. Now I have thought deeply otherwise. If a woman ignores these wrongs, then may women as a sex continue to suffer them; there is no help for any of us—let us be dumb and die. I have spoken therefore, and in speaking have used plain words—words which look like blots, and which you yourself would put away—words which, if blurred or softened, would imperil perhaps the force and righteousness of the moral influence. Still, I certainly will,

when the time comes, go over the poem carefully, and see where an of-
fence can be got rid of without loss otherwise. The second edition was
issued so early that Robert would not let me alter even a comma, would
not let me look between the pages in order to the least alteration. He
said (the truth) that my head was dizzy-blind with the book, and that,
if I changed anything, it would be probably for the worse; like arranging
a room in the dark. Oh no. Indeed he is not vexed that you should say
what you do. On the contrary, he was *pleased* because of the much more
that you said. As to your friend with the susceptible "morals"—well, I
could not help smiling indeed. I am assured too, by a friend of my own,
that the "mamas of England" in a body refuse to let their daughters read
it. Still, the daughters emancipate themselves and *do*, that is certain; for
the number of *young* women, not merely "the strong-minded" as a sect,
but pretty, affluent, happy women, surrounded by all the temptations
of English respectability, that cover it with the most extravagant praises
is surprising to me, who was not prepared for that particular kind of
welcome. It's true that there's a quantity of hate to balance the love, only
I think it chiefly seems to come from the less advanced part of society.
(See how modest that sounds! But you will know what I mean.) I mean,
from persons whose opinions are not in a state of growth, and who do
not like to be disturbed from a settled position. Oh, that there are faults
in the book, no human being knows so well as I; defects, weaknesses,
great gaps of intelligence. Don't let me stop to recount them.

The review in "Blackwood" proves to be by Mr. Aytoun; and com-
ing from the camp of the enemy (artistically and socially) cannot be con-
sidered other than generous. It is not quite so by the "North British,"
where another poet (Patmore), who knows more, is somewhat
depreciatory, I can't help feeling.

Now will you be sick of my literature; but you liked to hear, you
said. If you would see, besides, I would show you what George sent me
the other day, a number of the "National Magazine," with the most
hideous engraving, from a medallion, you could imagine—the head of
a "strong-minded" giantess on the neck of a bull, and my name under-
neath! Penini said, "It's not a bit like; it's too old and *not half so pretty*"—
which was comforting under the trying circumstance, if anything could
comfort one in despair.

(LEBB)

TO WILLIAM MAKEPEACE THACKERAY[12]

21 April [1861]
126 Via Felice, Rome

Dear Mr. Thackeray, — Pray consider the famous 'tooth' (a wise tooth!) as extracted under chloroform, and no pain suffered by anybody.

To prove that I am not sulky, I send another contribution, which may prove too much, perhaps — and, if you think so, dispose of the supererogatory virtue by burning the manuscript, as I am sure I may rely on your having done with the last.

I confess it, dear Mr. Thackeray, never was anyone turned out of a room for indecent behaviour in a more gracious and conciliatory manner! Also, I confess that from your 'Cornhill' standpoint (paterfamilias looking on) you are probably right ten times over. From mine, however, I may not be wrong, and I appeal to you as the deep man you are, whether it is not the higher mood, which on Sunday bears with the 'plain word,' so offensive on Monday, during the cheating across the counter? I am not a 'fast woman.' I don't like coarse subjects, or the coarse treatment of any subject. But I am deeply convinced that the corruption of our society requires not shut doors and windows, but light and air: and that it is exactly because pure and prosperous women choose to *ignore* vice, that miserable women suffer wrong by it everywhere. Has paterfamilias, with his Oriental traditions and veiled female faces, very successfully dealt with a certain class of evil? What if materfamilias, with her quick sure instincts and honest innocent eyes, do more towards their expulsion by simply looking at them and calling them by their names? See what insolence you put me up to by your kind way of naming my dignities — 'Browning's wife and Penini's mother.'

And I, being vain (turn some people out of a room and you don't humble them properly), retort with — 'materfamilias!'

(*LEBB*)

*   *   *   *   *

Review of *The Book of the Poets*[1]
1842

ON SHAKESPEARE

For the rest we must speak briefly of Shakespeare, and very weakly too, except for love. That he was a great natural genius nobody, we believe, has doubted—the fact has passed with the cheer of mankind; but that he was a great artist the majority has doubted. Yet Nature and Art cannot be reasoned apart into antagonistic principles. Nature is God's art—the accomplishment of a spiritual significance hidden in a sensible symbol. Poetic art (man's) looks past the symbol with a divine guess and reach of soul into the mystery of the significance,—disclosing from the analysis of the visible things the synthesis or unity of the ideal,—and expounds like symbol and like significance out of the infinite of God's doing into the finite of man's comprehending. Art lives by Nature, and not the bare mimetic life generally attributed to Art: she does not imitate, she expounds. *Interpres naturae*—is the poet-artist; and the poet wisest in nature is the most artistic poet: and thus our Shakespeare passes to the presidency unquestioned, as the greatest artist in the world. We believe in his judgment as in his genius. We believe in his learning, both of books and men, and hills and valleys: in his grammars and dictionaries we do not believe. In his philosophy of language we believe absolutely: in his Babel-learning, not at all. We believe reverently in the miracle of his variety; and it is observable that we become aware of it less by the numerousness of his persons and their positions, than by the *depth* of the least of either,—by the sense of visibility beyond what we see, as in nature. Our creed goes on to declare him most passionate and most rational—of an emotion which casts us into thought, of a reason which leaves us open to emotion: most grave and most gay—while we scarcely can guess that the man Shakespeare is grave or gay, because he interposes between ourselves and his personality the whole breadth and length of his ideality. His associative faculty,—the wit's faculty besides the poet's—for him who was both wit and poet, shed sparks like an electric wire. He was wise in the world, having studied it in his heart; what is called "the knowledge of the world" being just the knowledge of one heart, and certain exterior symbols. What else? What otherwise could he, the young transgressor of Sir

Thomas Lucy's fences, new from Stratford and the Avon, close in theatric London, have seen or touched or handled of the Hamlets and Lears and Othellos, that he should draw them? "How can I take portraits," said Marmontel, in a similar inexperience, "before I have beheld faces?" Voltaire embraced him, in reply. Well applauded, Voltaire! It was a *mot* for Marmontel's utterance, and Voltaire's praise—for Marmontel, not for Shakespeare. Every being is his own centre to the universe, and in himself must one foot of the compasses be fixed to attain to any measurement: nay, every being is his own mirror to the universe. Shakespeare wrote from within—the beautiful; and we recognise from within—the true. He is universal, because he is individual. And, without any prejudice of admiration, we may go on to account his faults to be the proofs of his power; the cloud of dust cast up by the multitude of the chariots. The activity of his associative faculty is occasionally morbid: in the abundance of his winged thoughts, the locust flies with the bee, and the ground is dark with the shadow of them. Take faults, take excellences, it is impossible to characterise this Shakespeare by an epithet: have we heard the remark before, that it should sound so obvious? We say of Corneille, the noble; of Racine, the tender; of Aeschylus, the terrible; of Sophocles, the perfect; but not one of these words, not one appropriately descriptive epithet, can we attach to Shakespeare without a conscious recoil. Shakespeare! the name is the description.

He is the most wonderful artist in blank verse of all in England, and almost the earliest. We do not say that he first broke the enchaining monotony, of which the Sackvilles and the Marlowes left us complaining; because the versification of "Hieronimo" ran at its own strong will, and the "Pinner of Wakefield" may have preceded his first plays. We do not even say, what we might, that his hand first proved the compass and infinite modulation of the new instrument; but we do say, that it never answered another hand as it answered his. We do say, this fingering was never learned of himself by another. From Massinger's more resonant majesty, from even Fletcher's more numerous and artful cadences, we turn back to his artlessness of art, to his singular and supreme estate as a versificator. Often when he is at the sweetest, his words are poor monosyllables, his pauses frequent to brokenness, and the structure of the several lines less varied than was taught after Fletcher's masterdom; but the whole results in an ineffable charming of the ear which we acquiesce in without seeking its cause, a happy mystery of music.

*   *   *   *   *

ON WORDSWORTH

It was not so—it was not in the projection of a passionate emotion—that William Wordsworth committed himself to nature, but in full resolution and determinate purpose. He is scarcely, perhaps, of a passionate temperament, although still less is he cold; rather quiet in his love, as the stockdove, and brooding over it as constantly, and with as soft an inward song lapsing outwardly—serene through deepness— saying himself of his thoughts, that they "do often lie too deep for tears"; which does not mean that their painfulness will not suffer them to be wept for, but that their closeness to the supreme Truth hallows them, like the cheek of an archangel, from tears. Call him the very opposite of Byron, who, with narrower sympathies for the crowd, yet stood nearer to the crowd, because everybody understands passion. Bryon was a poet through pain. Wordsworth is a feeling man because he is a thoughtful man; he knows grief itself by a reflex emotion; by sympathy rather than by suffering. He is eminently and humanly expansive; and, spreading his infinite egotism over all the objects of his contemplation, reiterates the love, life, and poetry of his peculiar being in transcribing and chanting the material universe, and so sinks a broad gulf between his descriptive poetry and that of the Darwinian painter-poet school. Darwin[2] was, as we have intimated, all optic nerve. Wordsworth's eye is his soul. He does not see that which he does not intellectually discern, and he beholds his own cloud-capped Helvellyn under the same conditions with which he would contemplate a grand spiritual abstraction. In his view of the exterior world,—as in a human Spinozism,—mountains and men's hearts share in a sublime unity of humanity; yet his Spinozism does in nowise affront God, for he is eminently a religious poet, if not, indeed, altogether as generous and capacious in his Christianity as in his poetry; and, being a true Christian poet, he is scarcely least so when he is not writing directly upon the subject of religion; just as we learn sometimes without looking up, and by the mere colour of the grass, that the sky is cloudless. But what is most remarkable in this great writer is his poetical consistency. There is a wonderful unity in these multiform poems of one man: they are "bound each to each in natural piety," even as his days are: and why? because they *are* his days—all his days, work days and Sabbath days— his life, in fact, and not the unconnected works of his life, as vulgar men do opine of poetry and do rightly opine of vulgar poems, but the sign, seal, and representation of his life—nay, the actual audible breathing of his inward spirit's life. When Milton said that a poet's life should be a poem, he spoke a high moral truth; if he had added a reversion of the saying, that a poet's poetry should be his life,—he would have spoken a critical truth, not low.

"Foole, saide my muse to mee, looke in thine hearte and write,"[3]—and not only, we must repeat, at feast times, fast times, or curfew times—not only at times of crisis and emotion, but at all hours of the clock; for that which God thought good enough to write, or permit the writing of, on His book, the heart, is not too common, let us be sure, to write again in the best of our poems. William Wordsworth wrote these common things of nature, and by no means in a phraseology nor in a style. He was daring in his commonness as any of your Tamerlanes may be daring when far fetching an alien image from an outermost world; and, notwithstanding the ribald cry of that "vox populi" which has, in the criticism of poems, so little the character of divinity, and which loudly and mockingly, at his first utterance, denied the sanctity of his simplicities,—the Nature he was faithful to "betrayed not the heart which loved her," but, finally, justifying herself and him, "DID"—without the "Edinburgh Review."

"Hero-worshippers" as we are, and sitting for all the critical pretence—in right or wrong of which we speak at all—at the feet of Mr. Wordsworth,—recognising him, as we do, as poet-hero of a movement essential to the better being of poetry, as poet-prophet of utterances greater than those who first listened could comprehend, and of influences most vital and expansive—we are yet honest to confess that certain things in the "Lyrical Ballads" which most provoked the ignorant innocent hootings of the mob, do not seem to us all heroic. Love, like ambition, may overvault itself; and Betty Foys of the Lake school (so called) may be as subject to conventionalities as Pope's Lady Bettys. And, perhaps, our great poet might, through the very vehemence and nobleness of his hero and prophet-work for nature, confound, for some blind moment, and by an association easily traced and excused, nature with rusticity, the simple with the bald; and even fall into a vulgar conventionality in the act of spurning a graceful one. If a trace of such confounding may occasionally be perceived in Mr. Wordsworth's earlier poetry, few critics are mad enough, to-day, to catch at the loose straws of the full golden sheaf and deck out withal their own arrogant fronts in the course of mouthing mocks at the poet. The veriest critic of straw knoweth well at this hour of the day, that if Mr. Wordsworth was ever over-rustic, it was not through incapacity to be right royal; that of all poets, indeed, who have been kings in England, not one has swept the purple with more majesty than this poet, when it hath pleased him to be majestic.

*   *   *   *   *

NOTES

Juvenilia and *Essay on Mind*

1. The transcript of this poem by Mary Moulton-Barrett indicates EBB wrote it at Fenham Hall, Newcastle, in September 1814 when she was eight years old.

2. Angelica Catalani (1780–1849), Italian opera singer, first appeared in England in 1806 and was an unrivaled prima donna there for many years.

3. Beginning in 1817, EBB worked on *The Battle of Marathon* for the next two years; she gave an old family friend, Miss Trepsack, a privately printed copy inscribed with the date March 6th, 1820, EBB's fourteenth birthday. Marathon was the scene of the great historical event of the Athenians' defeat of the Persians, 490 B.C.

4. Sallust (86–34 B.C.), Roman historian.

5. "We have one part in common with the gods, and one part in common with the brutes."

6. Alexander Pope (1688–1744), English neo-classical poet considered the master of the heroic couplet; he was both precocious and vain.

7. Pegasus, the winged steed symbolic of poetic inspiration; Parnassus, the mountain sacred to Apollo and the Muses.

8. Sappho (610–570 B.C.), celebrated Greek lyric poet of Lesbos.

9. George Gordon, Lord Byron (1788–1824), English Romantic poet.

10. Thomas Moore (1779–1852), national lyric poet of Ireland.

11. Sir Walter Scott (1771–1832), prolific Scottish poet and novelist of the Romantic period.

12. Marcus Tullius Cicero (106–43 B.C.), famous Roman orator noted for his perfection of the Latin language. "*Quò . . . fuerunt*": "Wherever the poets have had less honor, there has been less application to learning."

13. John Milton (1608–74), author of the epic *Paradise Lost* written in blank verse.

14. John Dryden (1631–1700), translator and English poet of the Restoration period noted for his high standards of versification.

15. "The sable night descends upon the sea," from Virgil's *Aeneid*, I, line 89.

16. "Oh, thrice, four times blessed," from *Aeneid*, I, line 94.

17. King Darius (c. 550–485 B.C.), builder of the great Persian empire.

18. Calliope, muse of epic poetry.

19. Another name for Venus or Aphrodite, goddess of love. She was the mother of Aeneas, the Trojan prince who founded Rome.

20. Venus, wife of Vulcan, god of fire and metalworking. She was caught in the act of adultery with Mars, god of war. EBB has her favoring the Persians here.

21. Ruler of Athens and son of Pisistratus, tyrant of Athens, c. 560 B.C. Expelled from Athens, Hippias went over to Darius who waged war against the Athenians to reinstate him.

22. Priam, King of Troy, slain by the Greek warrior, Pyrrhus.

23. Roman name for Pallas Athena, goddess of wisdom and battle and patroness of Athens. "Paphia's Queen" is another name for Venus.

24. One of the Greek generals opposing Darius.

25. Athenian of superb courage and tenacity, as the following lines indicate.

26. Dwelling place of happy spirits in Hades.

27. This mock epic, untitled by EBB but signed and dated "Monday evening March 8th 1819," illustrates her continued use of the heroic couplet, now with classical allusions and machinery reminiscent of Pope's "The Rape of the Lock."

28. A mountain sacred to the Muses and Apollo, hence, the source of poetic inspiration.

29. Mr. Daniel McSwiney, tutor who prepared EBB's eldest brother, Edward, or Bro, for Charterhouse.

30. Hector, son of King Priam and most valiant of the Trojans, slain in single combat by Achilles, the most valiant of the Greeks.

31. First published anonymously.

32. The epigraph reads "Desire much, hope little, and demand nothing." See Francis Bacon's "Of Dispatch" in *Essays or Counsels Civil and Moral*.

33. See *Midsummer Night's Dream* III. i. 17–47 for this allusion to the pompous rustic, Bottom, who, in directing the play "Pyramus and Thisbe," regards it as necessary to tell the audience in a prologue that any violence will be only make-believe.

34. Caius Cornelius Tacitus (54–110), Roman historian. The motto translates: "They are sustained by the subject."

35. Greek philosopher and astronomer (died 54 B.C.).

36. Byron, who had recently died.

37. Francis Bacon, Lord Verulam (1560–1626) whose scientific approach to knowledge did not stifle his imaginative style.

38. In Book X of the *Republic*, Plato denigrates the poet because his art does not affect the rational element of the soul.

39. EBB here groups the mathematician Isaac Newton (1642–1727), the philosopher John Locke (1632–1704), and the poet-critic Nicholas Boileau-Despréaux (1636–1711) to represent three different schools of thought which appear to denigrate poetry.

40. "Monument more durable than bronze," from Horace, Ode xxx, line 1.

41. Lucretius (95–51 B.C.), Roman author of "De Rerum Natura," and a natural rather than religious philosopher, hence, in EBB's eyes, "erring."

42. EBB pairs a famous rhetorician of antiquity, Marcus Fabius Quintilian (42–117), with a modern English historian, Edward Gibbon (1737–94), as supporters of the role of poetic imagination.

43. EBB misquotes Milton from "The Reason of Church Government Urged Against Prelaty," Introduction, Book II, by saying "reason" instead of "region"; nevertheless, EBB conveys Milton's general idea that poetry is a higher art than prose.

44. Quintus Horatius Flaccus (65–8 B.C.), Roman poet whose "Ars Poetica," based on Aristotle's "Poetics," sets forth principles of literary criticism which were the basis of Pope's and Boileau's poetry treating this subject.

45. "By no means with equal steps."

46. Here EBB appended a footnote as follows: "He is indebted to Aristotle, which, however, cannot be said to affect his poetical originality."

47. At the end of Book II of *Paradise Lost*, Satan, in his journey through chaos, sees the world hanging from heaven on a golden chain.

48. The river Halys flows from north-central Turkey into the Black Sea.

49. *The Faerie Queene*, I. xii. line 122.

50. Modeled on Pope's works, especially the "Essay on Criticism" and "An Essay on Man," EBB's poem argues for the compatibility of the poetical and philosophical powers of the mind and discusses two aspects of the philosophical (history and science).

51. The wings of Icarus, modeled in wax by his father Daedalus, which melted as he soared near the sun.

52. EBB contrasts two Romans of the same period: Marcus Tullius Cicero (106–43 B.C.), the senator, and Lucius Sergius Catiline (108–62 B.C.), the conspirator against the state whom Cicero denounced. The coupling technique is a clear echo of Pope's "Essay on Man," II, 195 ff. and IV, 145 ff.

53. Sir William Blackstone (1723–80), author of "Commentaries on the Laws of England." "Libel" here simply means a writing. Lines 31–38 present the mystery of individual talent by contrary examples: i.e., Dante might have used Petrarch's subject and vice versa; the liberal Paine might have been a monarchist; Byron might have written as did Edward, First Baron Thurlow (1732–1806), who opposed reforms; Robert Southey (1774–1843), a poet laureate, might have been a political philosopher like John Locke (1632–1704).

54. Book II deals with a third aspect of the philosophical mind—the metaphysical—and, finally, with the poetical mind which elevates Nature and expresses the ideal.

55. See Acts 26:31 for Paul's words on his status as prisoner of the Romans.

56. Ixion made love to Juno whereupon Jupiter tricked him by making a cloud in her shape which Ixion then embraced.

57. Thomas Hobbes (1588–1679) believed in sensation as the source of knowledge; Benedict Spinoza (1632–77) developed a pantheistic philosophical system. Both would have been in conflict with EBB's Christian-Platonic views.

58. See II Kings 2:1–13 which describes Elijah ascending to heaven in a chariot of fire, leaving behind his mantle to Elisha. EBB is exploring the paradox of expressing the inexpressible.

The Seraphim, and Other Poems

1. "The Seraphim" was composed in 1836.

2. In the first three pages of the Preface, here omitted, EBB states her desire, after working on her translation of Aeschylus' *Prometheus Bound*, to write a poem on a Christian theme as she believes Aeschylus might have done had he lived during the era of Christ. Thus the themes of revenge which appear in the classical work would have become themes of Christian love and forgiveness—entirely appropriate in her eyes, of course, for the poetic imagination. This desire eventually took the form of a "dramatic lyric" which consists mainly of a dialogue between two seraphim who decide to leave their angelic realm to view God incarnate and crucified. Looking down on the scene of the crucifixion, the two seraphs come to understand the meaning of redemptive love, that humans now can love God more than sinless seraphs can.

3. Jacob's dream of the ladder reaching from earth to heaven with the angels ascending and descending. See Genesis 28:12.

4. Nicolas Boileau-Despréaux, a translator of "The Treatise on the Sublime" by Longinus.

5. Robert Burns (1759–96), Scottish Romantic poet. His remark is found in a letter of 12 February 1788 to a Mrs. Dunlop.

6. Here EBB has a footnote which reads: "See his Phaedrus."

7. First published anonymously in the *New Monthly Magazine* of July 1836. The epigraph comes from the *Emblems*, xii, of Francis Quarles (1542–1644), based on Galatians 6:14: "But God forbid that I should glory, save in the cross of our Lord Jesus Christ, by whom the world is crucified unto me, and I unto the world."

8. Symbol of death.

9. Certainly.

10. Tournament.

11. A Wordsworthian poem (especially stanza IV), composed at Sidmouth and dated 17 August 1835. First published in the *Athenaeum* 2 July 1836.

12. The story told by the Second Royal Mendicant in *Arabian Nights' Entertainment*, I.

13. Stanza III suggests the twilight state of the potential moment of creativity or inspiration.

14. Another Wordsworthian poem in its emphasis on memory, nature and the child.

15. A reference to Edwin, a character in Goldsmith's melancholy "Edwin and Angelina. A Ballad." (1766).

Poems, 1844

1. Published August 1844 and in a separate American edition entitled *A Drama of Exile and Other Poems* the following October.

2. "Of fatherland, and of God, of poets, of the soul which exalts itself in praying."

3. William Congreve (1670–1729), English Restoration dramatist.

4. Giovanni Battista Andreini (1578?–1650), Italian actor and dramatist, author of the play *L'Adamo*, about the fall of man.

5. Honoré de Balzac (1799–1850), French novelist.

6. "The angelic patience of genius."

7. Begun in 1841 (as "A Day from Eden") and not completed until May 1844, this poem was published in two parts in July and August 1844 in the *United States Magazine and Democratic Review*. In the opening scene Lucifer taunts the angel Gabriel about man's sin and the Spirits of Eden lament the fall. Here, the Flower Spirits bid farewell to Adam and Eve.

8. An emblem of immortality, the amaranth grew in Paradise but was removed to heaven after man's fall.

9. Paleness.

10. A magical plant spoken of by Homer in the *Odyssey* and Milton in *Comus*.

11. In Greek myth the flower which grew in profusion in the Elysian Fields.

12. In the omitted passage the Earth Spirits gloat at their dominion over man, and Adam and Eve appeal to God for forgiveness.

13. A reference to man's possessing free will.

14. I.e., Christ as born of woman.

15. See Genesis 2:10: "A river went out of Eden to water the garden; and from thence it was parted and became into four heads." The four rivers were the Pison, Gihon, Hiddekel (Tigris) and Euphrates.

16. The poem ends, after Christ's transfiguration into suffering humanity, with the angel chorus comforting Adam and Eve and the sound of the defeated Lucifer's weeping.

17. First published in *Graham's Magazine* in July 1843, this poem was one of several EBB sent in response to a request from James Russell Lowell.

18. First published in *Graham's Magazine* in August 1843.

19. See Tobit 12:15 for "the seven holy angels which present the prayers of the saints, and which go in and out before the glory of the Holy One."

20. First published in the *Athenaeum* of 29 October 1842 as "Sonnet on Mr. Haydon's Portrait of Mr. Wordsworth." It was written earlier in October when the English historical painter Benjamin Robert Haydon (1786–1846) sent EBB his unfinished portrait of Wordsworth. EBB sent the sonnet to Haydon who showed it to Wordsworth, poet laureate at this time.

21. A mountain near Wordsworth's Grasmere home in the Lake District.

22. A reference to the Royal Academy of artists, i.e., formal and studied.

23. This poem, along with "Work and Contemplation," was first published, untitled, in *Graham's Magazine* in December 1842.

24. Venetian boat song suggesting a rowing rhythm.

25. See Luke 2:49 for Christ's allusion to his divine mission.

26. First published in *Graham's Magazine* in August 1844.

27. The satyr Marsyas who challenged Apollo to a flute contest.

28. Pen name of the French novelist Aurore Dudevant (1804–76), known for her bohemian life-style.

29. This poem, the most popular in the entire work, was completed in great haste in July 1844 to satisfy the publisher's demand that the two volumes of *Poems*, 1844 have an equal number of pages. (See her letter to H. S. Boyd of 22 September 1844, p. 215) The reference in lines 163–64 to Robert Browning encouraged him to initiate a correspondence with EBB. The poem's favorable reception caused EBB to begin planning a longer poem about modern society, a poem which eventually emerged as *Aurora Leigh*.

30. I.e., in so luxurious a room grief seems out of place.

31. The railroad, recently introduced into England.

32. The House of Commons in the English Parliament in which borough representation at this time was controlled by landed families.

33. An EBB coinage meaning "nymph-ensnared."

34. A reminder of the ancient feudal custom that required untitled persons to sit at the lower end of the table, below the salt.

35. White poplars.

36. Enchanted.

37. John Graham Lough (1806–76), English sculptor.

38. Symbol of silence; Cupid gave a rose to Harpocrates, god of silence, to keep him from betraying Venus' love affair.

39. Daisies.

40. Ash trees.

41. "The Shepheard's Calender" by the English Renaissance poet Edmund Spenser (1552–99).

42. Mary Howitt (1799–1888), minor English poet.

43. Browning's poetic series, *Bells and Pomegranates* (1841–46), the title of which indicates, he said, "an alternation, or mixture, of music with discoursing, sound with sense, poetry with thought."

44. A prophetic image of the electric cable, laid a decade later.

45. Luis de Camoëns (1524–80), Portuguese poet who wrote love poems to Doña Catarina de Atayde. See EBB's "Catarina to Camoëns," pp. 95–100.

46. Willow tree.

47. Inspired rage like that of Apollo's oracle, called "the Pythian."

48. Large bay window projecting from a wall.

49. The minstrel at Penelope's house in Homer's *Odyssey*.

50. From Paros, island noted for its marble.

51. Poem by William Browne (1591–1645), English pastoral poet.

52. A wood nymph.

53. The English poet John Keats (1795–1821) died in Rome and was buried there.

54. In the omitted passage the poet drinks and then finds himself with the lady before an altar on which stands an angel surrounded by a company of great poets of the past, led by Shakespeare and Homer. Each is named and described, beginning with the Greek and Latin poets and continuing with continental and English poets through the 17th century.

55. A line particularly admired by Browning, who called it "perfect."

56. A beautiful youth beloved by Aphrodite and killed by a boar. "Adonais" is the title of Shelley's elegy on Keats.

57. Literally, the Hebrew for "He blesses."

58. The poem concludes with the band of "true poets" accepting the vatic role of service to mankind, and the pilgrim-poet of the vision praising the "Poet-God." In an epilogue, the poet has died and his young son leads a procession of children honoring the poet's memory.

59. This poem, one of EBB's best known, was first published in *Blackwood's* in August 1843. Inspired by journalist R. H. Horne's parliamentary reports on conditions in the mines, it helped spur passage of child-labor reform laws.

60. "Woe, woe, why do you look upon me with your eyes, my children?"

61. Composed in November 1831 when EBB was reading the Portuguese poet Luis de Camoëns, this poem was revised and expanded for publication in *Graham's Magazine* in October 1843. Camoëns hoped to win the queen's maid of honor, Catarina de Atayde, but on his return from a campaign against the Moors in Africa he found that Catarina was dead. The title of EBB's "Sonnets from the Portuguese" was suggested by the character of Catarina.

62. Cithern or guitar.

63. EBB began this poem early in 1843 after reading John Kenyon's poem "The Gods of Greece," a paraphrase of "Die Götter Griechenlands" by the German poet and playwright Johann Friedrich Schiller (1759–1805). EBB refutes Schiller's view that the world's beauty and romance died with the passing of the Greek gods. By "Pan" she means not just the half-man, half-beast god of forests but all pagan nature deities.

64. Ancient name for Greece.

65. Wood nymphs, as are "Oreads" in line 51.

66. Plato's "Phaedrus" describes Jove in his winged chariot leading a procession of gods divided into eleven bands.

67. After her seven sons and seven daughters were all slain by Apollo, Niobe was turned to stone.

68. Athena, goddess of war, wore a helmet. The olive tree was sacred to her.

69. Bacchus, god of wine, rode on a panther and was attended by women called Maenads.

70. The Bacchanalian exclamation.

71. Ceres, goddess of grain and sowing, smiles at Pluto's misfortune because he had stolen her daughter Proserpina.

72. Venus, goddess of love, was born from the sea and wore an embroidered cestus or girdle. She loved the beautiful youth Adonis who was killed by a boar.

73. Frosty or frozen.

74. The gods' messenger, known for his trickery. His wand, or caduceus, was entwined with snakes and surmounted by wings.

75. Goddess of earth, attended in her lion-drawn chariot by Corybantes and crowned with turrets.

76. Goddess of the hearth, revered as oldest and worthiest of the Olympians.

77. Small Greek coin.

78. EBB's headnote to "The Dead Pan" quotes Plutarch's story in "De Oraculorum Defectu" that, at the hour of Christ's death, the cry that Pan was dead "swept across the waves in the hearing of certain mariners, – and the oracles ceased."

79. A reference to Jupiter's oracle at Dodona, the most ancient in Greece, where brazen kettles vibrating in the wind provided the oracle's responses.

80. Priestess of Apollo at the Delphic shrine.

81. Cf. Browning's line in Aprile's speech at the conclusion of Part II, in *Paracelsus*: "God is the perfect poet" and EBB's similar expression in "A Vision of Poets" (line 816): "Thou, Poet-God, art great and good!"

Poems, 1850

1. *Poems,* 1850 was the first volume EBB published after her marriage and move to Italy in 1846. It contained revised versions of many poems she had published earlier as well as several new works.

2. This poem was begun in 1845 in response to a request by the anti-slavery movement in America but was not completed until late in 1846. It was first published in the *Liberty Bell* of Boston in 1848. It was probably inspired by a slave story suggested as a poetic subject to EBB by her cousin Richard Barrett of Jamaica. Although "Pilgrim's Point" may be Plymouth Rock, landing site of the Pilgrim Fathers in Massachusetts, the poem suggests a Jamaican or semi-tropical setting.

3. Trouble or distress.

4. To the customary five wounds of Christ on the cross (in hands, feet and side), EBB is adding those made by the crown of thorns and the flogging.

5. This sonnet, probably written after EBB's move to Italy, was first published in *Blackwood's* in June 1847, as was the following sonnet, "The Poet."

6. Cf. Wordsworth's "Intimations Ode," line 64.

7. First published in *Household Words,* 26 October 1850. Hiram Powers (1805-73), an American sculptor with whom the Brownings became acquainted in Florence in 1847, had completed his statue of a Greek slave girl in 1843. It was shown at the Crystal Palace Exhibition in 1851.

8. First published, along with the two following poems, "A Woman's Shortcomings" and "A Man's Requirements," in *Blackwood's* in October 1846. EBB sent them with four other poems just before leaving England, in response to a request from the magazine.

9. See Matthew 12:20.

10. From "behoove": to be necessary and proper.

11. Composed in 1846.

12. This sonnet sequence, which has remained EBB's most popular work, was composed during the course of Browning's courtship in 1845-46. It traces the course of her victory over death through the power of love. The "Portuguese" was suggested by the woman beloved of the poet Camoëns; see EBB's "Catarina to Camoëns," pp. 000-000 and note, p. 000.

13. Greek poet (c. 315 B.C.) who celebrated in his Idyl XV the return of Adonis.

14. Cf. Athena's drawing Achilles back by the hair in *Iliad* I. 204.

15. Deprive, punish.

16. An allusion to the old custom of placing coins on a corpse's eyes to keep them closed.

17. Pledges.

18. In Aeschylus' *Oresteia* Electra received the funeral urn supposedly containing her brother Orestes' ashes.

19. Venetian glass was considered to be so fine that poison would shatter it.

20. An allusion to the ancient custom of tearing one's garments to express grief.

21. See Exodus 25:17-20 for a reference to the Jewish tabernacle's mercy-seat, regarded as the resting place of God, and located between the wings of golden angels sculptured above the Ark.

22. EBB and Browning each kept the letters written by the other, between his first letter of January 1845 and their marriage in September 1846. One letter of May 1845, in which Browning proposed marriage, was destoyed. See *LRB and ERB,* I, 72. After the death of both, the letters—some 573 in all—were published.

23. Browning first called on EBB 20 May 1845 and visited regularly thereafter.

24. A form of dote—to be excessively fond of.

25. By 1845 doctors were advising EBB to move to a warmer climate for her health

and Browning was urging her to go to Italy with him. After her marriage she occasionally visited England but had no contact with her father, who strongly opposed her marrying. These lines seem to anticipate the paternal estrangement as well as her own exile.

26. Those of her mother and her brothers Sam and Bro.

27. A just reward, or wage earned.

28. The opening line in her sonnet "Past and Future" in *Poems*, 1844 which Browning had told her moved him deeply. This Sonnet XLII was not included in the 1850 edition of *Poems* but was added to "Sonnets from the Portuguese" in 1856.

29. Her mother, brothers and other beloved dead.

Casa Guidi Windows, Part I

1. The first part of this poem was written in 1848, in the initial flush of optimism for Italy's future created by promised reforms by the Grand Duke Leopold II of Tuscany and the new pope, Pius IX. *Blackwood's* rejected it as being too political. The second part, written in 1851, expresses EBB's disillusionment at the failure of church and state to fulfill their promises. Casa Guidi was the Brownings' home in Florence, directly opposite the Pitti Palace, the Grand Duke's official residence.

2. "Oh beautiful liberty."

3. Vincenzio de Filicaja (1642–1707), Italian poet and patriot, who wrote lyrics about his country's unhappy history and "led on" others, like Alfieri and Byron, to do the same. The quotation in lines 25–26 is from Filicaja. Cf. also Byron's *Childe Harold* IV. 42.

4. Cybele, goddess of fertility, mourned perpetually over the dead youth Atys; Niobe, daughter of the Lydian king, mourned for the death of all her children, slain because of her pride in them.

5. I.e., like Shakespeare's Italian-born heroine, beautiful and star-crossed in love.

6. The river Arno which cuts through Florence, called golden because of its yellow silt.

7. The bell-tower, or campanile, of the Church of Santa Maria in Florence was designed by the artist Giotto di Bondone (1266?–1337).

8. Michelangelo Buonarroti (1475–1564), Tuscan painter and sculptor, whose statues known as *Night and Day* and *Dawn and Twilight* are part of the Medici chapel in San Lorenzo in Florence. The tombs of the Medici there include that of Lorenzo, the "princely Urbino" mentioned in line 93.

9. EBB's note on this line reads: "This mocking task was set by Pietro, the unworthy successor of Lorenzo the Magnificent."

10. EBB uses the word to suggest Italy's passion for a vision or an ideal.

11. Strips of parchment with scriptural passages worn by Jews during prayers—here symbolic of Italy's birthright now reduced to a mockery.

12. A French verse form with alternating long and short lines and interlocked rhyme scheme.

13. Girolamo Savonarola (1452–98), the Dominican monk martyred at the stake for his denouncement of corruption of the church and his advocacy of general reform.

14. The loyal ones.

15. See Genesis 4:21 for reference to Jubal as the "father of all such as handle the harp and organ."

16. Singer in the choir of David. See I Chronicles 6:39.

17. Moses' sister, who sang of the Israelites passing over the Red Sea and defeating the Egyptians. See Exodus 15:21–22.

18. The omitted passage (lines 320–441) describes the interior of Santa Maria Novella

and gives an extended commentary on Giovanni Cimabue's (1240–1300) "Madonna" as another example of the need of the present to acknowledge its debts to the past.

19. The omitted passage (lines 476–598) describes in detail the procession as it passed beneath the windows of Casa Guidi on 12 September 1847 in celebration of the Grand Duke's concession permitting the people to form a civic guard. The day also happened to be the first anniversary of the Brownings' marriage.

20. Located near the Piazza del Duomo. Dante, as a political exile, was buried in Ravenna (cf. line 616).

21. Santa Maria del Fiore, the cupola of which was designed by Filippo Brunelleschi (1377–1446).

22. A reference to Giotto's painting of Dante discovered in the nineteenth century on the walls of the Bargello Museum.

23. Prince Clemens Metternich-Winneburg (1773–1859), Austrian statesman, noted for his repressive policies.

24. A reference to the rape of Leda by Zeus in the form of a swan, resulting in the birth of Helen of Troy.

25. "Alas! me a sinner!"

26. Tomaso Aniello (1623–47), the fisherman who, revolting against the Duke of Arcos, became Master of Naples for a few days before he was assassinated. He is coupled with William Tell, the Swiss hunter, who helped free Switzerland from Austria in the fourteenth century.

27. Nicola di Rienzi (1310–52) who had tried to unify Italy but was murdered by conspirators. The "fasces," a bundle of fagots, was the emblem of the Tribune of Rome.

28. Giovanni Maria Mastai-Ferretti (1792–1875) acceded to the papacy as Pius IX in 1846 and began modernizing the institutions of the papal state. These acts of liberalism aided the Italian cause and alarmed the Austrians.

29. Silvio Pellico (1787–1854), Italian patriot and poet, suffered harsh imprisonment by the Austrian government in Spielberg fortress on a charge of plotting against the establishment in 1820. During his incarceration, he wrote several tragedies.

30. Attilio and Emilio Bandieri, officers in the Austrian army sympathetic to the Italian cause, were betrayed and killed as they tried to release some Italian political prisoners.

31. Deep pits or dungeons into which political prisoners were thrown and "forgotten."

32. Michael Servetus (1511?–53), Spanish theologian and physician, condemned to be burned at the stake for his Arian views by John Calvin (1509–64), who feared an assault on Trinitarian doctrine.

33. Roman coins of little value which were supposed to be the fee the dead paid for passing over the river Styx to the underworld.

34. The church councils of Nicaea (325 and 787) and of Trent (1545 to 1563) defined dogma of the Roman church.

35. Raphael Santi (1483–1520) whose paintings, like Michelangelo's sculpture, cry out for the cause of freedom.

36. Nicholas Poussin (1594–1665), French painter whose work was influenced by Italian artists after a six-year period in Rome. Louis XIII conferred the title of "first painter in ordinary" upon him.

37. The Brownings visited Vallombrosa outside Florence in the summer of 1847 and were reminded of Milton's lines from *Paradise Lost* I:303–04.

38. Guala Romanoni (1177?–1244), disciple of St. Dominic, who was forced to retire to the monastery at Vallombrosa because of a civil uprising.

Aurora Leigh, First Book

1. Cf. Ecclesiastes 12:11–12.

2. Finest and largest of the Franciscan churches in Florence, erected during the 13th and 14th centuries.

3. A village in the Apennines noted for its rural beauty.

4. A maid.

5. The Athanasian Creed is a post-Augustinian formulary of Christian belief; the Nicene Creed, a formulary of dogma arising at the Council of Nicaea (325). St. Bonaventura (1221–74), mentioned below, was known as the "Seraphic Doctor" and would have been too mystical for the aunt's taste.

6. Ironical allusion to the countermovement to ecclesiastical liberalism formulated in the "Tracts for the Times" by leaders of the Oxford Movement from 1833 to 1841.

7. Spanish historian (1478–1557) who accompanied Columbus on his voyages to America and who wrote on the genealogy of Spanish Grandees.

8. The first is a 21,424–foot mountain in the Andes; the second, in the Canary Islands, is 11,400 feet. Aurora is citing examples of trivia which made up her education. Lara and Klagenfert, towns located in Spain and Austria, respectively.

9. Aeschylus (525–450 B.C.), Greek dramatist who, according to legend, was killed by an eagle which, mistaking his bald head for a stone, dropped a tortoise on it to break its shell.

10. Marie Marguerite Marquise de Brinvilliers was beheaded in 1676 for poisoning her husband's relatives to gain their fortunes for her young lover. When, being questioned, she saw three buckets of water, she anticipated the water torture which consisted of forcing water down the throat.

11. Giotto di Bondone, (1266?–1337), the Florentine painter noted for his golden backgrounds.

12. Theophrastus (c. 372–287 B.C.), Greek philosopher and naturalist who wrote *Treatise on Plants* and *Moral Characters*.

13. Roman rhetorician (d. 222) noted for anecdotes of animal life frequently embodying a moral.

14. See I Samuel 11. Aurora is pointing out the child's difficulties in judging good and evil characters.

15. The Trojan prince carried off by Zeus's eagle to become cupbearer to the gods — standing here for poetry or poets.

16. Hera, queen of the gods, here stands as an appropriate symbol to receive the gift of the poets.

17. The French royal dynasty, here standing for kingship, generally.

18. A stringed instrument similar to a lyre.

Poems Before Congress

1. This slim volume, the last published in EBB's lifetime, contained eight poems, most of them political. It was completed while the Brownings wintered in Rome and was published in London in March 1860 to reviews highly critical of its pro-Italian sentiments, since England was refusing to help Italy. The "Congress" of the title refers to a meeting of the major powers scheduled to be held in Paris in January 1860 to settle the Italian question, a meeting that was never held.

2. "Even more."

3. The first poem in the volume hailed Louis Napoleon Bonaparte (1808–73), the first Napoleon's nephew who in 1852 had become Emperor Napoleon III of France, as a potential savior of Italy's independence.

4. See Luke 10:30–35 for the parable of the Good Samaritan who did not pass by the wounded man as did the priest and the Levite.

5. Cant and egotism, characteristics of the village of Little Peddlington in a satire by John Poole.

6. First published in the *Athenaeum* on 24 September 1859, without stanza VII which was composed in October 1859. Villafranca is the Italian town where a peace treaty was signed by Napoleon III and Emperor Franz Joseph of Austria in July 1859. Napoleon sued for a quick armistice without assuring Italy's total independence because he feared a Prussian attack.

7. The Brownings' child Robert ("Pen") was born in Florence in 1849.

8. The man was Napoleon III and the Deed, the liberation of Italy.

9. The Hebraic valley of refuse; hence, a place of misery.

10. First published in the anti-slavery *Liberty Bell* of Boston in 1856 where readers understood that the "curse" was directed at slavery in the American South. English reviewers of *Poems Before Congress* misread the "curse" as meant for England and sharply criticized EBB for lack of patriotism.

Last Poems

1. Immediately after EBB's death in June 1861, Browning left Florence for London where he prepared for publication this volume of her remaining poems.

2. EBB sent this poem to Thackeray in 1859, at his request, for publication in his new *Cornhill Magazine*, but he decided against publishing it on the grounds that readers might be offended at the poem's "account of unlawful passion." For EBB's reply, see her letter to Thackeray of 21 April [1861], p. 220.

3. A fabulous sea monster.

4. Armor made of metal links or plates.

5. "Thank you very much."

6. A container for the Host or the Eucharist; here portraying the speaker's devotion to her beloved.

7. "My good one."

8. Gaeta, north of the Bay of Naples, was the site of the last stand of Francis II of Naples against the forces of United Italy in 1861. The voice is that of the poet, Laura Savio of Turin. One of her sons had been killed at Ancona, on the Adriatic Sea, in September 1860; the other at Gaeta. EBB imagines her saying that no victory, even one that unites Italy, will compensate the loss of her sons.

9. The poem is based on the Greek myth, retold in Ovid's *Metamorphoses*, which explains the origin of the pipes of Pan. The wood-nymph Syrinx, wooed and pursued by the god of nature, Pan, fled to the water-nymphs who changed her into murmuring water-reeds which Pan grasped. As he breathed through them, they echoed his sighs in such charming music he cut them down to form his pipes.

Letters

1. EBB's eccentricities of spelling and punctuation have been purposely retained.

2. *Pippa Passes*, a dramatic lyric published in 1841. The lines EBB quotes are from the first section, "Morning."

3. Henry F. Chorley (1808–72), literary and music critic for the *Athenaeum* and friend of Mary Russell Mitford.

4. Walter Savage Landor (1775–1864), poet and author of the prose *Imaginary Conversations* (1824–29).

5. Tennyson's two-volume edition of poems published in 1842 contained "Locksley Hall," "Ulysses," and several other new poems which EBB admired.

6. See Isaiah 38:15.

7. Richard Monckton Milnes (1809–85), M.P., minor poet, and biographer of Keats.

8. "Image."

9. Pegasus, steed of the Muses.

10. Miss Mitford was planning a volume containing reminiscences of and works by poets she had known and had sought EBB's advice about whom to include.

11. *Aurora Leigh*.

12. William Makepeace Thackeray (1811–63), novelist and at this time editor of *Cornhill Magazine*. The Brownings became acquainted with him on a visit to Rome in 1853–54. In his letter of 2 April 1861 Thackeray had written about EBB's "Lord Walter's Wife" as follows: "In your poem, you know, there is an account of unlawful passion, felt by a man for a woman, and though you write pure doctrine, and real modesty, and pure ethics, I am sure our readers would make an outcry, and so I have not published this poem."

Review of *The Book of the Poets*

1. Written in response to a request from the editor of the *Athenaeum* for a review of an anthology of English poetry, *The Book of the Poets* (London: Scott, Webster, and Geary, 1841), editor unknown. EBB's review became a survey of English poetry in a series of five articles published in the June and August issues of 1842.

2. Erasmus Darwin (1731–1802), physician, botanist, and author of "The Botanic Garden," a poem in heroic couplets.

3. From a sonnet by Sir Philip Sidney (1554–86), Renaissance courtier and poet, and author of "Apology for Poetry."